Leadership for
Educational Renewal

Agenda for Education in a Democracy
Timothy J. McMannon, Series Editor

Leadership for Educational Renewal

Developing a Cadre of Leaders

Wilma F. Smith
Gary D Fenstermacher
Editors

Agenda for Education in a Democracy

Volume 1

Jossey-Bass Publishers
San Francisco

Jossey-Bass books and products are available through most bookstores. To contact Jossey-Bass directly, call (888) 378–2537, fax to (800) 605–2665, or visit our website at www.josseybass.com.

Substantial discounts on bulk quantities of Jossey-Bass books are available to corporations, professional associations, and other organizations. For details and discount information, contact the special sales department at Jossey-Bass.

 Manufactured in the United States of America on Lyons Falls Turin Book. This paper is acid-free and 100 percent totally chlorine-free.

Library of Congress Cataloging-in-Publication Data

Leadership for educational renewal : developing a cadre of leaders / Wilma F. Smith, Gary D Fenstermacher, editors. — 1st ed.
   p. cm. — (Agenda for education in a democracy series; v. 1)
  Includes bibliographical references and index.
  ISBN 0-7879-4558-7 (pbk.)
  1. School improvement programs—United States.
2. Teachers—Training of—United States. 3. Educational leadership—United States. I. Smith, Wilma F. II. Fenstermacher, Gary D. III. Series.
  LB2822.82.L42 1999
  370'.71—dc21

                           98-51242

PB Printing 10 9 8 7 6 5 4 3 2 1   FIRST EDITION

Contents

Series Foreword

In 1894, a young Theodore Roosevelt proclaimed, "There are two gospels which should be preached to every reformer. The first is the gospel of morality; the second is the gospel of efficiency."[1] The interplay of efficiency and morality in human institutions, particularly in the educational institutions we call schools, continues to intrigue.[2] On the surface, both morality and efficiency are good; *morality* denotes fairness, virtue, and good conduct, among other things, and *efficiency* bespeaks a high level of achievement or production with a minimal expenditure of effort, money, or time. Ideally, our schools, our governments, our places of employment, even our families would be both moral and efficient in their own ways.

Difficulties arise, however, when we attempt to move beyond generalizations to specifics. What is morality? Who decides? Philosophers far wiser than I have spent lifetimes trying to convince themselves and others that there are or there are not definitive answers to those brief but complex questions. How can efficiency be judged? What are the criteria? Again the questions point to no single, certain answers. Moreover, inefficiencies have frequently been imposed on human institutions in the name of efficiency, and immoralities promulgated in the name of morality. When we advance to another level of specificity and consider morality and efficiency in the schools, the questions not only retain their complexity but also become very personal and deadly serious: Should my child's school teach morality?

What exactly would that mean? How efficient is the schooling my child is experiencing? Do my child's grades reflect actual learning? These and similar questions shape debates and decisions about our nation's schools.

Neil Postman argues that we come to understand our lives and ascribe meaning to our actions by placing them in the context of a narrative: "a story . . . that tells of origins and envisions a future, a story that constructs ideals, prescribes rules of conduct, provides a source of authority, and, above all, gives a sense of continuity and purpose."[3] If Postman is right—and I think he is—then our chosen narratives help both to determine and to reveal what we are willing to work for, to live for, perhaps even to die for.

Rarely, if ever, are people called on to give their lives in defense of the institution of the school or the process of education. Some heroic teachers have, of course, given their lives in defense of their students. Clearly their narratives embraced selflessness and sacrifice. But for most educators, selflessness and sacrifice mean no more than forgoing other more lucrative and respected professions, giving up evenings and weekends to grade papers, or serving on interminable committees. Even these sacrifices represent hardships, however, and they raise questions about educators' narratives. What are teachers willing to work for, to give their lives *to?*

Educators in the sixteen settings of the National Network for Educational Renewal (NNER)—be they school faculty, teacher educators, or arts and sciences professors—have chosen to embrace a morally based narrative for education and schooling. They see schools as places where democracy is learned and practiced, where schooling is far more than job training, where education is a seamless process of self-improvement. To them, teaching must be guided by a four-part mission: enculturating the young in a social and political democracy, providing access to knowledge for all children and youths, practicing a nurturant pedagogy, and ensuring responsible stewardship of the schools. Each part of the mission is based on and permeated by moral dimensions.[4]

Because they perceive all levels of schooling to be interconnected, NNER educators insist that the improvement of the nation's schools and the improvement of its teacher education programs must proceed simultaneously. Having better schools requires having better teachers; preparing better teachers requires having exemplary schools in which to prepare them. And the word *reform* rarely enters NNER educators' vocabularies: that term implies a finite process with corruption at one end and completion at the other. Faculty members at NNER settings prefer to think of educational improvement as a process of *renewal* by which they continuously remake good schools and teacher education programs into better ones through inquiry and hard work. NNER participants work toward the simultaneous renewal of schooling and the education of educators.

Without a plan, simultaneous renewal would be no more than a slogan. In other words, it would be morality without efficiency. The plan, or agenda, by which NNER educators pursue simultaneous renewal has come to be called the Agenda for Education in a Democracy. No creation of momentary inspiration, the Agenda emerged over several years as a product of inquiries into schools and teaching, and it was disseminated by means of several books written or edited by John Goodlad and his associates. Goodlad's *A Place Called School* (1984) began the process of explicating the Agenda, and four books published in 1990—*The Moral Dimensions of Teaching, Places Where Teachers Are Taught, Teachers for Our Nation's Schools*, and *Access to Knowledge*—further developed the essential concepts.[5] These concepts were clarified for implementation as nineteen postulates, which describe conditions that must be established in order to achieve the four-part mission for educators and the schools in which they teach.[6] The postulates guide the efforts of school and university leaders as they work together to establish new organizational structures and processes to advance their institutions on the path of simultaneous renewal.

The books in the Agenda for Education in a Democracy series explore key ideas underlying the Agenda and describe strategies for pursuing the simultaneous renewal of schools and the education of educators. This volume, the first, examines the history, philosophy, pedagogy, and evolution of the Institute for Educational Inquiry's Leadership Program and NNER settings' programs modeled on it. The Leadership Program provides a forum through which participants, or Leadership Associates, inquire into important educational and social issues, build their own leadership capacities, and advance the Agenda in their own settings and across the nation. The other volumes in the series investigate national and local education policy, renewal within a teacher education program, professional development schools, and centers of pedagogy. Together, these books offer a hopeful narrative of schools and teacher preparation programs as increasingly connected, increasingly moral, and increasingly efficient educational institutions.

TIMOTHY J. McMANNON
Series Editor
Agenda for Education
in a Democracy

Notes

1. Theodore Roosevelt, "The Manly Virtues and Practical Politics," *Forum* 17 (July 1894): 551.

2. I explored this relationship in *Morality, Efficiency, and Reform: An Interpretation of the History of American Education*, Work in Progress Series no. 5 (Seattle: Institute for Educational Inquiry, 1995).

3. Neil Postman, *The End of Education: Redefining the Value of School* (New York: Vintage, 1996 [orig. Knopf, 1995]), pp. 5–6.

4. John I. Goodlad, *Educational Renewal: Better Teachers, Better Schools* (San Francisco: Jossey-Bass, 1994), pp. 4–6.

5. John I. Goodlad, *A Place Called School: Prospects for the Future* (New York: McGraw-Hill, 1984); John I. Goodlad, Roger Soder, and

Kenneth A. Sirotnik (eds.), *The Moral Dimensions of Teaching* (San Francisco: Jossey-Bass, 1990); John I. Goodlad, Roger Soder, and Kenneth A. Sirotnik (eds.), *Places Where Teachers Are Taught* (San Francisco: Jossey-Bass, 1990); John I. Goodlad, *Teachers for Our Nation's Schools* (San Francisco: Jossey-Bass, 1990); and John I. Goodlad and Pamela Keating (eds.), *Access to Knowledge: An Agenda for Our Nation's Schools* (New York: College Entrance Examination Board, 1990).

By 1997, four more books contributed to the growing literature associated with the Agenda: John I. Goodlad, *Educational Renewal: Better Teachers, Better Schools* (San Francisco: Jossey-Bass, 1994); Roger Soder (ed.), *Democracy, Education, and the Schools* (San Francisco: Jossey-Bass, 1996); John I. Goodlad and Timothy J. McMannon (eds.), *The Public Purpose of Education and Schooling* (San Francisco: Jossey-Bass, 1997); and John I. Goodlad, *In Praise of Education* (New York: Teachers College Press, 1997).

6. The postulates were first defined in Goodlad, *Teachers for Our Nation's Schools*, pp. 54–64, and later refined in Goodlad, *Educational Renewal*, pp. 70–94. This latter version of the postulates is the reference for the Leadership Program and is reprinted in Appendix A in this book.

Introduction

Two major themes constitute the warp and woof of Timothy J. McMannon's general introduction to a series of books addressing the connection between education and democracy. The first pertains to an educational narrative drawn from this connection intended to guide school and university colleagues in their collaborative efforts to renew both the schools and the preparation programs for those who work in schools. The second theme pertains to the translation of this narrative into an agenda, referred to in this and other volumes in the series as the Agenda for Education in a Democracy. This theme embraces part of the strategy for implementing this agenda, specifically through a leadership program for the preparation of key participants in the process. To shorten and simplify the wording, we refer to the first theme as "the simultaneous renewal of schooling and the education of educators" and the second as "the Leadership Program."

In his role as general editor, Tim McMannon provides a historical and contemporary context that is essential to readers of any of the books in this series. The editors of this volume describe both the genesis and characteristics of the Agenda (Gary Fenstermacher in Chapter One) and the Leadership Program (Wilma Smith in Chapter Two). Subsequent chapters focus on major components of the Agenda or on experiences with implementing them, with particular attention to the Leadership Program.

Renewal Rather Than Reform

As observers of and participants in the so-called school reform era of the 1980s and 1990s, my colleagues and I have come to differentiate sharply between reform and renewal. *Reform* is designed to correct behavior or circumstances in individuals or institutions perceived externally to be misguided, inadequate, delinquent, or perhaps even dangerous. Accountability rests almost entirely on those to be reformed. Those pushing the reforms step into the circle of accountability when they commit resources that might be otherwise used. By the time the verdict is in, they usually have left this circle. But those to be reformed are still there to take the blame. Hence, in school reform, the schools, not the reforms, are seen as having failed and become, once again, the targets of reform. There is much repetition but little learning.

Renewal, in contrast, is self-initiated, involves learning from experience, and is a high-order educational endeavor of replacing or adding to behavior or circumstances that the individual or collection of individuals perceives as inadequate and less than satisfying. It rarely is self-renewal because renewing organisms and ecosystems tend to seek out relevant support from others. Responsibility, in contrast to accountability, is built in, not imposed. There are lessons learned and lessons to pass on to others challenged by the prospects of renewal.

My colleagues and I have watched the frequent comings and goings, with little evidence of their passing, of reform proposals for both schools and teacher education. We have watched with much greater interest the comings and stayings of initiatives in educational renewal that carry with them no mandates, no threats other than those of possible failure, little or no financial inducements, and the expectation of hard work and some trying times. The inducements have been connecting with some ideas that appear to be relevant to ongoing work, some nonthreatening technical and (for want of a better word) spiritual support, and affiliation with a community of like-minded participants in renewal. Several of those initiatives with which we have been in association and from which we have learned are referred to in this and other volumes.

We have noticed in the initiatives that appear to experience the most success and engender the greatest enthusiasm two major characteristics: some semblance of an agenda of ideas that participants find attractive or even compelling and an infrastructure that offers both a sense of belonging and opportunities for social interaction, such as provision for networking. In reflecting on our work, we note the degree to which the human and financial resources of the Center for Educational Renewal and the Institute for Educational Inquiry (see McMannon's commentary on this series of books in the Series Foreword) have focused on the conceptual grounding of the Agenda for Education in a Democracy and the social and political infrastructure of the National Network for Educational Renewal (NNER) through which this Agenda is interpreted, implemented, and tested.

About Agendas and the Genesis of Ours

It appears that the longevity and robustness of an initiative in educational renewal correlates with the depth and comprehensiveness of the inquiry underlying and driving the agenda and accompanying its implementation. Over the years, I have seen schools latch onto sloganized panaceas for improvement, such as "back to basics" or "education for the space age," that promise much and deliver little. Probing reveals the absence of solid inquiry to support either the rhetoric of justification or the effort of implementation. Indeed, the attractive simplicity of the rhetoric ensures little effort and little effect. By contrast, the school renewal efforts inspired by the inquiries of Theodore Sizer and his colleagues into secondary schools and Howard Gardner's theory of multiple intelligences, to take two highly visible examples, are demanding of effort, time, and intellect. They stimulate the inquiry, collegiality, and conversation that are essential to continuing individual and institutional renewal.

Our focus on the simultaneous renewal of schooling and the education of educators preceded by several years our development and implementation of the agenda designed to guide and drive the process. While conducting our comprehensive study of elementary and secondary schools in the late 1970s into the 1980s, many persisting problems of schooling were becoming increasingly apparent to us, as were the challenges these present to teachers and their preparation programs. By 1985, we were engaged in conversations with key representatives of both schools and universities around the concept of joining these two sets of institutions in partnerships for purposes of addressing the problems and the challenges they present to teacher educators. Our agenda was defined as one of simultaneous renewal. The substance of this agenda—that is, the specific array of pressing problems and issues—became the major focus of discourse in the meetings of persons representing the ten school-university partnerships that constituted by April 1986 the NNER.

The absence in the agenda of any prespecification of this array of problems and issues was, in my judgment, the cancer that grew to be inoperable in a few years. Although the document agreed to by all ten settings as a condition of membership in the NNER put forward an initiative in which the concept of advancing *simultaneous* renewal was nonnegotiable, some participants made it abundantly clear that renewal on the higher education side was off the table (and, some said, unnecessary). The frustration of those for whom teacher education was of major concern was palpable. With each meeting, the prospect that a common agenda would emerge became increasingly dim.

What I have briefly described is, I believe, more the norm than the exception in educational improvement agendas. The concept of a group of well-intentioned people with highly diverse purposes coming together from time to time to hammer out common purpose and common commitment of time and energy to fulfilling that purpose is naive. It is democratic only in the sense of respecting everyone's right to an opinion, but the democratic principle of wise use of intelligence, for example, too often is sacrificed to and ultimately savaged by the struggle among conflicting opinions. Freedom to choose is another important democratic principle, but choice frequently begets mischief when the nature of the choice to be made is vague or, even if clear, carelessly observed.

It is in most people's best interests not to let initiatives drift to collapse but, rather, to terminate them when dissatisfaction is widespread or to confront and deal with major reconstruction. By 1988, those of us who had created the NNER were deeply immersed in our comprehensive study of teacher education in the United States that, we were convinced, would produce specifics regarding the problems of teacher education paralleling those of schooling uncovered in our earlier inquiry. We would be able to fill in the missing half of the simultaneous renewal process and draw attention to the connection between the conduct of schooling and that of educating educators to work in schools.

Taking the course of major reconstruction, we announced in 1989 an eighteen-month period of low maintenance of the NNER during which we would all rethink our priorities and commitments. In 1990, the trilogy of books on the study was published. One of these contained much more than identification of troublesome problems to add to the array of school problems that our earlier research identified. For the first time, we described in detail an agenda of mission, conditions to be put in place for the advancement of this mission, and the conceptual grounding for understanding and implementing this agenda. Membership in the new iteration of the NNER that followed required several months of intellectual engagement with the Agenda for Education in a Democracy and, from this, thoughtful attention to its nature and expectations.

Experiencing the Agenda

This volume and those that follow in the series recount the experiences and perceptions of individuals who, with others, have provided much of the leadership for a sustained educational improvement initiative dependent on a unique collaboration of school and university personnel—the latter from the often-feuding domains of education and of the arts and sciences disciplines. My intent in this introduction to the first of the volumes in the series (relevant, I hope, to the others) is to shed some light on what has engaged the interest, time, energy, and commitment of diverse groups of participants over a period of years—long enough to put in place many of the daunting conditions of the Agenda for Education in a Democracy. An assessment process is under way. Until the results are in, it is encouraging to note that a disproportionately large percentage of teacher education programs selected recently as outstanding—by, for example, the National Education Association—are embedded in NNER settings.

Our experience with the first iteration of the NNER was a wake-up call regarding the significance of agendas in sustaining an educational improvement initiative. There must be an agenda. It must be comprehensive with respect to its encompassing a very large number of what I call "commonplaces": those characteristics and conditions that unavoidably accompany the endeavor or domain. A commonplace of teacher education is guided practice. Absent attention to field experiences, student teaching, or internships of some kind, an agenda for the improvement of teacher education is incomplete. An agenda addressed to some but not most or all commonplaces should so state and should endeavor to connect with the others. To downplay or attempt to simplify an agenda's demands is to court trouble down the road. The process of determining participation in an initiative guided by an agenda should ensure for the applicant authentic preadmission experiences with it and ensure for the initiative's stewards authentic interest and commitment on the part of the applicant. "Trophy" memberships and "trophy" members tend to become liabilities. I am convinced that nourishing, sustaining agendas possess an onion-like quality. They can be peeled back and peeled back, again and again, with each pull revealing new nuances of understanding and stimulating new activity. But little is known about this relatively unstudied quality. Clearly, there are agendas of so little substance that participants rarely refer to them for guidance. The initiative becomes stalled in controversy, splinters, or is abandoned. Agendas possessing the onion-like quality are complex; complexity virtually invites differing perceptions and often stimulates controversy. What is the potential that even this type of agenda will become dysfunctional?

The Agenda for Education in a Democracy has been widely discussed within and, we are learning, beyond the NNER. "Unpacking" the postulates—that is, dissecting them for meaning—is an activity required of applicants for admission. Each postulate is a comprehensive statement of necessary conditions for attaining robust, coherent teacher education programs; the entire set of nineteen postulates specifies several dozen such conditions. Some NNER settings report two-hour discussions focused on just one postulate—sometimes a year or two after meeting the admission requirements. Some key actors in settings outside the NNER but desiring admission refer to wanting to participate in "The Conversation"—that is, the conversation through which the Agenda for Education in a Democracy (both mission and postulates) is understood. At annual meetings of the NNER, it is not uncommon for persons engaged in lively discussion to say, "Let's go back to the moral grounding of our work." And, of course, sessions of the Leadership Program are characterized by intense conversations around both the mission of the Agenda and the conditions for attending to it embedded in the nineteen postulates. But to repeat: When, if ever, does the nature and intensity of critical inquiry into such an agenda become dysfunctional?

Exploring the Agenda's Ideas

During the planning for this series of books, there was considerable discussion of whether I should, one more time, describe the Agenda for Education in a Democracy. The decision to give this task to someone else who has studied and worked with it over a period of years (especially as a member of the faculty of the Leadership Program) was a good one. Gary Fenstermacher has done a superb job in Chapter One. Those of us who read the initial manuscript are much clearer than we were before on the distinctions between reform and renewal, for example. Similarly, he has clarified the presence of both mission and the necessary conditions for its advancement in the Agenda and the difference between this substantive agenda and the strategy of simultaneous renewal (which some participants refer to, from time to time, as the Agenda). As a result, Chapter One provides conceptual grounding for the entire initiative. Similarly, Wilma Smith, in Chapter Two, sets out the necessary contextual orientation to the Leadership Program that we believe is essential to the advancement of any long-term, complex educational improvement effort.

So long as one stays at the relatively comprehensive level necessitated in encompassing a great deal of descriptive analysis, the interested inquirer is likely to seek understanding of the whole rather than points of likely controversy. This usually is the case with a set of educational aims, for example. We readily agree with what appears to be intended virtue at a general level, but quickly disagree during processes of unpacking the specific meaning of each. For example, at first blush, I move readily outward from Donna Kerr's conception of a public pedagogy of nurture (Chapter Six) into Benjamin Barber's domain of particular interest—that of civic and civil communities (discussed in his chapter in one of our books outside this series, *The Public Purpose of Education and Schooling*). But in a symposium we sponsored several years ago, Kerr and Barber were in sharp disagreement and moved away from rather than toward one another during the discussion.

In this volume, those of us who read the first draft of Chapter One were so much in agreement that we converged on only a few suggested clarifications, to which the author readily agreed. Chapter Four, however, which digs deeply into one of the four major components of the Agenda's mission, provoked controversy and evoked suggestions calling for some fundamental revisions, only some of which the author regarded as acceptable. And whereas I had glided so easily and agreeably through the paragraphs of Chapter One, I found myself grinding to a puzzled halt more than once in Chapter Four.

Gary Fenstermacher and I have interacted with one another (as both friends and colleagues) over commonplaces of the human conversation for more than three decades. Now I find, from reading Chapter Four, that we are in fundamental disagreement over a significant part of the preceding sentence. He seeks to correct my use of the words "the human conversation" by adding an "s" to the last word. This would produce a profound change in my conception of what it means to be human, a conception I have put forward in sessions of the Leadership Program described in Chapter Two and in writing, especially in my book *In Praise of Education* (1997). Indeed, I summarized this conception in my "Response" included in Gary Fenstermacher's *On Knowledge and the Human Conversation* (Number 6 in the Work in Progress Series of the Institute for Educational Inquiry), an earlier (1997) version of some of what is dealt with in Chapter Four of this book. Clearly, we have a conceptual difference not easily reconciled. Nevertheless, I do not consider it dysfunctional to advancing our Agenda for Education in a Democracy.

As the bull I apparently have by the horns (with respect to my interpretation of knowledge) became more ferocious with the turning of the pages of Chapter Four, I began to wish that I had stayed with the initial formulation of the mission element this chapter addresses. The four-part mission emerged first as the four-legged stool of teaching and teacher education developed by Kenneth Sirotnik, Roger Soder, and me during the conceptualization of our Study of the Education of Educators in the late 1980s. It entered the public domain in 1990, in several short paragraphs on pages 43 and 44 of my *Teachers for Our Nation's Schools*, as our recommended moral grounding of teacher education, the professional teacher, and the teaching profession.

Unfortunately, there always seems to be some loss in translation when narrative becomes specifically intentional and is converted into an agenda for widespread, collective action. The initial place-holder for the knowledge component in the four-part mission described in Chapter One was "the human conversation." It appears on page 44 of *Teachers* in the sentence, "Teachers should participate widely in the human conversation and, in doing so, provide models of good judgment and clear communication"—a sentence convey-ing much more than is implied by the canon of the modernists with which Gary aligns me. Indeed, the word *knowledge* does not appear in any of the paragraphs introducing what later became the Agenda's four-part mission. The shift from "participation in the human con-versation" to "access to knowledge" (the subject of Chapter Five) presumably was made in deference to communication, but it is one I now regret. Since, from my perspective, the ongoing debate and controversy over modern and postmodern conceptions of knowl-edge (pursued primarily in academe) is but a part—admittedly a sig-nificant part—of the human conversation, discourse regarding the Agenda for Education in a Democracy could be better served by our addressing the incredible gulf in meaning between "human con-versations" and "*the* human conversation." There is little hope of a place for each of all the variations and nuances characterizing the human conversation until the educative process succeeds in teach-ing us that we are one people in one habitat engaged in a conver-sation that is universal.

Searching for Origins

Determining origins is fraught with challenge and sand traps, as his-torians well know. Fenstermacher writes in convincing language that the idea of the human conversation in our agenda came from the political philosopher Michael Oakeshott. Not so. Although I knew a little about Oakeshott before 1990, I did not read any of his works until 1992 (in a collection of his writings published in 1991).

I was formally introduced to Oakeshott by Josiah Auspitz in his piece in the *American Scholar* (Summer 1991), which begins, "Michael Oakeshott would have enjoyed his funeral." Earlier in this foreword, I noted our initial use of "the human conversation" in developing the Agenda's mission statement and my reference to it on page 44 of *Teachers for Our Nation's Schools*, published in 1990.

In her opening sentence of Chapter Two of this volume, Wilma Smith refers to the February 1992 meeting in Seattle (shortly after the Institute for Educational Inquiry was founded) in which we envisioned the Leadership Program. During the months following that meeting, several of us hammered out the substance and structure of a curriculum that remained surprisingly stable for each successive cohort for six years. When we got down to the question of how we should open the first session of the first cohort in the summer of 1992, I thought of the Auspitz piece—mostly from a pedagogical perspective. Although well written, the article requires careful reading and, although it evoked for me metaphorical extrapolations regarding the human conversation, I saw pedagogical utility in its implications for the art of conversation.

We discussed the routine with which a group coming together for the first time handles the matter of introductions. One after another, moving clockwise or counterclockwise around the table, each person introduces herself or himself, usually reaching for a cute phrase to ease the tension. Once finished, one might become a listener, but before then one is too busy figuring out what to say. We decided on a quite different approach, using Oakeshott as a way to get into our various perspectives through a reading (the Auspitz piece) that we rightly predicted would be new for everyone while simultaneously providing opportunities for the desired personal introductions. Roger Soder quite vividly recreates this process in Chapter Three.

There may be other pieces that would serve pedagogical purpose just as well, but we have not yet come up with one. Because the article is about Oakeshott but by Auspitz, and because we endeavored to focus on the latter's words, we lessened the danger that someone in the group who knew Oakeshott well would dominate a discussion for which the others would not be prepared. All had read the Auspitz piece. And because it said much about the way Oakeshott participated in conversation, it was relatively easy for us to move to questions regarding conditions appropriate and perhaps necessary for the many conversations we would be having.

And what about the genesis of the concept of the human conversation in our work and as an element of the Agenda? I can speak only for myself and with little confidence. There were stirrings, I think, as a consequence of novels I read quite early in my life. Recollection of a first "aha!" experience connects with the late Gerhard Hirschfeld who, appalled by the many holocausts that were World War II, created the Council for the Study of Mankind, which today would be the Council for the Study of Humankind. Some of his vision of oneness or unity among all inhabitants of the world appears in Chapter One of a book edited by several colleagues and me published in 1974, entitled *Toward a Mankind School*. The "aha!" experience of reading about Michael Oakeshott turned my attention to his take on the human conversation and, in the early 1990s, to some of his writing.

Ideas as Change Agents

I have chosen to focus here on differences between Gary Fenstermacher and me regarding our perceptions of the Agenda for Education in a Democracy primarily because his was the task of explaining it to those who will read the books of this series. Consequently, although there are points of disagreement with other authors (and with other statements in Chapter Four), it is important to highlight those that are fundamental. I do not perceive the complexity of ideas that promote such disagreement as dysfunctional. Rather, the ideas in themselves became virtually change agents because of the degree to which the process of working through them stimulates renewed attention to the implications of the agenda for renewal.

What I am trying to say becomes clear to me in the concluding pages of Gary Fenstermacher's Chapter Four. Early in the chapter, he brought to bear his epistemological insights in the kind of critique that is commonplace among philosophers and within which he endeavors to place some of my views. Then he moves outside this disciplined process to address the human conversation rather than "disciplined encounters" and "subject matters" (where our differences are considerable). Now, in spite of our differences over "human conversations" and "*the* human conversation," he finds a good deal of common ground—ground we share with thousands of others within and beyond the National Network for Educational Renewal. It is my hope and expectation that our readers too will come to this common ground and perhaps have more than one "aha!" in experiencing renewal.

Seattle, Washington   JOHN I. GOODLAD
December 1998

Acknowledgments

This book could not have been written if John Goodlad, Roger Soder, Richard Clark, David Imig, and Kenneth Sirotnik had not met with us to brainstorm and design the Leadership Program for the sixteen National Network for Educational Renewal (NNER) settings. Indeed, without the critically important ideas of John Goodlad, we would not have been nearly so determined to take on the daunting challenges of renewing our nation's schools and the programs that prepare and encourage their teachers.

Each year we have been renewed by coming to know another cohort of educational leaders from the sixteen NNER settings. Their influence on the work of educational renewal is making a decided difference in the lives of thousands of schoolchildren and young adults, and we thank them for their determination to make it happen.

The chapter authors are authentic, renewing leaders who care profoundly about the future of our nation's schools and are dedicated to taking action that will strengthen the linkages between education and democracy. We deeply appreciate their demonstrated commitment to both the theory and the practices that underlie the critical work of developing better teachers and better schools.

One of our major funders, the Philip Morris Companies Inc., provided initial support for the Leadership Program, contributed toward the expenses for graduate Associates to attend our annual meetings, and underwrote the production of this book. We appreciate the Companies' financial backing as well as their belief in our work, as evidenced by their support throughout the past six years.

Our colleagues at the Institute for Educational Inquiry, Amanda Froh and Paula McMannon, have been consistently supportive of our efforts, and we thank them for their efficient work and unflagging encouragement. We especially thank Timothy McMannon for his meticulous editing and his guidance in making the individual chapters fit together to tell the story of the Leadership Program.

Our long-suffering spouses advised, cajoled, encouraged, and assisted us in our writing and editing tasks. Thank you, John and Virginia, for staying the course with us.

December 1998   WILMA F. SMITH
                                                      GARY D FENSTERMACHER

About the Sponsor

The National Network for Educational Renewal (NNER) was established in 1986 to put into practice the belief that the improvement of schooling and the renewal of teacher education must proceed simultaneously. In short, good schools require good teachers, and good teachers learn their profession in good schools.

The NNER presently embraces sixteen member settings in fourteen states: California, Colorado, Connecticut, Hawaii, Maine, Missouri, Nebraska, New Jersey, Ohio, South Carolina, Texas, Utah, Washington, and Wyoming. Member settings work to build collaboration among three main groups that play a vital role in the preparation of new teachers: education faculty in colleges and universities; arts and sciences faculty; and faculty in elementary and secondary schools. All told, there are thirty-three colleges or universities, over one hundred school districts, and about five hundred partner schools in the NNER.

The NNER extends the work of the Center for Educational Renewal (CER), which was founded in 1985 by John I. Goodlad, Kenneth A. Sirotnik, and Roger Soder to study and facilitate "the simultaneous renewal of schooling and the education of educators."

To support the work of the NNER and the CER, Goodlad, Soder, and Sirotnik established the independent, nonprofit Institute for Educational Inquiry (IEI) in Seattle in 1992. The IEI oversees leadership training programs for key personnel from NNER settings, administers grants from philanthropic organizations to the NNER, conducts research and evaluation studies, and publishes a series of Work in Progress papers. The IEI is the sponsoring agency for the Agenda for Education in a Democracy series.

About the Editors

Wilma F. Smith is a senior associate of the Institute for Educational Inquiry and of the Center for Educational Renewal at the University of Washington. A public school educator for thirty-three years, she served in six school districts as teacher, principal, special educator, and area superintendent, ending her public school career as superintendent of the Mercer Island (Washington) School District. For ten years, she taught graduate-level educational leadership courses at the University of Washington and at Western Washington University. She now facilitates all aspects of the Institute's leadership programs, which serve to build cadres of leaders committed to the simultaneous renewal of schools and the education of educators.

Gary D Fenstermacher is professor of education at the University of Michigan, Ann Arbor. His specialty is the philosophy and politics of education, particularly as these pertain to teaching and teacher education. He serves as both a senior associate for the Center for Educational Renewal and a senior fellow of the Institute for Educational Inquiry. His work with renewal initiatives dates back to 1968, when he was appointed assistant professor in the Graduate School of Education at the University of California at Los Angeles. Fenstermacher later served as dean of the College of Education at the University of Arizona, which participated in the first iteration of the National Network for Educational Renewal.

About the Contributors

Mona H. Bailey is a senior associate of the Institute for Educational Inquiry and of the Center for Educational Renewal at the University of Washington, focusing on issues of minority recruitment and retention into teaching. She has served as assistant state superintendent for Washington and in a variety of roles in the Seattle Public Schools. She is currently serving as director of the National Faculty's western region.

John I. Goodlad is president of the Institute for Educational Inquiry and codirector of the Center for Educational Renewal at the University of Washington. Throughout his career, he has been involved in an array of educational renewal programs and projects and has engaged in large-scale studies of educational change, schooling, and teacher education. In addition to advancing a comprehensive program of research and development directed to the simultaneous renewal of schooling and teacher education, he is inquiring into the mission of education in a democratic society to which such renewal must be directed.

Barbara L. Gottesman was for seven years state site director for the South Carolina Network for Educational Renewal, a consortium of five institutions of higher education, more than ten school districts, and over thirty partner schools collaborating to improve teacher education in South Carolina. She also served as director of the South Carolina Center for the Advancement of Teaching and School Leadership and chair of the education department at Columbia College in Columbia, South Carolina. Her areas of research and writing interest include peer coaching for educators and collaboration for school renewal.

Marilyn B. Hadley is former executive director of the Nebraska Network for Educational Renewal and is professor and interim dean of the College of Education at the University of Nebraska at Kearney. She taught for seven years in public schools and for more than twenty years in higher education. While at the University of Nebraska at Kearney, she has held various administrative positions and taught in the teacher education program. Her professional interests include developing and examining partnerships between teacher education programs and P–12 schools.

Kathleen H. Hughes is the executive director of the Center for the Improvement of Teacher Education and Schooling at Brigham Young University. She was formerly the assistant superintendent for curriculum and instruction in the Provo (Utah) City School District. Prior to becoming a district administrator, she taught at all levels in public schools. One of her main educational interests is the unification of educational programs to produce a seamless system that meets all students' needs.

Tina Jacobowitz is professor of education in the Department of Reading and Educational Media and Coordinator of the Agenda for Education in a Democracy at Montclair State University, Upper Montclair, New Jersey. She teaches courses in literacy and critical thinking and serves on the advisory board of Montclair State's center of pedagogy. She is actively involved with the New Jersey Network for Educational Renewal and its nineteen member districts. She began teaching at the elementary school level in 1967 in Bedford Stuyvesant, Brooklyn, which was, and continues to be, one of the poorest inner-city neighborhoods in New York City.

Donna H. Kerr is professor of education at the University of Washington and a senior fellow of the Institute for Educational Inquiry. Kerr has taught at all levels of the educational system, served as vice provost of the university, and was dean during the launching of the University of Washington's branch campuses. Her current interests focus on philosophical questions regarding domination and nurture in interpersonal relations and institutional structures.

Timothy J. McMannon is a senior associate of the Institute for Educational Inquiry and of the Center for Educational Renewal at the University of Washington and teaches history at colleges and universities in the Seattle area. His main areas of interest include recent U.S. history, the history of American education, and the public purpose of education and schooling.

Nicholas M. Michelli is dean of the College of Education and Human Services at Montclair State University, Upper Montclair, New Jersey. He provided leadership in launching the nation's first center of pedagogy, joining arts and sciences faculty, teacher educators, and members of the New Jersey Network for Educational Renewal at Montclair State. His interests include critical thinking, school-university partnerships, faculty roles and rewards, and professional development for P–12 and college faculty. He chairs the American Association of Colleges for Teacher Education's Governmental Relations Committee and works in that role to develop state and federal policy to support the education of educators.

Robert S. Patterson is dean of the David O. McKay School of Education at Brigham Young University (BYU) and director of the Center for the Improvement of Teacher Education and Schooling at BYU. Prior to joining the faculty at BYU in 1992, he taught at the University of Alberta for twenty-five years, where he also served as dean for eight years. His interests include the history of teacher education and the role of partnerships in educational change.

Antonette Port is codirector of the Hawaii Institute for Educational Partnerships at the University of Hawaii at Manoa. Formerly the director of the Hawaii School University Partnership, she has provided leadership in developing and implementing the partner school concept in Hawaii and in restructuring the teacher education programs at the College of Education. Port has been an educator at elementary, high school, and college levels and has held key positions in the Hawaii State Department of Education in teacher education and certification, staff development, and curriculum development. Her broad-based experiences as an educator in the United States and West Africa have stimulated her interest in the development of communities of lifelong learners who are informed, responsible, and caring citizens in a democratic and global society.

Katharine D. Rasch is the dean of the School of Education at Maryville University in St. Louis. She has been a teacher for twenty-four years, fourteen of them as a teacher educator at Maryville University. She has been instrumental in developing the Metropolitan St. Louis Consortium's Center for Inquiry and Renewal, a unique collaborative entity that brings together cohorts of preservice students from Maryville University and Harris-Stowe State College. She recently completed a term as president of the American Association of Independent Liberal Arts Colleges for Teacher Education and is an active participant in the National Council for Accreditation of Teacher Education and the American Association of Colleges for Teacher Education.

Roger Soder is codirector of the Center for Educational Renewal at the University of Washington and vice president of the Institute for

Educational Inquiry. Formerly an administrator in the Cape Flattery School District on the Makah Indian Reservation at Neah Bay, Washington, and education director of the Seattle Urban League, Soder now focuses on the ethics and politics of rhetoric and education and the role of the university in a free society.

Jeanne Surface is a 7–12 principal at Wakefield Community School in rural northeast Nebraska. A former teacher, Surface taught family and consumer sciences and was a drug-free-schools coordinator. A major focus of her administrative efforts has been to create a learning environment that capitalizes on the rural nature of her school and community. She has also worked to build a partnership with Wayne State College in Wayne, Nebraska, to prepare teachers for rural schools.

Leadership for
Educational Renewal

Part I

Background and Mission

Agenda for Education in a Democracy

Gary D Fenstermacher

W hy do we have public schools in the United States? This question is closely linked to another: Do we really need them? These are compelling questions, particularly in these times when the advocates for public schooling appear to be on the defensive and calls for vouchers and other forms of privatization of schooling are increasing in frequency and intensity. As the debate unfolds and the pros and cons of public schooling are examined, one voice seems more muted than others. It is the voice of democracy.

It is as if Americans participating in the debate have taken one of the central rationales for public education for granted. It is as if the voice of democracy is not the crucial voice. Instead, the voices of economic strength, global competitiveness, equal opportunity, and high standards and high achievement are prominent and powerful, while that of democracy is barely audible. The near absence of this voice may be why David Mathews found that "despite a long tradition of thinking of public education as a sacred trust, Americans today are halfway out the schoolhouse door."[1] Although the American public still gives lip service to public education, Mathews states that the broad mandate for public schools "has lost its power to inspire extensive commitment."[2] The reason that this has happened may be that many of today's Americans have forgotten or perhaps never really understood the vital links between public education and the ideals of democracy.

A central purpose of the work of John I. Goodlad, his colleagues at the Center for Educational Renewal and the Institute for Educational Inquiry, and the hundreds of participants at the various settings of the National Network for Educational Renewal (NNER) is to restore the links between education and democracy, to ground the work of the public schools in the moral and political ideals of democratic life. That is why this restorative work is called the Agenda for Education in a Democracy. The overarching purpose of the endeavor is to strengthen the voice of democracy in the ongoing discussion of the purpose and the future of public education in the United States.

It would not be the first time that the point and purpose of public education in the United States have been grounded in democratic ideals. The history of public schooling in America has gone through several phases, with the voice of democracy strong in some and quite weak in others. The earliest schools in what would become the United States, those in the Massachusetts Bay Colony of the mid-1600s, had decidedly religious purposes.[3] As we embarked on building a new nation after the American Revolution, the formation of an independent political identity brought democratic ideals to the fore. Then came industrialization, with its attendant need for a workforce that could no longer be prepared at home, as had been the case in a more agrarian economy. On the heels of industrialization, the Civil War so divided the fledgling nation that restoration of the republic became a critical task in the latter half of the nineteenth century. Democratic aspirations were at the heart of much of this national restoration, but within a few decades of the Civil War, waves of immigrants would refocus the efforts of schools to the multiple tasks of establishing a common language, teaching common skills, and building a common culture. U.S. participation in two world wars, with a massive economic depression between them, served as a strong argument for schools that prepared the young to take their places in a workforce that was competitive and productive. As we move closer to the present, however, it is less easy to discern the point of our endeavors, for historical perspective is far more difficult to attain.

Although the purpose and effects of public schooling in these times are not easy to ascertain, it appears clear enough that across the broad historical sweep of public schooling in the United States, two very strong strains go a long way toward explaining why we have schools. The first of these is democratic community; the second, economic opportunity. These twin purposes appear to enjoy prominence at different times in the history of public education, depending on what is valued and sought after in American life. What distinguishes the present cycle from previous ones is the distinct possibility, as Mathews suggests, that public schooling will not survive the current inattention to democratic ideals. With economic opportunity so prominent in the current cycle, and democratic community so muted, the rationale for why we have schooling that is common, popular, and public is nearly lost.

The Agenda for Education in a Democracy aims at renewing our common and collective commitment to public education in the United States. How it does so is what this book and others in the series are about. What the Agenda for Education in a Democracy is, and why it has the form it does, is what this chapter is about. Before moving directly to the Agenda, it will prove useful to say just a bit more about how the concept of democracy is understood in this context.

The idea of democracy means more than simply the rule of the people. It also refers to a way of living wherein each individual holds an entitlement to envision an ideal future for himself or herself and is ensured sufficient freedom to pursue that vision. Inasmuch as the unrestrained pursuit of thousands of different visions can yield chaos, and sometimes outright physical harm, the government or state exercises a measure of responsibility to regulate these pursuits.[4] The state exercises this responsibility through the passage of laws, by fostering communities that depend on the cultivation of norms and mores rather than the enforcement of laws, and through public schools, where the content, norms, and values required for a productive, fulfilling life in a democracy are cultivated.

Law, community, and school are important and powerful forces for sustaining democracy.[5] Communities are aided in their democratic endeavors by schools that prepare the young for various roles in their respective communities, including those of citizen, worker, and neighbor.[6] These links are critical to the Agenda for Education in a Democracy, wherein schools, as the primary force for the formal education of the young, carry an enormous responsibility for fostering democratic character, which is vital to democratic governance (which, in its turn, is vital to sustaining democratic community, thus quickly leading us to the near-obvious insight of a strong ecological relationship among schools, communities, and democratic governments). With this backdrop of the role of communities and schools in the construction of a robust, enlivened democracy, it is possible to explore in greater detail what is involved in the Agenda for Education in a Democracy.

Simultaneous Renewal

The core initiative of the Agenda for Education in a Democracy is quite simple—so simple it requires only sixteen words to state: To foster the simultaneous renewal of places that educate children and programs that educate their teachers—so simple it seems as if its accomplishment would be a snap. Yet it turns out that it is one of the most challenging aspects of the entire Agenda. The challenge becomes apparent as each of the terms in the expression *simultaneous renewal* is studied more carefully.

Simultaneity is the end-in-view that characterizes the relationship between elementary and secondary schools, on the one hand, and colleges and universities, on the other. The task that faces both is to revitalize, in concert with one another, conceptions of their work, the conduct of their practice, and the outcomes of their endeavors. The words "in concert with one another" slip easily into this text, but making cooperation of this kind happen is quite another matter. In the United States, elementary schools are different from secondary schools, and both are very different from institutions of higher education (often abbreviated "IHEs"). Bringing the three sectors of the educational system together is hard and often frustrating work (although tremendously gratifying for all when it succeeds). To complicate this work, the renewal efforts of the IHEs must involve members of the faculties of *both* schools of education and colleges of arts and sciences. That makes the work even more difficult, for the divide that separates faculties in the arts and sciences from faculties in education may be as wide as the separation sometimes observed between education faculty and elementary and secondary school personnel.

Simultaneous renewal is understood to mean that both sides of the relationship—P–12 schools[7] and IHEs—get better at their requisite tasks in ways that further their mutual interests. Thus, the interest of the school, college, or department of education (SCDE) in selected P–12 schools cannot simply be for the purpose of finding training sites for student teachers. Simultaneous renewal requires that some substantive and renewing endeavor takes place between the IHE and the selected schools and that the preparation of teachers be an integral part of that endeavor. Similarly, selected P–12 schools cannot seek affiliation with an SCDE merely to gain a supply of adults for classrooms or because the schools want to initiate prospective teachers "the right way." Again, there must be a substantive endeavor under way between the sites, an endeavor that creates a worthwhile occasion for the further development of prospective teachers *as well as* experienced teachers and collegiate faculty members.

Just as the adjective *simultaneous* is important, so is the noun *renewal*. One way to gain a sense of the significance of this term is to draw a distinction among three types of institutional change: repair, reform, and renewal. *Repair* is fixing something that is broken, typically without alteration of its underlying structure or function.

Reform is extensive revision, perhaps massive reformulation, of an enterprise, with a corresponding overhaul of structure and function. *Renewal* is a reinvigoration of and reengagement with what is often already in place but little used. The Agenda's attention to renewal rather than repair or reform is quite intentional; Goodlad has discussed it on more than one occasion.[8]

Renewal is a process of capitalizing on the strengths of what is already in place, while also acknowledging the challenges facing those who populate the organization or system undergoing renewal. In the case of the Agenda, renewal is a process of attentive listening and careful telling. That is, the Agenda contains a great deal to which its adherents are asked to conform, but it is also predicated on the view that these adherents have minds of their own, that they are generally engaged in doing good work, and that they must bring their own local characteristics and interests to bear on the implementation of the Agenda. In other words, renewal is an activity sustained by mutual understanding, by all parties' taking one another seriously and acting together in good faith.

Reform, by contrast, is frequently associated with imposition, with compliance, with persons or parties in power altering the circumstances of those not similarly situated. I do not mean that reform is always bad or that renewal is always good. Good things can and do emerge from reform, and poor results may certainly stem from renewal. The reason for placing emphasis on renewal rather than reform is to make clear the vital importance of attending carefully to the lived experiences and structural contexts of those who participate in renewal. It is to make clear that the work of the Agenda has nothing to do with bringing refined ideas to untutored practitioners, but everything to do with blending the wisdom, skills, contexts, and constraints of the participants with the ideals, ideas, and conditions of the Agenda.

Part of the appeal of the term *renewal*, in contrast to *repair* or *reform*, is that, for those involved in the Agenda, renewal is primarily an educational endeavor. That is, in order to effect the change called for in renewal, the agent of renewal openly, reasonably, and fairly engages the interested inquirer in consideration of the terms of renewal, so that the inquirer can grasp these terms and make an unfettered decision whether to engage in the renewal endeavor. Furthermore, if the endeavor is educative, the inquirer also gains, through study and experience, influence in altering the terms of the renewal. It is easy enough to read these words without fully grasping their import. There is an enormous difference between change initiatives that are attained through policy, regulation, or law and those that are attained through education. In a democratic society, there are substantial grounds for both forms of change. What is important here is that the change strategy of the Agenda depends far more on education than on the promulgation of policy or law. As such, those involved with the Agenda aspire to its serving as an example of the very forms of change congruent with the education of this nation's teachers and their education of this nation's children.

The Leadership Program sponsored by the Institute for Educational Inquiry for the members of the NNER, which is described in greater detail in the next chapter, is different from what, in school settings, is called "staff development." It is an occasion for deep examination of the fundamental ideas undergirding the Agenda, with a great deal of give-and-take in the examination of these ideas. If done as successfully as its planners aspire to do it, it becomes a model for how to educate, in the noblest and most general sense of the term.

Simultaneous renewal, then, is a bringing together of educational partners who are participating in the instruction of schoolchildren and their teachers in ways that honor the realities of everyday experience and the ideals of transcendent thought, for the purpose of revitalizing the place and purpose of schools in a democratic society. What makes it *simultaneous* is that all partners to the relationship are engaged together in pursuit of the Agenda for their mutual and shared benefit. What makes it *renewal* is that it is attentive to who the partners are, the contexts of their endeavors, and their aspirations for their sites, while also holding firm to a set of ideals that ground and conditions that foster the sought-after change.

This invigorating and challenging work is anchored in two ways. The first is with a clear, compact specification of ideals, collectively known as the mission for teaching in a democracy. The second is with an extensive set of conditions for how simultaneous renewal can be achieved, that is, the postulates.

The Four-Part Mission

One of the most compelling features of the Agenda for Education in a Democracy is that it is far more than a scholarly treatise or a research program. It is also a change effort taking place in many of this nation's P–12 schools and colleges and universities. When scholarly ideas, research programs, and institutional practices come together in a sustained effort at change, a number of tensions arise. One of the more challenging of these tensions is how to maintain fidelity to basic concepts and principles while acknowledging the need to adapt to time, place, and circumstance. Anyone participating in efforts to change large, complex human systems soon learns that rigidity in the application of ideals can easily wreck a promising effort at change. Yet too much flexibility in the application of the ideals soon overwhelms them, absorbing them so deeply into everyday realities that they no longer serve as valued destinations or even as maps for the journey.

Some parts of the endeavor to promote change must be bedrock; other parts are more flexible and adaptable. The four-part mission is the bedrock of the Agenda for Education in a Democracy. It is a nonnegotiable set of commitments that all participants agree to as part of their voluntary affiliation with the Agenda. Although it is encompassed in four brief statements, it is better understood as an extended argument for what the education of teachers and their students ought to be about. Its purpose is to correct a serious omission in so many proposals for change: the absence of "a vision that encompasses a good and just society, the centrality of education to the renewal of that society, the role of the schools in bringing this education equitably to all, and the kind of preparation teachers require for their stewardship of the nation's schools."[9]

The first two components of the mission statement specify worthy ends for schooling:

1. To facilitate the critical enculturation of the young into a social and political democracy

2. To provide to all children and youths disciplined encounters with all the subject matters of the human conversation

The third and fourth components stipulate essential teaching practices for attaining the ends defined in the first two parts:

3. To engage in pedagogical practices that forge a caring and effective connection between teacher and student

4. To exercise responsible stewardship of our schools[10]

This four-part mission is inseparably bound up with the moral dimensions of education. Often referred to as the grounding for the Agenda, the moral dimensions are the principles and arguments on which the mission is based. These principles and arguments are alluded to in descriptions of the components of the mission presented below, and are developed more extensively in Chapters Three through Seven of this book. Understanding why these moral dimensions are included is critical to understanding the Agenda and therefore worthy of brief comment.

Education, as conceived in the Agenda for Education in a Democracy, is both an epistemic and an ethical undertaking. In other words, it is rooted in matters of knowledge and matters of morality. Too often, when the idea of education is translated into the activity of schooling, the point of the endeavor turns away from learning to become a person of a certain kind to having a person learn certain kinds of things. The latter, epistemic, considerations are very important, but so are the former, moral, considerations. These moral considerations pertain to the ends we have for schooling and how we go about determining these ends and what means we will use to achieve them. Within the Agenda, education is understood as the provision of means to one's fellow human beings to enlarge their knowledge, skill, understanding, autonomy, authenticity, and sense of place in the past, present, and future of the human race. Harvard philosopher Israel Scheffler put the challenge eloquently, contending that the aims of education "must encompass . . . the formation of habits of judgment and the development of character, the elevation of standards, the facilitation of understanding, the development of taste and discrimination, the stimulation of curiosity and wonder, the fostering of style and a sense of beauty, the growth of a thirst for new ideas and visions of the yet unknown."[11]

These moral views of education ground both the ideals and the practice of the Agenda. In concert with John Dewey, participants in the Agenda believe that democratic governance and democratic community offer unparalleled opportunities to realize the moral dimensions of education. This is one reason that the first part of the mission statement pertains to democracy, stressing as it does the preparation of children and youths for productive life in a social and political democracy. As we turn to a brief consideration of each component of the mission, it will become increasingly clear how the moral dimensions of education constitute the framework for the Agenda's four-part mission.

Enculturating the Young into a Democracy

The first part of this mission is the enculturation of the young into a social and political democracy. This purpose encompasses many ideas commonly held to be important objectives of schooling in a democracy: responsible conduct, critical reflection, reasoned argument, civic participation, and integrity and decency in dealings with others. And there is a good deal more. Democracy is not a natural state of the human species. It requires intentional, discerning effort to achieve and then maintain.[12] The young must be prepared to do that work. In the same way that a vocational school might train auto mechanics to care for vehicles, the public schools engage in preparing citizens who will be worthy caretakers of democracy.

Preparing the upcoming generation for this work involves more than preparing them for democratic governance, that is, for such tasks as reading ballots, casting votes, serving as jurors, and writing to their legislators. Democracy, to function well, requires persons of a particular character, as well as of particular skills and understandings.[13] A few examples of the traits of democratic character are tolerance, fairness, caring, openness, critical judgment, and a due regard for evidence. Without these and other related traits, democracy cannot be a way of living and, not being a way of living, can then hardly be a form of political life. This last point appears too little understood in discussions of the place of democracy in the work of the schools. Readying the young for democratic participation requires more than offering lessons in civics; it also entails offering lessons in the formation of character essential to the maintenance and the advancement of democratic life. Hence, the task of readying the young for democratic life is the business of all educators. Teachers cannot be prepared for this work in professional schools alone; this preparation must be part of the larger academic education they receive in elementary and secondary schools and in the academic and professional programs of colleges and universities.[14]

Renewing the responsibilities of public schooling for enculturating the young into a social and political democracy is no minor task. As we once took the air we breathe for granted, believing it would always be pure and wholesome no matter what we poured into it, we appear today to take democracy for granted, assuming that no matter what we do with our schools, democracy will always be there, pure and wholesome. Recent scholarship cautions against this view. Democracy is not a low-maintenance endeavor. Among its requirements is a system of education that prepares people for it—not only to operate it, in the sense of knowing civics, but to *constitute* it, in the sense of practicing civility. Hence the premier position of democratic ideals in the Agenda.

Providing Disciplined Encounters with All Subject Matters

The second major part of the mission underlying the Agenda is providing to all children disciplined encounters with all of the subject matters that comprise the human conversation. This component calls for attention to the many disciplines of human knowledge and understanding so that children become acquainted with these in ways that not only permit their understanding of them, but also lay the groundwork for their eventual contributions to these disciplines. Attention to the disciplines is not all that is demanded by this second purpose, however. It also calls on educators to attend to the disciplines in ways that offer all willing learners fair and equal access to the accumulated knowledge and wisdom of humankind.

Equality of access and ample opportunity to learn are critical features of this second part of the mission statement. Forms of tracking or streaming that would deny equal access and opportunity to learn are alien to this purpose, as are ways of teaching that would, for example, favor the academically motivated with critical inquiry and exploratory discretion while burdening the less motivated with incessant engagement in drill and practice, accompanied by virtually no choice in what to study or how to study it. To obligate schools to provide all children with disciplined encounters with all the subjects of the human conversation is to assert that schools should not be willing instruments for sorting, selecting, and legitimating children into social classes and occupational roles, but rather that schools must provide the young with authentic opportunities to break away from the stereotyping and stratifying influences of class, race, gender, and other similar chance aspects of birth or environment.

In these times of postmodern critiques of conventional conceptions of human knowledge, as well as constructivist conceptions of learning and teaching, a call to provide all children with encounters to the full range of human knowledge may seem unfashionable, perhaps even wrongheaded. That is a risk run by any statement of purpose that aspires to be both brief and clear. However, nothing in this second part of the mission statement prohibits cognitive or constructivist psychologies of learning or teaching. Indeed, to the extent that such approaches assist more children in learning to converse within and across different communities of discourse, and thereby to think and act well within and across these communities, such approaches are highly consistent with the larger purpose of the Agenda. There is, however, some tension between the modernist versions of knowledge implied by the Agenda and the postmodern critiques so much discussed in academia today. This tension is addressed in Chapter Four.

To achieve the ideals contained in the first two parts of the mission, it is vital that educators engage in conduct of a certain kind. The last two parts of the mission statement identify practices essential to that conduct. They are to teach in a manner that nurtures the relationship between teacher and learner, and to serve one's school in a responsible manner. A brief description of each is offered here, with more detail provided in Chapters Six and Seven.

Engaging in a Nurturant Pedagogy

A nurturant pedagogy calls attention to the relational character of teaching and learning and to the demands for sustaining all parts of that relationship. In a genuinely nurturing pedagogy, the teacher is prohibited from retreating exclusively into the confines of content or subject matter, leaving it detached from the life experiences and potential of the learner. The teacher is also prohibited from offering instruction that engages only one dimension of the student, such as the cognitive or the affective aspects of learning. Instead, the teacher must engage the student as both a student and as a fellow human being.

Effecting connections with the student as a person calls for instructional practices of high sophistication—practices that engage all the dimensions of the child's capacity to learn and develop, to the ends of facilitating enculturation into a social and political democracy and providing disciplined encounters with all the subject matters of the human conversation. Such practices cannot be learned in a few methods courses in the college setting, or in a few months of observation and practice in the school setting. A far more integrated and seamless set of connections between P–12 schools and IHEs is needed to cultivate and sustain the competence required for practicing nurturant pedagogy. This task calls for the support of faculty members in arts and sciences, who in their provision of academic instruction can do much to model the acquiring of knowledge and understanding in settings that exhibit high levels of regard for learners and teachers and the connections between them. This task also calls on the schools of education to work with professional practice or partner schools to ensure that a nurturant pedagogy is a feature of both settings and widely modeled for teaching candidates in training at these sites.

To practice a nurturant pedagogy is not, for example, to care more for the student's feelings than for her academic standing, or more for his personal situation than for his mastery of content. A nurturant pedagogy requires attention to all these and more, for it emphasizes the *quality* of the relationship that obtains between student and teacher. This relationship is rooted in the simple realization that teacher and student are co-inhabitants of multiple, interdependent worlds of engagement. Reduced to its simplest terms, the forging of such relationships is why it takes a whole village to raise a child. For the village to raise that child well, it must nurture. A vital part of that nurture is the relationship between the teachers in the village and the children in the village.

Exercising Responsible Stewardship for One's School

Many of us who have worked in schools, or in virtually any other organization, are familiar with the lament that some problem or other is the fault of the "system" (but not of anyone in it). Often tacked on to the gripe is the admonishment, "Why don't they do something about this?" To exercise responsible stewardship is to understand oneself as being among the "they." In the case of schools (elementary, secondary, and collegiate), it is to perceive oneself as occupying more than a classroom or an office. That additional something is the organizational unit of which one is a part—the school or the college or university. To exercise responsible stewardship is to see oneself as part of the larger unit, a unit that advances or declines depending on the commitment its participants make to its health and welfare.

In Chapter Seven, Wilma Smith describes this connection to the organization as "moral stewardship"; others sometimes call it "responsible stewardship." Whatever term is used, the intended meaning is the same: all participants in the unit are individually and collectively obligated to the welfare of the whole as well as to themselves and to selected others who constitute the whole. This vital commitment is easily lost in the isolation that schoolteachers frequently experience behind the classroom door and that college professors experience in the often lonely realm of scholarship. In his discussion of the voices of conscience, Thomas F. Green reminds us that the voice of membership and the voice of sacrifice are essential elements of a moral community.[15] The voice of membership calls on us to understand how our identity and our character are shaped by the groups to which we belong (family, church, neighborhood, workplace) and therefore how dependent we are on the goodness of these units to cultivate identity and character that are worthy. The voice of sacrifice calls on us to forgo constant self-interest, to give up things for ourselves so that others may gain. Green puts this last point eloquently, revealing much of what is meant by responsible stewardship: "The moral practices of promise keeping, truth telling, keeping contracts, preserving confidences—these are the paradigm practices in which the voice of conscience as sacrifice speaks most firmly. The performance of perfectly gratuitous acts of grace and kindness among friends and fellow members offers experiences in self-indifference that may point, in turn, to experiences of self-sacrifice."[16]

The mission is the bedrock of the Agenda. It sets forth two central purposes of schooling and two vital forms of teacher conduct, each and all essential to the work of simultaneous renewal. To say that one is committed to the Agenda for Education in a Democracy is to say that one is committed to this mission. Having a mission, however, is not the same as having a way to carry it out. The mission stipulates the ends, but not the means. For the means, it is necessary to look elsewhere.

The Nineteen Postulates

Perhaps no other gap in the affairs of life looms larger than the one between the ideal and the real. The difference between our most devout desires and what actually lies before us is often so great that we have no idea how to close the gap. The four themes described above, and their associated moral dimensions, make up the ideals of the Agenda for Education in a Democracy. The nineteen postulates attend to the real world before us, stipulating the means for narrowing the gap between the real and the ideal. Calling these conditions *postulates*, as Goodlad does, might lead some to infer that they possess the assurance and coherence of formulaic lines in a geometric proof. That is not the meaning intended. Consider this more hospitable notion of *postulate*, from the *American Heritage Dictionary* (third edition): "a fundamental element; a basic principle."

This definition captures well the meaning of *postulate* intended here. After examining teacher education programs around the nation in the late 1980s, Goodlad and his colleagues argued that certain fundamental conditions must be in place if the education of teachers is to attain the possibilities envisioned in the Agenda for Education in a Democracy.[17] There are nineteen postulates detailing approximately fifty conditions that should be in effect within and across institutions of higher education and partner schools at the elementary and secondary levels. (Appendix A contains a complete list of the postulates.) Inasmuch as these nineteen postulates are described at length in Goodlad's book, *Educational Renewal*, as well as commented on frequently throughout this book, they will not be explored in depth in this chapter. However, it is essential to review them in some modest detail if one is to have a complete picture of the Agenda.

The first three postulates describe what might be thought of as structural or organizational conditions that are required for renewing programs for the education of educators. These postulates stipulate that programs for the education of educators must (1) be adequately supported and vigorously advanced by the institution's top leadership; (2) enjoy parity with other professional education programs, including rewards for participating faculty members; and (3) be autonomous and secure in their borders, with stable budgets and personnel. Given the history of teacher education and school renewal programs in higher education institutions, these conditions are considered essential to undertaking simultaneous renewal in a manner consistent with the mission. All too often the education of teachers has carried a low priority in institutions of higher education, as well as in the competition for resources in P–12 school districts. As such, when leadership changes or funds become tight or new initiatives outside this arena catch the eye of the top administrators, programs for the education of educators are often diminished. Typically programs for the education of educators are in an especially poor position to respond to this reduction in assets because they are not clearly and securely identified within the institution's own table of organization. Postulates One, Two, and Three are designed to correct these problems by stipulating the key institutional conditions necessary if the education of educators and the work of simultaneous renewal are not only to survive, but to thrive.

Postulates Four, Five, and Six establish the necessary conditions for faculty members participating in the education of educators, whether these faculty members are located in schools of education, departments within the arts and sciences, or in partner schools. The conditions stipulate that there must be a clearly identifiable and responsible group of academic and clinical faculty members who are (4) responsible and accountable for selecting diverse groups of students and monitoring their progress, offering the full curriculum sequence, continuously evaluating and improving programs, and facilitating the entry of graduates into teaching careers; (5) fully cognizant of the aims of education and the role of schools in our society and fully committed to selecting and preparing teachers to assume the full range of educational responsibilities required; and (6) engaged in recruiting and selecting a fixed number of candidates who reveal an initial commitment to the moral and enculturating responsibilities of teaching.

As Postulates Four through Six set the conditions for faculty members in the program, Postulates Seven through Twelve describe conditions pertaining to the teacher preparation program and students enrolled in it. These six postulates cover the gamut from who should be considered for admission and what should be included in the program to what kinds of experiences students ought to have and how they ought to be judged in the course of these experiences. Postulate Seven sets out the critical and reflective capabilities of teacher education students, requiring that all candidates possess or acquire the literacy and the critical-thinking abilities associated with the concept of an educated person. Postulates Eight through Twelve make a series of demands on the programs provided to prospective teachers, requiring, in the case of Postulates Eight and

Nine, that there be extensive opportunities for future teachers to make the transition from being persons who acquire knowledge (students) to persons who inquire into knowledge and into pedagogy (teachers). Postulate Ten places on teacher education programs the very heavy burden that they exemplify the same conditions for teaching and learning that future teachers are to establish in their own schools and classrooms. Postulate Eleven calls on preparatory programs to initiate and sustain an attitude of continuous inquiry into the nature of teaching and learning, an attitude that teacher candidates carry over to their own work as teachers. Postulate Twelve addresses one of the most important dimensions of this inquiry, the issues emerging out of the tension between the rights and interests of individual parents and interest groups, on the one hand, and the role of the schools in transcending parochialism and advancing democratic community, on the other.

The twelve postulates examined thus far break down into several categories. Postulates One through Three impose obligations on the top administrators of institutions engaged in the preparation of educators. Postulates Four through Six impose obligations on faculty members participating in programs for the education of educators. Postulates Seven through Twelve outline the purposes and responsibilities of preparation programs with respect to the students enrolled in them.

The next five postulates, numbers Thirteen through Seventeen, impose obligations on the programs themselves, stipulating content, curricula, and practicums. Postulate Thirteen focuses attention on equal access to knowledge, calling on programs to support the preparation of teachers who can ensure equitable access to and active engagement in the best possible P–12 education for all children and youths. Postulate Fourteen calls for the exploration of alternatives, wherein teachers are prepared not only for the schools as they find them, but also as they might be, given various morally grounded theories of education. Postulate Fifteen makes two programmatic demands: first, that there be a wide array of opportunities for observation, simulation, internships, and residencies; and second, that no more students be admitted to the program than can be reasonably accommodated in the available laboratory settings. Postulate Sixteen calls on the program to prepare future teachers for the difficulties of merging theory and practice, for understanding that what seems to work in practice may not be justified in theory or research, and that what seems logically implied by theory or research may not work well in practice. The final postulate in this set, Postulate Seventeen, charges programs for the education of educators to do what far too few actually do: to maintain a connection to the graduates of the program for the purpose of gathering evaluative data to be used for program revision, and to assist the graduates in making an effective transition from inexperienced to experienced teachers.

The eighteenth and nineteenth postulates set forth the necessary social and political contexts needed to sustain strong, renewing programs for the education of educators. Although each of the nineteen postulates has implications for educational policy, these two final postulates are intended specifically to guide policymaking in the area of the education of educators. They require that those engaged in regulating and accrediting teacher education programs, or in the licensing or certificating of teachers, act in ways that do not limit or circumscribe any of the conditions required for attaining the seventeen prior postulates. Further, these postulates call for policies that permit programs for the education of educators to work continuously to improve on the conditions embedded in the postulates without jeopardizing program funding or support.

These nineteen postulates are believed, on the basis of empirical evidence[18] and theory,[19] to delineate the conditions necessary to simultaneous renewal as framed within the Agenda for Education in a Democracy. With the description of these postulates, the fabric of the Agenda should now be fully evident. Knowing what makes up the Agenda and having a grasp of its operation are, however, quite different species of understanding. Let us turn now to what is involved in putting these ideas into practice.

Engaging the Agenda

In a nutshell, the Agenda consists of a single core activity—the simultaneous renewal of schooling and the education of educators—guided by a four-part mission. The success of the endeavor is measured, to a considerable extent, by the seriousness with which the nineteen postulates are observed. These three features should now be familiar to the reader. There is another feature of the Agenda that, although mentioned previously, may not have received the attention it deserves: the connection among elementary, secondary, and tertiary schools or, in more familiar parlance, between grade schools and high schools, on the one hand, and colleges and universities, on the other. The connection was referred to in the earlier discussion of simultaneous renewal, when the notion of renewing both levels of our system of education through collaboration was presented. What was left unstated there was an explanation for *why* it is so important that P–12 schools and IHEs be engaged in simultaneous educational renewal.

Forging connections between P–12 schools and colleges and universities has long been a hallmark of John Goodlad's approach to educational renewal, and it permeates the Agenda. The importance stems from unique and important contributions that each institution makes to the other. Colleges and universities, as sites for the creation and dissemination of disciplinary knowledge and ideas, are essential contributors to the curriculum and the instruction offered in elementary and secondary schools. In order to teach this disciplinary knowledge, elementary and secondary schools must structure, interpret, and present it in ways that enable the young to acquire it. In so doing, the P–12 sector contributes to the general fund of knowledge about learning and teaching. As the schools make these modifications and adaptations, they do far more than merely shape the minds of learners bound for colleges and universities (an important enough reason for colleges and universities to take a great interest in what happens in schools); they ready their students to be citizens, parents, workers, and taxpayers, all of whom affect not only the vitality of our democratic institutions as a whole but also the vitality of our institutions of higher education within the larger democracy.

Elementary and secondary schools, on the other hand, have a considerable stake in how colleges and universities conduct themselves, because the IHEs are among the few formal constituencies in a political economy of democratic capitalism charged with representing truth in relation to power, reason in relation to profit, and justice in relation to efficiency. These representations are essential features of educational theory in a democratic society. As such, institutions of higher education carry obligations to assist the public schools collaboratively to effect a reasonable and often delicate balance between the capitalist values of success and wealth, and the democratic values of liberty and justice. It is no accident that our schools are confronted with effecting this often precarious balance between economic opportunity and democratic community. It has been characteristic of public schooling in America from the time of its founding more than 150 years ago.

At the heart of simultaneous renewal is the call for elementary and secondary schools to work with colleges and universities on common purposes, thereby forging, sustaining, and advancing the larger purposes of both educational sectors in a democratic society. Bringing about this kind of collaboration is a challenging, indeed sometimes herculean, undertaking. Despite its difficulties, it is the journey that all the participants in the Agenda agree to undertake. Yet it remains a journey so fraught with its own kind of perils that those who take it find that having some help along the way is a real advantage. Among the forms of help, one of the most powerful and useful is the Leadership Program, which is the occasion for both this chapter and this book.

The Leadership Program brings together faculty from the public schools, the colleges of education, and the colleges of arts and sciences. During each iteration of the Leadership Program, spanning four sessions in the period of one year, colleagues from all three sectors explore the principles and possibilities of simultaneous renewal, reflect on the meaning and application of the four-part mission, and delve deeply into the postulates in order to understand how they relate to the mission and the objective of simultaneous renewal.

Much of the work of the Leadership Program involves reculti-vating the connections between P–12 schools and higher education institutions, for in some places these bonds have become quite ten-uous, if not altogether torn asunder. The point to be made here is that the Agenda involves more than a set of ideas; it also involves a set of relationships. In order to engage the Agenda, in the sense of bringing it into being, both the ideas and the relationships are essential.

Once assembled as Associates in the Leadership Program, par-ticipants begin their own remarkable journeys. These journeys are described in Parts Three and Four of this book, where participants at selected sites describe their efforts to attain the aspirations of the Agenda for Education in a Democracy. In combination with the deeper analyses of the Agenda described in Part Two, readers will find here a quite extraordinary story of efforts to realize "a vision that encompasses a good and just society, the centrality of educa-tion to the renewal of that society, the role of schools [in] bringing this education equitably to all, and the kind of preparation teach-ers require for their stewardship of the nation's schools."[20]

Notes

1. David Mathews, "The Lack of a Public for Public Schools," *Phi Delta Kappan* 78 (June 1997): 741.

2. Mathews, "Lack of a Public," p. 741.

3. This brief description of the historical challenges facing America's schools is based on Henry J. Perkinson, *The Imperfect Panacea: American Faith in Education, 1865–1990*, 3rd ed. (New York: McGraw-Hill, 1991).

4. On the manner in which the liberal state exercises restraint on con-flicting conceptions of the good life, see Barry L. Bull, "The Limits of Teacher Professionalization," in John I. Goodlad, Roger Soder, and Kenneth A. Sirotnik (eds.), *The Moral Dimensions of Teaching* (San Francisco: Jossey-Bass, 1990), pp. 87–129. See also Kenneth A. Strike, "Professionalism, Democracy, and Discursive Communi-ties: Normative Reflections on Restructuring," *American Educa-tional Research Journal* 30 (Summer 1993): 255–275; and Kenneth A. Strike, "The Moral Role of Schooling in a Liberal Democratic Society," in Gerald Grant (ed.), *Review of Research in Education*, vol. 17 (Washington, D.C.: American Educational Research Asso-ciation, 1991), pp. 413–483.

5. Among those who would vouch for this claim are John Dewey, *Democracy and Education* (New York: Macmillan, 1916); Robert Nisbet, *Community and Power* (New York: Oxford University Press, Galaxy Book, 1962); Robert Putnam, *Making Democracy Work: Civic Traditions in Modern Italy* (Princeton, N.J.: Princeton Univer-sity Press, 1993); and Alexis de Tocqueville, *Democracy in America*, trans. George Lawrence, ed. J. P. Mayer (New York: Harper Peren-nial, 1969).

6. On the relation of education and communities, see John I. Goodlad, *In Praise of Education* (New York: Teachers College Press, 1997).

7. The expression "P–12" refers to school systems that cover pre-kindergarten through grade 12.

8. See, for example, John I. Goodlad, *Educational Renewal: Better Teachers, Better Schools* (San Francisco: Jossey-Bass, 1994), particu-larly chap. 8.

9. Goodlad, *Educational Renewal*, p. 4.

10. For the evolution of these mission statements, see John I. Goodlad, "The Occupation of Teaching in Schools," in Goodlad, Soder, and Sirotnik (eds.), *Moral Dimensions of Teaching*, pp. 17–27; John I. Goodlad, *Teachers for Our Nation's Schools* (San Francisco: Jossey-Bass, 1990), pp. 46–53; and Goodlad, *Educational Renewal*, pp. 4–5.

11. Israel Scheffler, "Basic Mathematical Skills: Some Philosophical and Practical Remarks," *Teachers College Record* 78 (December 1976): 206.

12. Benjamin Barber calls democracy "an extraordinary and rare contrivance of cultivated imagination" (*An Aristocracy of Everyone* [New York: Ballantine Books, 1992], p. 5).

13. On this point, see Barber, *Aristocracy of Everyone*, and Jean Bethke Elshtain, *Democracy on Trial* (New York: Basic Books, 1995).

14. A compelling argument to this effect is offered by Roger Soder in "Teaching in a Democracy: The Role of the Arts and Sciences in the Preparation of Teachers," Occasional Paper no. 19 (Seattle: Center for Educational Renewal, College of Education, University of Washington, 1994).

15. Thomas F. Green, "The Formation of Conscience in an Age of Technology," *American Journal of Education* 94 (November 1985): 1–32. See also Green's forthcoming book, *Voices*, to be published by the University of Notre Dame Press.

16. Green, "Formation of Conscience," pp. 19–20.

17. The study and the first version of the postulates are reported in Goodlad, *Teachers for Our Nation's Schools*. An extended and modestly revised set of postulates is discussed at length in Goodlad, *Educational Renewal*.

18. Such evidence is found in John I. Goodlad, Roger Soder, and Kenneth A. Sirotnik (eds.), *Places Where Teachers Are Taught* (San Francisco: Jossey-Bass, 1990), and in Goodlad, *Teachers for Our Nation's Schools*.

19. For the undergirding theory, see Goodlad, *Educational Renewal* and *In Praise of Education*. In addition, see Goodlad, Soder, and Sirotnik (eds.), *Moral Dimensions of Teaching*; Roger Soder (ed.), *Democracy, Education, and the Schools* (San Francisco: Jossey-Bass, 1996); and John I. Goodlad and Timothy J. McMannon (eds.), *The Public Purpose of Education and Schooling* (San Francisco: Jossey-Bass, 1997).

20. Goodlad, *Educational Renewal*, p. 4.

2

Developing Leadership for Educational Renewal

Wilma F. Smith

Early in February 1992, six senior associates of the Institute for Educational Inquiry (IEI) met in Seattle with the Institute's president, John Goodlad, to ponder the possibilities for strengthening the capacity of leaders in the National Network for Educational Renewal (NNER) settings.[1] Deeply committed to the Agenda for Education in a Democracy—its mission and the conditions necessary for its implementation—we seven were well aware that educators from schools and colleges were the key actors in bringing about renewal. Schoolteachers, principals, and central office administrators, together with professors, deans, and university administrators, were setting forth to develop entirely new organizational structures to nurture collaboration among school and university partners. These educational leaders, personally committed to the beliefs and ideas of the Agenda, would certainly face innumerable challenges as they sought to forge new relationships and to engage their colleagues and officials in the work of simultaneous renewal.

What support could we at the IEI offer them? We decided early in our deliberations that providing an intensive program of study, conversation, reflection, and critical inquiry would be an effective approach, but other questions rapidly arose. What kind of capacity building would be of most value? What core of knowledge would be essential to educational leaders? We put forth ideas and argued about their pros and cons. We wrestled with notions of audience.

Should we gather the deans together for extended sessions around the Agenda? What would the content of such sessions include? How intensive should the development be? How would participants be selected?

Purpose and Themes

Throughout our deliberations, we kept returning to our purpose: to advance the Agenda for Education in a Democracy through the simultaneous renewal of teacher education and P–12 schools. By the close of this brainstorming session, we had crafted a statement of purpose for the Leadership Program: "To empower a cadre of leaders deeply committed to the Agenda who will work to carry out the vision of renewing simultaneously America's schools and the education of educators."

Our rationale for this statement was that leaders from the schools and colleges who immersed themselves in the ideas of the Agenda, inquired deeply into its grounding principles, and developed a common language would maximize their effectiveness as change agents advancing simultaneous renewal. Participants in the Leadership Program would do the following:

- Develop a deeper understanding of the moral dimensions of teaching in a democracy

- Collaborate with P–12 educators, education professors, and arts and sciences professors toward the simultaneous renewal of schools and the education of educators

- Become effective agents of change in their institutions and settings

- Conduct inquiry into the nature of simultaneous renewal in the NNER

- Contribute to the work of simultaneous renewal by serving as presenters, advisers, facilitators, and friendly critics to the sixteen settings of the NNER

Once we had clearly enunciated the Leadership Program's statement of purpose and enumerated our goals for it, design elements began to evolve: the size and composition of cohort groups, the process for securing nominations of participants (called "Leadership Associates"), the number and duration of program sessions, the themes of the curriculum, the readings to be explored, and the nature of the inquiry project. These program elements continue to characterize the Institute's Leadership Program, six years after the first cohort began its journey together. Table 2.1 summarizes the design elements of the Leadership Program.

Throughout the design process, we sought to model our Leadership Program on the conditions described in Goodlad's nineteen postulates (see Appendix A).[2] We believed that constructing a program for leaders of simultaneous renewal efforts should extend our own learning as well as the learning of participants. Further, we wanted this program to make a significant difference in the hearts and lives of the participants from the settings. We did not want the experience to be just one more conference, seminar, inservice session, or faculty development event.

We reviewed a number of studies and theoretical pieces that had something to tell us about creating and sustaining leadership for renewal. For example, we revisited Seymour Sarason's writings on school change and teacher education change,[3] as well as John Goodlad's earlier writings about school renewal.[4] It was important for the participants in our Leadership Program to understand the ecological nature of school change efforts and that the responsibility for engaging others in renewal is a shared one. We wanted to emphasize that renewal is a long-term process that requires changes in attitudes and commitment to the mission of teaching in a democracy.

We also thought deeply about the way our program was being designed and the ways that the Associates would be "improving from within" their school and university cultures, including relationships and "regularities"—the way institutions conduct their day-to-day business.[5] We studied Kenneth Sirotnik's ideas about the school as the center of change,[6] gaining insights into how we could construct

Table 2.1. Leadership Program Design Elements

Element	Description	Rationale
Purpose	Develop at each setting a cadre of leaders who are committed to the Agenda for Education in a Democracy and willing to engage others in the collaborative work	Site leaders who have immersed themselves in the Agenda, together with others from A&S, P–12, and SCDE, will maximize their effectiveness as change agents.
Agenda	Simultaneous renewal of schools and the education of educators	Foundation for the work of the NNER, CER, and IEI
Cohort size	18–21 Associates	Individuals develop trust and understanding in small groups and can participate more.
Associates	Diverse cohort composition in terms of A&S, SCDE, and P–12 representation; gender; ethnicity; experience; and so forth	Collaboration is developed as Associates share language, meaning, and perspectives, and solve common problems.
Nominations	Sought from NNER settings and requiring commitment from individual and from institutional sponsor	Settings can build a cadre of leaders representing the tripartite membership.
Sessions	Four five-day sessions conducted over a year in Seattle	Five days allow time for seminars, conversations, informal networking, reading, thinking; four sessions allow special focus on themes.
Themes of the curriculum	• Enculturating the Young in a Democracy • Access to Knowledge • A Nurturing Pedagogy • Stewardship of Schools . . . each infused with moral dimensions	Cornerstones of the mission of teacher education in a democracy, the grounding of the Agenda for Education in a Democracy
Readings	Writings in education and the arts and sciences, literary pieces, journal articles, and others	Read by Associates before sessions, these form the bases for focused conversations and expression of informed opinions.
Inquiry project	Intensive year-long investigation into an aspect of educational renewal	Furthers the work of the Associate and the NNER as a whole

Note: P–12 = School; SCDE = School, College, Department of Education; A&S = Arts and Sciences.

experiences in the program that would help the Associates think more deeply about whole-school renewal. Michael Fullan's comprehensive reviews of change forces in action reminded us that those who seek to renew schools must have a compelling moral purpose coupled with the skills of an effective change agent.[7] Practical ideas about individual responses to change, developed by Shirley Hord and her colleagues, inspired us to use a simulation entitled, "Making Change for School Improvement."[8] Bruce Joyce and Beverly Showers's work on effective staff development was helpful to us as we considered how to arrange the readings, the sessions, and the inquiry projects so as to maximize the participants' learning over the course of the year.[9] We reviewed Ann Lieberman's edited volume on teacher leadership, finding Part Two, "Building Collaboration and Expanded Leadership Roles and Responsibilities," to be particularly helpful in thinking about the new roles that professors and teachers would be taking on as they led efforts in school renewal and teacher education.[10] Recent works by Thomas Sergiovanni[11] and Roland Barth[12] highlighted their perspectives on the moral leadership required to improve schools from within. These authors helped us think of ways we might introduce meaningful applications of the moral dimensions of teaching into the day-to-day work lives of school and university faculty and administrators.

Jerry Patterson's redefinition of leadership[13] and, during year 3 of the Leadership Program, David Chrislip and Carl Larson's excellent work on collaborative leadership in the larger community helped us to consider the critical nature of the collaborative roles our Associates would play in their work at the settings. We especially appreciated Chrislip and Larson's definition of collaboration as "a mutually beneficial relationship between two or more parties who work toward common goals by sharing responsibility, authority, and accountability for achieving results."[14] We also considered Allan Cohen and David Bradford's work, *Influence Without Authority*, which clarified principles of persuasion and the use of influence for people who do not hold positions of authority within organizations.[15] Robert Kegan and Lisa Lahey reminded us that adults benefit from a constructivist approach to leadership development,[16] and Chris Argyris and Donald Schön affirmed our inclination toward helping the Associates design and carry out interventions that could free their institutions from perpetuating the status quo. Particularly, we sought to provide opportunities for knowing-in-action, reflection-in-action, and reflective practice.[17] To be perfectly honest, we knew that our program would evolve and change if we were to take to heart the advice of these authors. In the words of Karl Weick, "People should visualize organizations as evolutionary systems."[18]

Our next consideration was to identify the themes of the curriculum for the Leadership Program. The moral dimensions of the four components of the teaching mission—enculturating the young in a social and political democracy, providing access to knowledge for all children and youths, engaging in a nurturing pedagogy, and serving as moral stewards of schools—would serve as the overarching foci for the curriculum.[19] We would immerse the setting leaders in readings, conversations, reflection, and inquiry centered on the conditions identified in the nineteen postulates as being necessary to carry out the four-part mission of teaching.

Cohort Size, Participants, and Nominations

Because our pedagogy was intended to enhance conversation and develop respect and camaraderie among the participants from the schools, colleges of arts and sciences, and schools, colleges, or departments of education (SCDEs), we limited the cohort size to eighteen to twenty-one, a group that could be accommodated around a good-sized table within a classroom. The cohort could be subdivided into three groups of six or seven, or two groups of nine to ten. We also took to heart the concept of cohort, as indicated for preservice teachers in Postulate Nine: "Programs for the education of educators must be characterized by a socialization process through which candidates transcend their self-oriented student preoccupations to become more other-oriented in identifying with a culture of teaching."[20] We asked ourselves, for example, how our Leadership Program might give deliberate attention to the socialization of a group of diverse professionals so that they might benefit from one another's expertise and viewpoints in coming to understand the Agenda in new ways. How could we build an atmosphere of trust and collegiality among schoolteachers, school administrators, college faculty, and college administrators from Hawaii to Maine? From differing ethnic, age, gender, and experiential backgrounds? From urban and rural, private and public, small and large schools and universities? We believed that a special relationship would grow among the participants in each cohort as they engaged in substantive conversations about the Agenda over the course of a year's intensive work together and that they would not only renew themselves but find new motivation and understanding through the synthesis of perspectives and ideas of the group.

We debated for some time about who the participants (called the Leadership Associates) should be. Some of us thought that the NNER deans of education should be the initial target group, since they were essentially inaugurating the partnership efforts at the settings. Others argued that the superintendents or school principals should constitute the first leadership cohorts in the program. After some intense deliberation, we agreed that our cohort composition should model the tripartite collaboration described in the postulates: we would design a cohort to include diverse participation from the schools, the colleges of arts and sciences, and the SCDEs. Further, we would seek representation that reflected diversity with respect to gender, professional experience, age, ethnicity, geographic location, and so forth. Table 2.2 shows the diversity and composition of each of the six cohorts of Leadership Associates from 1992 to 1998.

For the selection process for the Associates in the Leadership Program, we sought nominations from the NNER settings. We sent a description of the program and asked for individuals who would not only benefit professionally from the program but would also be in positions of leadership to help advance the work of simultaneous

Table 2.2. Composition of Cohorts in the Institute's Leadership Program

Cohort (Number in Cohort)	Male	Female	White	Nonwhite	P–12	SCDE	A&S	S/U P
Cohort I (19)	10	9	13	6	5	12	1	1
Cohort II (18)	9	9	13	5	6	10	2	0
Cohort III (21)	7	14	9	12	9	8	3	1
Cohort IV (18)	11	7	12	6	6	7	5	0
Cohort V (18)	8	10	17	1	4	8	3	3
Cohort VI (19)	13	6	14	5	6	7	6	0
Total (113)	58	55	78	35	36	52	20	5

Note: P–12 = School; SCDE = School, College, Department of Education; A&S = Arts and Sciences; S/U P = School/University Partnership.

renewal in the settings. In our invitation, we asked the institutional sponsor to make a commitment to supporting the nominee with released time and travel expenses to and from Seattle. We asked the individual nominee to make a commitment to the mission and goals of the Leadership Program, attend all four sessions in full, and prepare for each session by completing the required readings and other assignments.

Sessions, Curriculum, and Readings

We divided the year-long program into four intense sessions, each focusing on the moral dimensions of one of the four themes of teaching and each four and one-half days in duration. A residential program of that length, we thought, would allow the Associates to remove themselves from their day-to-day work, putting them in a retreat situation for an extended period of time, during which they would be able to concentrate on the themes, participate in conversations (formal and informal) with their colleagues, and have time for reflection, a scarce commodity in the lives of most educators. Exhibit 2.1 contains a sample outline of the four sessions centered on the themes of the curriculum.

We wanted the Associates to build on their own diverse experiences while studying an extensive set of common readings to generate new understandings about the renewal of teacher education and schools. Readings were diverse and challenging; they included Mortimer Adler's *We Hold These Truths*, John Goodlad's *Teachers for Our Nation's Schools*, Amy Gutmann's "Democratic Education in Difficult Times," Robert Putnam's *Making Democracy Work*, Alex Kotlowitz's *There Are No Children Here*, and Kazuo Ishiguro's *The Remains of the Day*.[21]

Over the six years of the Leadership Program, we added new texts and struggled with the difficult task of deleting others. For example, Neil Postman's 1995 book, *The End of Education*, was a timely complement to Roger Soder's edited volume, *Democracy, Education, and the Schools*, published in 1996.[22] Jonathan Kozol's

Exhibit 2.1. Outline of Leadership Program Session Themes and Topics

	Day 1	Day 2	Day 3	Day 4	Day 5
Session 1	Meaning of Conversation	Moral Dimensions	Unpacking the Postulates	The Public Purpose of Education and Schooling	The Human Conversation
	Moral Dimensions	Simultaneous Renewal	Partner Schools		Implications for Practice
	The Inquiry Project	Implications for Practice: A Scenario	Issues of Simultaneous Renewal	Enculturating the Young in a Democracy	Debriefing the Session

	Day 6	Day 7	Day 8	Day 9	Day 10
Session 2	Reflections from Session 1	Access to Knowledge: Jigsaw Activity	Persuasion and Argument	Access to Knowledge: Children at Risk	Implications: A Scenario
	Access to Knowledge	Unpacking the Postulates	Constructing a Language of Collaboration	Access to Knowledge: Multiple Intelligences	Synthesis and Debriefing the Session
	Examining Our Practices	Inquiry Projects	Visit: Partner Elementary Schools	Implications for Our Work	

	Day 11	Day 12	Day 13	Day 14	Day 15
Session 3	Reflections from Session 2	A Nurturing Pedagogy: Implications for Practice	Visit: Partner Secondary Schools	Collaborating for Educational Renewal	Implications for Our Work
	A Nurturing Pedagogy	Unpacking the Postulates	Debriefing School Visit	Inquiry Projects: Critique One Another	Debriefing the Session
	Small Groups: Persuasion Activity	Collaborating for School Renewal	Collaborating for Curriculum Renewal		

	Day 16	Day 17	Day 18	Day 19	Day 20
Session 4	Reflections from Session 3	The Educative Community	Inquiry Project Reports: Round I	Creating a Renewing Community	Predicting the Work of Change in Our Settings
	Moral Stewardship of the Schools	Making Democracy Work	Inquiry Project Reports: Round II	Becoming Agents for Change: A Simulation	Planning to Stay Connected
	Small Groups: Implications for Practice	Creating a Center of Pedagogy: A Scenario	Inquiry Project Reports: Round III		Final Debriefing and Evaluation of the Program

Amazing Grace challenged us in powerful ways to ensure equal access to education for all children.[23] And John Goodlad's most recent book, *In Praise of Education*, synthesized many aspects of simultaneous renewal in today's democracy.[24] One of our readings, Josiah Auspitz's "Michael Oakeshott: 1901–1990," served as the text through which we introduced every cohort to the elements of "conversation," as practiced throughout our Leadership Program.[25] This article was not easy to conceptualize, and Associates had a wide variety of reactions to it. However, it stood the test of time and became our standard opener for everyone. Today, a number of Associates have used this same article to introduce "conversation" to others at their settings. Our biggest challenge with the readings was to allocate enough time to discuss them specifically and to relate key concepts to the overarching Agenda for Education in a Democracy: its mission, its relation to the postulates, and the implications it held for the Associates in their home partnerships.

Inquiry Project

The final design element, the inquiry project, was incorporated into the program through having each participant design and carry out a year-long inquiry into some aspect of simultaneous renewal. Associates were asked to examine their current educational practices and analyze whether these practices advanced the four-part mission of teaching for simultaneous renewal. The project would fulfill four goals: (1) enhancing the individual's learning through reflection, research, discussion, and writing about critical issues related to the simultaneous renewal of schools and the education of educators; (2) extending the individual's knowledge through collaboration with other members of the cohort; (3) supporting renewal efforts at each NNER setting; and (4) providing opportunities to share the knowledge derived from the project through presentations and publication. Each year, the Associates have presented their inquiry projects at the annual meeting of the NNER, which brings together representatives from each of the sixteen settings and all of the graduates of the Leadership Program cohorts. In this way, the third goal of the Leadership Program—benefiting the work of the entire net-work—is supported. Over the course of the six years, Associates have inquired into nearly every aspect of simultaneous renewal, including school-university partnerships, involvement of the arts and sciences, partner schools (professional development schools), renewing teacher education, curriculum and assessment, new orga-nizational structures such as centers of pedagogy, infusing the moral dimensions into the curriculum for educators, policy development at local and state levels, developing democratic community, and reflective practice. A number of the inquiry projects have resulted in publications and presentations at major conferences.

The "teaching staff" for the Leadership Program has included as regular presenters and facilitators senior associates John Goodlad, Richard Clark, Wilma Smith, and Roger Soder of the Center for Educational Renewal and the Institute for Educational Inquiry. Other senior associates—Mona Bailey, Phyllis Edmundson, Robert Egbert, Calvin Frazier, Donna Hughes, and Kenneth Sirotnik—have shared particular aspects of their expertise.

Seven leaders in educational reform have accepted appointments as senior fellows of the Institute for Educational Inquiry, sharing their written work and participating as keynote presenters for the Lead-ership Program: James Comer (child psychology and development, Yale University), Linda Darling-Hammond (educational policy, Stanford University), Gary Fenstermacher (educational policy and philosophy, University of Michigan), Howard Gardner (education and psychology, Harvard University), Donna Kerr (philosophy of education, University of Washington), Henry Levin (economics and higher education, Stanford University), and Theodore Sizer (edu-cation, Brown University).[26]

A Continuing Story

Having completed the design for the Leadership Program and secured philanthropic support, we began in August 1992 with our first cohort of nineteen Associates. The seven of us who began this journey together have seen the results of this program expand and succeed beyond our wildest imagination. The Leadership Program has become a vital force for change and renewal among the Associates, evidenced by their own words and by those of others across the NNER and beyond. Since 1993, graduates of the program have replicated its design in their own settings, creating local leadership programs for educators and community members to engage increasing numbers of others in the work of simultaneous renewal. In order for the renewal process to thrive and build momentum over time, leadership capacities must be developed in a critical mass of educators within each setting. School and university leaders must continually seek to share leadership so that the agenda permeates every facet of their collaborative work.

Notes

1. The seven senior associates who participated in this meeting were Richard Clark, former deputy superintendent of the Bellevue (Washington) School District; Gary Fenstermacher, professor of education at the University of Arizona (now at the University of Michigan); John Goodlad, professor of education at the University of Washington, director of the Center for Educational Renewal at the University of Washington, and president of the Institute for Educational Inquiry; David Imig, executive director of the American Association of Colleges for Teacher Education; Kenneth Sirotnik, professor of education at the University of Washington; Wilma Smith, former superintendent of schools, Mercer Island (Washington) School District; and Roger Soder, associate director of the Center for Educational Renewal and vice president of the Institute for Educational Inquiry.

2. We were especially concerned with fulfilling the conditions of Postulate Ten, which states: "Programs for the education of educators must be characterized in all respects by the conditions for learning that future teachers are to establish in their own schools and classrooms."

3. We gained much from three of Seymour Sarason's many writings on change and renewal: *The Culture of the School and the Problem of Change,* 2nd ed. (Boston: Allyn & Bacon, 1982); *The Case for Change: Rethinking the Preparation of Educators* (San Francisco: Jossey-Bass, 1993); and *School Change: The Personal Development of a Point of View* (New York: Teachers College Press, 1995).

4. In addition to Goodlad's *Teachers for Our Nation's Schools* (San Francisco: Jossey-Bass, 1990) and *Educational Renewal* (San Francisco: Jossey-Bass, 1994), we found great value in two earlier books: *The Dynamics of Educational Change* (New York: McGraw-Hill, 1975) and his edited book, *The Ecology of School Renewal* (Chicago: University of Chicago Press, 1987).

5. See Seymour B. Sarason, *Revisiting "The Culture of the School and the Problem of Change"* (New York: Teachers College Press, 1996), p. 4. *The Culture of the School and the Problem of Change* was originally published in 1971 by Allyn & Bacon.

6. Kenneth A. Sirotnik, "The School as the Center of Change," in Thomas J. Sergiovanni and John H. Moore (eds.), *Schooling for Tomorrow: Directing Reforms to Issues That Count* (Boston: Allyn & Bacon, 1989) is particularly helpful in emphasizing the idea that "educators in schools must become empowered agents in their own school improvement process" (p. 90).

7. In the first two years of the Leadership Program, we referred often to Michael G. Fullan and Suzanne Stiegelbauer, *The New Meaning of Educational Change,* 2nd ed. (New York: Teachers College Press, 1991). In 1993 we were delighted with Fullan's synthesis of school and teacher education reform efforts and his linking "moral purpose and change agentry" (p. 8), in Michael Fullan, *Change Forces: Probing the Depths of Educational Reform* (Bristol, Pa.: Falmer Press, 1993).

8. Shirley M. Hord, William L. Rutherford, Leslie Huling-Austin, and Gene E. Hall, *Taking Charge of Change* (Alexandria, Va.: Association for Supervision and Curriculum Development, 1987). The simulation board game, Making Change for School Improvement, was produced by The NETWORK, Inc. (Andover, Mass., 1988).

9. Bruce R. Joyce and Beverly Showers, *Power in Staff Development through Research on Training* (Alexandria, Va.: Association for Supervision and Curriculum Development, 1983).

10. Ann Lieberman (ed.), *Building a Professional Culture in Schools* (New York: Teachers College Press, 1988).

11. Thomas J. Sergiovanni, *Moral Leadership: Getting to the Heart of School Improvement* (San Francisco: Jossey-Bass, 1992).

12. Roland S. Barth, *Improving Schools from Within: Teachers, Parents, and Principals Can Make the Difference* (San Francisco: Jossey-Bass, 1990).

13. Jerry L. Patterson, *Leadership for Tomorrow's Schools* (Alexandria, Va.: Association for Supervision and Curriculum Development, 1993).

14. David D. Chrislip and Carl E. Larson, *Collaborative Leadership: How Citizens and Civic Leaders Can Make a Difference* (San Francisco: Jossey-Bass, 1994), p. 5.

15. Allan R. Cohen and David L. Bradford, *Influence Without Authority* (New York: Wiley, 1991). Particularly useful were the ideas related to "currencies frequently valued in organizations" (p. 79). When considering how the three partners in simultaneous renewal—the faculties of the schools, the colleges of education, and the colleges of arts and sciences—might collaborate to achieve better teachers and better schools, it is useful to be candid about legitimate self-interests of the parties and to identify how each may benefit from the collaboration.

16. Robert Kegan and Lisa L. Lahey, "Adult Leadership and Adult Development—A Constructivist View," in Barbara Kellerman (ed.), *Leadership: Multidisciplinary Perspectives* (Englewood Cliffs, N.J.: Prentice-Hall, 1984).

17. Chris Argyris and Donald Schön, *Theory in Practice: Increasing Professional Effectiveness* (San Francisco: Jossey-Bass, 1992). Particularly helpful were discussions of five central issues for professional practice and education: whom professionals serve, whether professional schools prepare competent practitioners, whether professionals

benefit from cumulative learning, whether reform is possible, and whether self-actualization is possible in professional practice (pp. 139–145).

18. Karl E. Weick, *The Social Psychology of Organizing* (Reading, Mass.: Addison-Wesley, 1979), p. 260.

19. See Goodlad, *Teachers for Our Nation's Schools*, pp. 46–53, 250–256; and John I. Goodlad, "The Occupation of Teaching in Schools," in John I. Goodlad, Roger Soder, and Kenneth A. Sirotnik (eds.), *The Moral Dimensions of Teaching* (San Francisco: Jossey-Bass, 1990), pp. 20–27.

20. Goodlad, *Educational Renewal*, p. 83.

21. Mortimer J. Adler, *We Hold These Truths* (New York: Macmillan, 1987); John I. Goodlad, *Teachers for Our Nation's Schools* (San Francisco: Jossey-Bass, 1990); Amy Gutmann, "Democratic Education in Difficult Times," *Teachers College Record* 92 (Fall 1990): 7–20; Robert D. Putnam, *Making Democracy Work: Civic Traditions in Modern Italy* (Princeton: Princeton University Press, 1993); Alex Kotlowitz, *There Are No Children Here: The Story of Two Boys Growing Up in the Other America* (New York: Doubleday, 1991); and Kazuo Ishiguro, *The Remains of the Day* (New York: Vintage, 1990). We have used *Remains of the Day* at the end of each cohort year to elicit reflection on professional and personal aspects of our lives and the meaning of our work.

22. Neil Postman, *The End of Education* (New York: Random House, 1995); Roger Soder (ed.), *Democracy, Education, and the Schools* (San Francisco: Jossey-Bass, 1996).

23. Jonathan Kozol, *Amazing Grace* (New York: Random House, 1996).

24. John I. Goodlad, *In Praise of Education* (New York: Teachers College Press, 1997).

25. Josiah L. Auspitz, "Michael Oakeshott: 1901–1990," *American Scholar* 60 (Summer 1991): 351–370. See Roger Soder's discussion of this piece in Chapter Three.

26. Over the six-year life of the Leadership Program, Associates have read the following writings of the senior fellows: James P. Comer,

School Power (New York: Macmillan, 1982); Linda Darling-Hammond, "Education for Democracy" (inaugural lecture, William F. Russell Professor in the Foundations of Education, Teachers College, Columbia University) and "Developing Professional Development Schools: Early Lessons, Challenge, and Promise," in Linda Darling-Hammond (ed.), *Professional Development Schools: Schools for Developing a Profession* (New York: Teachers College Press, 1994); Gary D Fenstermacher, *On Knowledge and Its Relation to the Human Conversation*, Work in Progress Series no. 6 (Seattle: Institute for Educational Inquiry, 1997); Howard Gardner, *Frames of Mind* (New York: Basic Books, 1983) and, with Veronica Boix-Mansilla, "Teaching for Understanding—Within and Across the Disciplines," *Educational Leadership* 51 (February 1994): 14–18; Donna H. Kerr, *Beyond Education: In Search of Nurture*, Work in Progress Series no. 2 (Seattle: Institute for Educational Inquiry, 1993) and "Democracy, Nurturance, and Community," in Roger Soder (ed.), *Democracy, Education, and the Schools* (San Francisco: Jossey-Bass, 1996); Henry M. Levin, "Accelerated Schools After Eight Years," in Leona Schauble and Robert Glaser (eds.), *Innovations in Learning: New Environments for Education* (Mahwah, N.J.: Erlbaum, 1996); and Theodore R. Sizer, *Horace's School* (Boston: Houghton Mifflin, 1992) and *Horace's Hope* (Boston: Houghton Mifflin, 1996).

Part II

Advancing the Agenda

The Core Curriculum

3

"To Ourselves and Our Posterity"
Enculturating the Young into a Democracy

Roger Soder

Echoing a biblical sentiment, the narrator of *The Great Gatsby* tells us that "conduct can be founded on the hard rock or the wet marshes." Nick Carraway is tolerant, though: "After a certain point I don't care what it's founded on," he says.[1] But I suspect Nick cares a good deal more than he lets on—that, after all, is a central point of his narrative—and we must care too. There is a lot of difference between hard rock and wet marshes and between the two considerably various ways of viewing the goods of the world and how we deal with others in terms of prudence or practical wisdom. Choices must be made. And within the realm of education and educational leadership, it is particularly important not only that we understand that we do indeed have to choose but also that we understand the bases of what we demand of others in terms of their conduct and what we need to demand of ourselves.

These are matters of central concern in the constitution of our Leadership Program. Choice is necessary, but in order to choose well we must have grounding. With Camus, we must say, "To live is also to act. To act in the name of what?"[2] The work of the Institute for Educational Inquiry and the Center for Educational Renewal has as its chosen grounding the moral and political dimensions of teaching and learning in a democracy. Part of that grounding is an argument about the relationship of democracy and education and schools that runs along the following lines.

First, do we want to have a democracy? This is not an idle question by any means. Many people in many parts of the world do not think democracy is a good form of government. But assuming that our Associates plump for democracy, then the next question we must ask is, Are there conditions necessary for the functioning of a healthy democracy? That is, are there some conditions that have to be in place, or can a democracy somehow exist without recourse to context? Here, Dewey provides a useful guide. He talks of the need for

> discussion of cultural conditions, conditions of science, art, morals, religion, education and industry, so as to discover which of them in actuality promote and which retard the development of the native constituents of human nature. If we want individuals to be free we must see to it that suitable conditions exist:—a truism which at least indicates the direction in which to look and move.
>
> It tells us among other things to get rid of the ideas that lead us to believe that democratic conditions automatically maintain themselves, or that they can be identified with fulfillment of prescriptions laid down in a constitution.[3]

Assuming that there are conditions requisite to a healthy democracy, then what are they? During the course of the Leadership Program sessions, we discuss eleven such conditions, recognizing that the eleven do not constitute an exhaustive list.

1. *Trust.* Without trust, people will not be able to enter into the kinds of long-term relationships necessary for political and social interaction in a democracy.[4]

2. *Exchange.* People must be able to exchange goods and services in order to survive in a democracy. The act of exchange is a way of building and sustaining relationships.[5]

3. *Social capital.* People need to have social and political skills in order to work together, as opposed to simply accepting orders.[6]

4. *Respect for equal justice under law.* If there is no justice, we have no recourse other than self-interest, which is ultimately self-defeating.[7]

5. *Respect for civil discourse.* If people cannot talk to each other, advance ideas, adduce evidence, and weigh and consider alternatives, all without resorting to physical or verbal violence, democracy will not survive.[8]

6. *Recognition of the need for e pluribus unum.* The American democracy is not experienced by isolated groups, each celebrating its own peculiar identity. There must be some sort of glue that holds the whole together. But there must be respect for individual and group differences as well. The trick here is to acknowledge and deal with the constant tension between the *unum* and the *pluribus*.[9]

7. *Free and open inquiry.* How can we talk intelligently if we cannot inquire into what is going on—and not just at the margins, but at the core?[10]

8. *Knowledge of rights.* If we do not know what our rights are, we will have difficulty exercising them. A people without knowledge of its rights can hardly be expected to participate effectively in a democracy.[11]

9. *Freedom.* As has been said by many, one must have the power to exercise freedom and the insight to value it. Both conditions are necessary.[12]

10. *Recognition of the tension between freedom and order.* As Leo Strauss reminds us, we have to deal with the "liberty that is not license and the order that is not oppression."[13]

11. *Recognition of the difference between a persuaded audience and a more thoughtful public.* We must know this difference ourselves and we must demand that our leaders know it too.[14]

If these conditions (or a similar set) are necessary for a healthy democracy, then the next question we must ask is: Are people born knowing about these conditions and how to create and maintain them, or do they have to learn about them? Assuming that there is no genetic programming that enables us to know about such matters as justice and law and freedom from the time of birth, and assuming that we choose learning, then the next question is obvious: How are people to learn these things? And given the nature of a democracy and that we want all people to have a working knowledge of how to create and maintain the necessary conditions, then we have to determine probabilities—specifically, where is it most likely that the greatest proportion of the people will be able to gain such a working knowledge? In *Rights Talk*, Mary Ann Glendon indicates a similar concern: "Where do citizens acquire the capacity to care about the common good? Where do people learn to view others with respect and concern, rather than to regard them as objects, means, or obstacles? Where does a boy or girl develop the healthy independence of mind and self-confidence that enable men and women to participate effectively in government and to exercise responsible leadership?"[15]

It comes as no great surprise that our argument leads us to schools—public schools—performing their public function.[16] Moreover, in their structure and actions, schools and the people in them must themselves exemplify democratic practice and the conditions necessary for democracy.

If we are going to take seriously the implications of this argument and claimed grounding, then we must focus on the conduct, on the *character*, of those who would be educators. We must recall John Henry Newman's observation that "in morals, as in physics, the stream cannot rise higher than the source."[17] Even more so, we must focus on our own conduct, our own character, and not be too preoccupied with those of distant others. We must, in short, apply to our own lives the commentary of Robert Coles on George Eliot and *Middlemarch*: "George Eliot can't seem to stop pressing the strange notion that the only kind of moral imagination that matters is the kind given expression by our daily lives, and that such a moral imagination is by no means the exclusive property of those who have acquired university degrees, reputation, money, or power."[18]

As educators, then, concerned about our own character and ultimately about that of the young, we need to pay particular attention to the enculturating function of schools. The young are not genetically programmed to take on their responsibilities for living and working in a democracy. As we have seen, these responsibilities, and a willingness to assume them, must be taught. If they are going to be taught, then we have to attend to the character of those who would do the teaching. What do educators need to know, and how do they need to behave in order to fulfill their responsibilities? How are schools and classrooms to be structured to help create the conditions for democracy? These questions, and related ones, guided us in planning and implementing the Leadership Program overall and, in particular, those parts of the program that center on enculturation of the young into a democracy.

During the six years of the Leadership Program, we have used more than one hundred texts as sources for framing and considering these questions. Of these, about one-fourth deal directly with democracy, the moral and political dimensions of teaching, and enculturation of the young. We use the texts to introduce content. We also talk about how to approach and analyze the texts in order to help participants gain a better understanding of textual analysis and close reading, as well as a sense of the kinds of community created by an author and a collection of readers. We talk, too, about an ethics of reading. We argue that it is difficult—and unethical— to comment in any depth on a text one has not read, or has not read very carefully. Moreover, we consider Goethe's notion that "if we wish to reproach an author with obscurity let us first look within ourselves to see if everything is quite clear there. Very plain writing becomes illegible at dusk."[19]

Beyond the reading and analysis of texts, we offer Leadership Associates opportunities to participate in experiences that we trust will lead to a deeper understanding of democracy and enculturation. We spend a great deal of time in talking about how to talk—about texts, about ourselves, about our colleagues, about what we think is going on that we like, about what is going on that we do not like. This is not idle chatter, nor is it specious hairsplitting. Talking is a critical element in a democracy; it is, in the end, what we mean by civil discourse: a way of conversing about the world that increases respect for individual difference and concern for the common weal. "The mutual understanding and communication discovered by rebellion can survive only in the free exchange of conversation. Every ambiguity, every misunderstanding, leads to death; clear language and simple words are the only salvation from this death."[20] We also subscribe to Camus's notion that "our words commit us and . . . we should remain faithful to them. Naming an object inaccurately means adding to the unhappiness of this world."[21]

It is from this argument, particularly the list of hypothesized conditions, that we derive our texts, our approaches to them, and the other kinds of experiences participants in the program share. What we are about, then, is very close to what Ralph Lerner suggests we might well be about: "Speaking and listening, thinking and judging, in other words, learning to behave like a people who deserve a free society and are capable of sustaining it."[22]

We place considerable emphasis on all four of Lerner's designated activities. In particular, in our approach to texts, we place considerable emphasis on how we are going to talk—about both the text in question and how to talk with each other about the text. In addition to reading and discussing texts, all Leadership Associates participate in a particular kind of talk, namely, a persuasive speech. During the second session, Associates are introduced to a key element of leadership: the persuasion of others. They consider persuasion in terms of its ethical and ecological implications and in terms of some of the conditions necessary for a democracy (for example,

respect for civil discourse and the need to distinguish between a persuaded audience and a more thoughtful public). During the second
session, they are introduced to the persuasion exercise: a speech
they will give to their colleagues during the third session.

In what follows, I consider selected texts that undergird the
democracy and enculturation part of the Leadership Program; I then
discuss the persuasion exercise and conclude with a short commentary on the whole.

Texts

Of the twenty-four texts dealing with aspects of democracy and
enculturation, five are particularly illustrative of the content and
pedagogical approaches.

Josiah Lee Auspitz, "Michael Oakeshott: 1901–1990"

This charming and insightful essay on political philosopher Oakeshott
appeared in the *American Scholar* not too long before the first cohort
of Leadership Associates gathered in Seattle.[23] Several of us had read
the essay, but John Goodlad recognized its particular pedagogical
potential. He started off the first cohort with Auspitz's gentle but
penetrating consideration of Oakeshott's work and way of living and
has used it with all subsequent cohorts, with little variation in
approach and always to good end. Were the essay not used at the
beginning of each cohort's first session—when the new cohort is
getting itself sorted out, with participants trying to determine who
they are, who they are going to be, and who everyone else is and is
going to be—it would be most useful to videotape Goodlad and the
group as they begin to talk about Oakeshott, themselves, and how
they are going to talk.

What happens in each of these opening sessions is quite different from what most of us have experienced in similar settings. Most
of us have sat around the table during an introductory session, with
each member taking a minute or two to tell where he or she is from,

his or her institutional affiliation, favorite books or flowers (or whatever the facilitator has asked of us to help break the ice). As the "tell who you are" task moves from person to person, there often is less listening to others and more private calculation as to what each of us wants to say. The task is, after all, a daunting one. What should I decide to say about myself? Should I tell a joke, come up with a clever quip or, even better (or worse), a pun? Should I make reference to some of my writings—or would that appear too self-serving? Should I comment on what the previous person said—it was curious and thought provoking, after all—or would that appear off-task?

The approach Goodlad uses with the piece on Oakeshott eschews this traditional approach. Goodlad, in fact, tells the participants that they will not be using that approach. Rather, he says, they will begin a conversation about Oakeshott and about Auspitz's essay. Participants have had several months to read the essay. They are ready to begin. Goodlad outlines the rules of discourse: anyone who speaks about the text first needs to tell the others his or her name, job function, and institutional affiliation. Goodlad then frames a general question about some aspect of the piece, looks around, selects a person to provide an opening response, and for the next two hours Leadership Associates are enthralled by Auspitz, Oakeshott, Goodlad, and each other. One way or another, all participants speak up, either voluntarily or because they are called on. By the end of the discussion, much has happened.

First, participants have gained some sense of the distinction between casual off-the-cuff opinions and viewpoints that have been developed with some attention to logic, reflection, analysis, and consideration. They have, in effect, begun to engage in serious conversation about a text and about how to engage in serious conversation.

Second, because the focus of the conversation is on the text, participants have learned that careful reading is required if they are to participate on the "informed opinion" level. My own sense is that as the years progressed, so did the level of careful reading of the text in advance of the discussion. Perhaps because many of the later participants had talked with earlier members about the program (and about this first session in particular), some socialization took place.

Third, members have learned quite a bit about their colleagues by being able to identify this person or that with a given argument or position on the text. I suspect that it is probably easier to get to know people through active intellectual engagement than through trying to remember who told the chicken joke or the bad pun or who was the associate dean at whatever institution.

The opening of the first session, surely one of the most important parts of any kind of group work, is by all accounts very effective. It remains salient years later and is often imitated. My own sense is that for Goodlad the text is not the critical factor. That is, armed with any text of any reasonable depth and significance and thus open to a variety of interpretations, Goodlad could accomplish what he set out to do.[24]

George Orwell, "Politics and the English Language"

Orwell's "Politics and the English Language" is used in the second session.[25] Given that a major theme running through the program is the fundamental relationship of language, politics, and morality, the choice of this particular Orwell essay appeared obvious to us. "Politics" probes this theme, making the reader feel (we trust) uncomfortable in the recognition that one's own use of language can easily lead to immoral ends and, indeed, be immoral itself. Orwell says that words are important, the meanings of words are important, and how words are put together is a moral matter for both author and reader. Orwell is close to Camus in many respects, and certainly in his sense of the potential for language to obscure evil. Camus, for example, wrote, "It is worth noting that the language peculiar to totalitarian doctrines is always a scholastic or administrative language."[26]

Much of the task of addressing the texts focuses on the task itself. In each cohort, some participants are not accustomed to close textual reading—the kind of reading Orwell demands if we are to make sense of his arguments. Beyond the difficulties of approaching a text in an unfamiliar way, we are on unfamiliar terrain once we start to deal with content. We use language in habitual ways—it hardly could be otherwise—and Orwell's blunt thesis of the relationship between sloppy thinking and sloppy writing takes many people by surprise. We use the Orwell text in a somewhat stealthy way. Just when you think it is safe not to have to think about language and its relationship to politics and morality, Orwell stops you cold, flinging his propositions at you in a way difficult to avoid.

We try to link the texts chosen for the program with other texts by the same authors or dealing with similar ideas. Thus, the conversations about Orwell and "Politics" move on to *Animal Farm* and *1984*. We are now starting to use some of Orwell's other essays too—such as "Shooting an Elephant," his brutal account of his own willingness to behave badly just because he is a bureaucrat and does not want to play the fool—as examples of how Orwell puts his own strictures about clear writing into practice. We will be using his "A Hanging" for similar reasons.

James Boyd White, "Constituting a Culture of Argument: The Possibilities of American Law"

Less familiar to most than the Orwell essay, this selection, by a professor of law, professor of English, and adjunct professor of classical languages, provides a startlingly new reading of an old and familiar text, the Declaration of Independence, to show again the relationship of language, politics, and morality.[27]

We could have used any number of White's brilliant analyses of texts—he treats, among others, the *Iliad*, Plato's *Gorgias*, and Austen's *Emma*—but we thought it made more sense to take a familiar old piece, one comfortable, even platitudinous, and let White work his magic. By looking at the Declaration in new and exciting ways, we reasoned, participants might become a bit more aware of the moral and political implications of their own familiar writing.

White argues that "social and political institutions . . . are not objects, although that is how we often talk about them, but complex sets of understandings, relations, and activities. They are ways of talking that can be learned and understood."[28] Further, echoing Lerner, he asks us to be better judges: "If we can find a way to describe and understand the relations established by [texts] with their readers, we shall have a ground for judging more moral and explicit political relations as well."[29] White also argues that the reader, of both texts and people, changes as he or she reads: one is always learning to see more clearly what is there and to respond to it more fully, or at least differently, and in the process, one is oneself always changing, in relation to friend or to text. The reader who knows Jane Austen well, for example, will not be like every other reader who knows her well, but he will be deeply different from what he would have been had he never read her at all. The meaning of a text is not simply to be found within it, to be dug out like a kind of mineral treasure, nor does it come from the reader as if he were a kind of movie projector. It resides in the life of reading itself, to which both text and reader contribute.[30]

Participants generally take to the White essay. Many are surprised to find a familiar text much more complex than they had thought. Others have difficulty moving beyond their personal opinions about Jefferson, his hypocrisy, his sexism. Airing these difficulties and opinions sometimes leads to useful conversation as to how we might reasonably and fairly judge a text and its author. The conversation sometimes strays from engaging White's particular arguments, but we nonetheless talk about how we are going to talk—a matter of considerable concern to White—and thus we are on target. In other instances, the difficulties and personal opinions are impossible to transcend, and the conversation stops.

We also use the White excerpt to entice thoughtful participants into a further exploration of *When Words Lose Their Meaning* and other of White's books.[31] White wears his learning lightly in helping us become better, more ethical, readers. (If this appears to be an unabashed attempt to get you to stop right now and turn to White, you have the sentiment right.)

Robert Putnam, *Making Democracy Work:*
Civic Traditions in Modern Italy

In the early 1970s, Italy changed from a central government to a collection of some thirty states. Over the next fifteen years, Robert Putnam and his colleagues studied what happened. How did people come to govern themselves? What contributed to different practices of government? What accounts for different patterns of participation? *Making Democracy Work* provides in just two hundred pages the results of Putnam's research, a chapter on the history of Italy and its governmental styles since the 1200s, and a chapter on general themes and implications.[32]

We used *Making Democracy Work* as part of the program for Cohorts I through IV. It is a superb book, and the review of it in the *Economist* is quite on the mark: "Here is a book that masquerades as a routine study of Italian Regional Government but is actually a great work of social science, worthy to rank alongside de Tocqueville, Pareto, and Weber."[33] Even if one disagrees with Putnam's specified conditions for a healthy democracy (trust, exchange, and social capital are key variables for him), thoughtful readers are still left with the task of defining *some* set of conditions and defining further whether those conditions are mutable and sustainable.

I do not know if the text was useful to participants in the Leadership Program. For a variety of reasons, and despite a wide variety of pedagogical approaches, most members of Cohorts I through IV did not warm to Putnam. It is a curious business. Putnam's methodology seems reasonable enough. The text is easy to read. We are not dealing with, say, the interminable regression analyses found in most articles in the *American Political Science Review*. Perhaps the lack of resonance has to do with the data sources. Some of the Associates publicly (and more of them privately) asked why we were talking about Italy—either historic Italy or Italy in the 1970s. What did

Italy have to do with American schools? I fear that for all the insistence about diversity and multiculturalism, we have not moved very far beyond clearly obvious ethnic balancing in textbook photos or the bloodlines of authors. Perhaps we are still learning, as Mary Catherine Bateson argues in *Composing a Life*, that

> human beings tend to regard the conventions of their own societies as natural, often as sacred. One of the great steps forward in history was learning to regard those who spoke odd-sounding languages and had different smells and habits as fully human, as similar to oneself. The next step from this realization, one which we have still not fully made, is the willingness to question and purposefully alter one's own conditions and habits, to learn by observing others.[34]

Putnam has written shorter pieces, including "Bowling Alone," and "What Makes Democracy Work?"[35] His ideas are provocative and certainly worth discussing; perhaps these shorter essays might serve to stimulate conversation without the apparent barriers that the longer work poses. At the very least, Putnam must be recognized for his important reminder, à la Dewey, that democracy has conditions attached to it and we need to give extended thought to those conditions and how to create and sustain them.

Roger Soder (ed.), *Democracy, Education, and the Schools*

We began to use chapters from this volume with Cohort VI and with those who attended annual meetings of all the cohorts.[36] Two essays, contrasting in style and content, have been particularly useful. In "The Meanings of Democracy," Nathan Tarcov examines fifth-century B.C.E. Greek understandings of classical democracy; he considers democracy at its best and at its worst. Tarcov also discusses modern democracy, beginning with the mixed republic advocated by Machiavelli, moving on to Locke's liberalism, and concluding with a consideration of the American representative democracy through an examination of *The Federalist*. It is in some respects a difficult chapter; Tarcov's syntax demands—more than most writing, even among our several texts—an extremely close and careful reading. Added to the syntax is a combination of things not said (often more important than what is said) and irony, making the demands on the reader even greater.

Concerned with many of the same issues as Tarcov, but taking a different perspective, is Donna Kerr in "Democracy, Nurturance, and Community." Kerr argues in this chapter that democracy needs to be considered in relationship to the nurturance of self. She wants us to understand that democratized family relations and civic society are instrumental to the nurturance of self and that we should encourage associations, such as families and community groups and agencies, that bring mutual respect and trust to human relationships. Kerr's syntax and style are at first glance relaxed—artfully so, in my opinion—leading the reader along until he or she is truly obligated to confront fundamental issues of ethics and politics. Those coming up for air after a difficult struggle with Tarcov find temporary succor with Kerr, only to discover that the demands on them are equally great.

Other texts are discussed and recommended in Leadership Program sessions. Although we no longer use Mortimer Adler's succinct analysis, *We Hold These Truths: Understanding the Ideas and Ideals of the Constitution*,[37] we continue to urge participants to read it. Other texts we recommend include Francis Fukuyama's *Trust: The Social Virtues and the Creation of Prosperity*, Amy Gutmann's *Democratic Education*,[38] and, more recently, John Goodlad and Timothy McMannon's edited book, *The Public Purpose of Education and Schooling*, and Goodlad's *In Praise of Education*.[39]

The Persuasion Exercise

To lead is to persuade. Those who are unable or unwilling to persuade others eventually are replaced by those who can and will. Accordingly, a significant chunk of time in the Leadership Program is devoted to helping participants become better at persuading others and, more than that, better at creating a more thoughtful public.[40]

The conceptual frame for this part of the program is derived in large part from rhetoric, particularly the work of Richard Weaver in his *The Ethics of Rhetoric*. Weaver argues that "the choice of one's source of argument" is "the most critical undertaking of all."[41]

In discussing rhetoric and persuasion, we consider the basic sources or types of arguments (definition, similitude, circumstance, consequence, and authority, among others) and the ethical and ecological implications of choosing one type of argument over another. The implications are profound. As Weaver tells us, "If a leader asks only consequences, he will find himself involved in naked competition of forces. If he asks only circumstance, he will find himself intimidated against all vision. But if he asks for principle, he may get that, all tied up and complete, and though purchased at a price, paid for. Therefore it is of first importance whether a leader has the courage to define. Nowhere does a man's rhetoric catch up with him more completely than in the topics he chooses to win other men's assent."[42]

We ask Leadership Associates to consider the kinds of responses they might make to a student asking why she should study. Each reason given ("If you don't study, I'll hit you," or "Because I told you to") can be seen as an example of a type of argument (consequence, authority). Through discussions of familiar examples, participants explore the ethics of choice of grounding.

Following the discussion, we talk at length about putting the concepts into practice—the persuasion exercise that takes place during the third session. Sometime between the second and third sessions, each participant prepares a five- to ten-minute speech on some aspect of simultaneous renewal. During the third session, each Leadership Associate gives the speech to a group of five or six colleagues. At the conclusion of each speech, the audience acts as a critical friend, noting strengths and weaknesses. A critical friend does not flatter, as Tocqueville knows. In the preface to the second volume of *Democracy in America*, he tells us that "it may seem surprising that this book expresses such severe criticism of [democracy]. My answer is simply that, being no enemy of democracy, I want to treat it with sincerity."[43]

The response to the persuasion exercise has varied within and between groups, ranging from enthusiastic to quite negative. The overall level of negativity was highest in the first cohort. Perhaps part of the reason for the less-than-enthusiastic response was that we introduced the speech assignment on a Monday, with participants to be prepared to give their speeches two days later. And perhaps part of the reason for the negative response stemmed from the newness of the entire business. The persuasion exercise had not been conceived months in advance; it was developed on the fly, and perhaps some members of the first cohort felt (quite rightly) that we were using them as test subjects.

With each succeeding cohort, response to the persuasion exercise grew ever more positive. Perhaps, in part, the positive reaction reflected our efforts to improve the rules of the game. Instead of springing the exercise on them, for example, we discussed it in the second session, thus giving them several months to prepare. We also improved understanding of the exercise by role playing: three senior associates modeled the assignment by giving speeches and having the Leadership Associates critique them.

The persuasion exercise takes a lot of collective time. Was it worth it? If we agree that learning better ways of "speaking and listening, thinking and judging" is important for leaders in schools in a democracy, then the exercise has much potential. Participants who thought they knew all there was to know about public speaking (and some did seem to think this way, justified or not) some-times learned that even they had some things to learn, some refine-ments to make. Others who had not given the matter much thought sometimes came to realize that there are profound implications as to how they speak, that is, on what grounds they choose to advance their case.

Perhaps one difficulty with carrying out the persuasion exercise is helping people to act as genuine critical friends during the de-briefing session after a speech. It is sometimes difficult to get people to be critical. A number of participants viewed the persuasion exer-cise as a threat. Some people do not like to speak in a formal set-ting, especially when the setting is self-consciously critical, as was the case with the persuasion exercise. They do not think they are good at it, and they are acutely aware of what they think are their deficiencies. Others in the "audience" are aware of the speaker's struggles (they might have similar difficulties), and thus debriefing sessions can slide from critical-friends analysis to generalized sup-port sessions. As usual, what happens first is of the greatest impor-tance. If the first speaker gives a solid performance and the group really attends to its tasks, then a high standard is set and subsequent debriefing sessions will be lively and critical. But if the first speaker struggles, struggles, and brings the performance to a quiet and unin-spired end (somewhat like Tom Sawyer in his "Give me Liberty or give me Death" speech at the school graduation event: in the mid-dle of the soaring rhetoric, he forgets, falters, and fades, and the audience responds with sympathy and silence), then the audience might very well lay off, with colleagues saying "great speech," "good effort," and such in attempts to support the discouraged speaker, while ignoring the reason for the exercise in the first place. Under these circumstances, it is unlikely that subsequent debriefing ses-sions will rise above generalized expressions of support, no matter how strong the next speakers might be.

The difficulties we have experienced are not an argument against the persuasion exercise. We believe the exercise is productive. In follow-up assessments, most participants indicated that (at least after the fact) they thought the exercise was productive, too.

Concluding Thoughts

After all the readings and speeches (and other parts of the program that are relevant but not touched on here), we hope that participants have begun to see in better ways the importance and fragility of democracy and the need to take active measures to sustain it. "Better ways" means ways that go beyond rote patriotism and meaningless ritual, and transcend current binary and Manichaean ways of talking (for example, "sexist," "racist," "classist," and other conversation stoppers).

We hope that participants have begun to understand that wisdom does not repose in the narrow confines of one's generation or one's people, but is formed through careful conversation with thoughtful people across the ages. Just as Machiavelli wrote that he converses with the ancients,[44] we hope that participants will come to understand that wisdom comes, too, from a variety of sources and not just from empirical research written up in narrowly focused research journals.

We hope that participants will have developed a better understanding of the conditions necessary to sustain a healthy democracy. It is not necessary that participants agree with the conditions outlined in this chapter, but we want them to be able to weigh and consider the relationships among democracy, the conditions necessary for democracy, education, and schooling.

It is not enough that participants develop a better personal understanding of what is required to sustain a social and political democracy. Such understanding is necessary but not sufficient. Personal understanding must be joined with action. We fully expect Leadership Associates to return to their institutions prepared to put into practice their understanding of what it means to enculturate the young into a social and political democracy. That understanding, we trust, will lead to better institutional structures that will enhance democratic character and be more consonant with democratic ideals. We believe that that understanding will foster respect in interpersonal relationships and lead to better ways of selecting and focusing on content, perplexing and potentially dangerous as that selection and focus might be.

Struggling with these issues conceptually and practically is a difficult task, to be sure. It might be tempting to forgo the struggle, but I do not think we really have that choice. Our guide here is once again Nick Carraway, this time ruminating, near the end of his narrative, on the conduct of two major *Gatsby* characters: "They were careless people, Tom and Daisy—they smashed up things and creatures and then retreated back into their money or their vast carelessness, or whatever it was that kept them together, and let other people clean up the mess they had made."[45] There are lots of people who carelessly mess with schools, turning them for whatever reason, political or personal, into narrow places devoid of spirit and devoid of any connection to democracy. It is our responsibility to clean up the mess, to restore the human spirit, and to bring to the fore the role of schools in sustaining healthy people in a healthy democracy. We must assume the responsibility for building our conduct on the hard rock, not the wet marshes, if we are indeed to secure the blessings of liberty to ourselves and our posterity.

Notes

1. F. Scott Fitzgerald, *The Great Gatsby* (New York: Charles Scribner's Sons, 1925), p. 2.

2. Albert Camus, *The Rebel* (New York: Vintage International, 1991 [orig. Knopf, 1956]), p. 57.

3. John Dewey, *Freedom and Culture* (New York: Putnam's Sons, 1939), pp. 34–35.

4. See Diego Gambetta (ed.), *Trust: Making and Breaking Cooperative Relations* (New York: Blackwell, 1988).

5. For a useful discussion of exchange, see Marcel Mauss, *The Gift: Forms and Functions of Exchange in Archaic Societies* (New York: Norton, 1967), and Alfred North Whitehead, *Adventures of Ideas* (New York: Free Press, 1967), chap. 5.

6. In *Making Democracy Work: Civic Traditions in Modern Italy* (Princeton, N.J.: Princeton University Press, 1993), Robert Putnam argues that the three conditions so far stated (trust, exchange, social capital) are critical to a healthy democracy.

7. Useful here is James Boyd White, *The Legal Imagination* (Chicago: University of Chicago Press, 1987).

8. See, among others, Mary Ann Glendon, *Rights Talk: The Impoverishment of Political Discourse* (New York: Free Press, 1991).

9. Conversations about these matters might best begin (and end) with Alexis de Tocqueville, *Democracy in America*, trans. George Lawrence (New York: Anchor, 1969).

10. For this matter of free and open inquiry, there are myriads of texts and there are no texts. Socrates and Galileo come to mind. One might also consult Herbert Muller, *The Uses of the Past* (New York: Oxford University Press, 1952), chap. 3.

11. A most useful discussion is found in Philip B. Kurland and Ralph Lerner (eds.), *The Founders' Constitution: Major Themes* (Chicago: University of Chicago Press, 1987), vol. 1, chap. 14.

12. Donald Treadgold, *Freedom: A History* (New York: New York University Press, 1990).

13. Leo Strauss, *Persecution and the Art of Writing* (Chicago: University of Chicago Press, 1988 [orig. Free Press, 1952]), p. 37.

14. For the notion of the distinction between the two, see Ralph Lerner, *Revolutions Revisited: The Two Faces of the Politics of Enlightenment* (Chapel Hill: University of North Carolina Press, 1994), p. 59.

15. Glendon, *Rights Talk*, p. 129.

16. For useful discussions of the distinction between public and private purpose, see John I. Goodlad and Timothy J. McMannon (eds.), *The*

Public Purpose of Education and Schooling (San Francisco: Jossey-Bass, 1997), and John I. Goodlad, *In Praise of Education* (New York: Teachers College Press, 1997).

17. John Henry Newman, *Discussions and Arguments on Various Subjects* (London: Longmans, Green, 1899), p. 272.

18. Robert Coles, "The Virtues of *Middlemarch*," in *That Red Wheelbarrow* (Iowa City: University of Iowa Press, 1988), p. 37.

19. Friedrich Bruns (ed.), *Goethe's Poems and Aphorisms* (New York: Oxford University Press, 1932), p. 203.

20. Camus, *The Rebel*, p. 283.

21. Albert Camus, *Lyrical and Critical Essays*, ed. Philip Thody, trans. Ellen Conroy Kennedy (New York: Vintage, 1970), p. 238.

22. Lerner, *Revolutions Revisited*, p. 44.

23. Josiah Lee Auspitz, "Michael Oakeshott: 1901–1990," *American Scholar* 60 (Summer 1991): 351–370.

24. Goodlad and others suggest further exploration of Oakeshott's work. The most accessible volume is Michael Oakeshott, *Rationalism in Politics and Other Essays*, exp. ed. (Indianapolis: LibertyPress, 1991).

25. George Orwell, "Politics and the English Language," in Sonia Orwell and Ian Angus (eds.), *The Collected Essays, Journalism and Letters of George Orwell*, vol. 4: *In Front of Your Nose, 1945–1950* (New York: Harcourt, Brace & World, 1968).

26. Camus, *The Rebel*, p. 238.

27. James Boyd White, "Constituting a Culture of Argument," in *When Words Lose Their Meaning* (Chicago: University of Chicago Press, 1984), pp. 231–240.

28. White, *When Words Lose Their Meaning*, p. 11.

29. White, *When Words Lose Their Meaning*, p. 18.

30. White, *When Words Lose Their Meaning*, p. 19.

31. The essays in White's *Heracles' Bow: Essays on the Rhetoric and Poetics of the Law* (Madison: University of Wisconsin Press, 1985) are uniformly insightful; of particular interest are chap. 1, "Persuasion

and Community in Philoctetes," and chap. 7, "Fact, Fiction, and Value in Historical Narrative: Gibbon's Roads of Rome." *The Legal Imagination: Studies in the Nature of Legal Thought and Expression* (Boston: Little, Brown, 1973) is what the title says; it is also an excellent text on learning to write better. In *Acts of Hope: Creating Authority in Literature, Law, and Politics* (Chicago: University of Chicago Press, 1994), White gives us more astonishing readings of texts, ranging from *Richard II* to Austen's *Mansfield Park*, to poems of Emily Dickinson.

32. Putnam, *Making Democracy Work*.

33. Review of *Making Democracy Work*, *Economist*, February 6, 1993, p. 96.

34. Mary Catherine Bateson, *Composing a Life* (New York: Atlantic Monthly Press, 1989), p. 57. Similarly, in his *Persian Wars*, Herodotus notes that "if one were to offer men to choose out of all the customs of the world such as seemed to them the best, they would examine the whole number, and end by preferring their own; so convinced are they that their own usages far surpass those of all others" (III, 38).

35. "Bowling Alone," *Journal of Democracy* 6 (January 1995): 65–78; and "What Makes Democracy Work?" *National Civic Review* 82 (Spring 1993): 101–107.

36. Roger Soder (ed.), *Democracy, Education, and the Schools* (San Francisco: Jossey-Bass, 1996).

37. Mortimer J. Adler, *We Hold These Truths: Understanding the Ideas and Ideals of the Constitution* (New York: Collier Books, 1987).

38. Francis Fukuyama, *Trust: The Social Virtues and the Creation of Prosperity* (New York: Free Press, 1995); and Amy Gutmann, *Democratic Education* (Princeton, N.J.: Princeton University Press, 1987).

39. See note 16 for publication information.

40. I am currently developing these notions for a book to be published by Jossey-Bass.

41. Richard Weaver, *The Ethics of Rhetoric* (Chicago: Regnery, 1953), p. 84.

42. Weaver, *Ethics of Rhetoric*, p. 114.

43. Alexis de Tocqueville, *Democracy in America*, trans. George Lawrence, ed. J. P. Mayer and Max Lerner (New York: Harper & Row, 1966), Preface to vol. 2.

44. In a letter to Francesco Vettori dated December 10, 1513, Machiavelli talks to his friend (and to us) about talking (and about much more): "On the coming of evening, I return to my house and enter my study; and at the door I take off the day's clothing, covered with mud and dust, and put on garments regal and courtly; and reclothed appropriately, I enter the ancient courts of ancient men, where, received by them with affection, I feed on that food which only is mine and which I was born for, where I am not ashamed to speak with them and to ask them the reasons for their actions; and they in their kindness answer me." *The Letters of Machiavelli*, ed. and trans. Allan Gilbert (New York: Capricorn Books, 1961), p. 142.

45. Fitzgerald, *Great Gatsby*, pp. 180–181.

4

On Knowledge and Its Place in the Human Conversation

Gary D Fenstermacher

The second part of the four-part mission of the Agenda for Education in a Democracy calls on the schools to provide to all children disciplined encounters with all the subject matters of the human conversation. In this chapter, I examine such phrases as "disciplined encounters," "subject matters," and "the human conversation," to the end of supporting equal access to knowledge. In the next chapter, Mona Bailey examines the "to all children" portion of this mission statement, describing what impedes and what assists educators in the challenging task of providing equal access to the various subject matters of the human conversation. Inasmuch as the concept of knowledge is at the heart of such notions as "disciplined encounters" and "subject matters," this chapter begins with that concept, looking first at the problems encountered in gaining a clear understanding of what is meant by *knowledge*.

Some Difficulties with Our Ideas About Knowledge

The word *knowledge*, which slips so easily off the tongue, provides one of the most enduring puzzles in all of philosophy. For a concept that is so filled with both power and ambiguity, it is a wonder that we continue to make any sense of it at all. Indeed, making sense of the concept of knowledge is precisely the challenge we face.

There is currently a grand debate taking place among scholars. In a nutshell it comes down to this: Shall we hold fast to some definitive, tightly grounded conception of knowledge or allow "a thousand flowers to bloom," whereby your knowledge, my knowledge, and their knowledge may all be different but equally respectable? This debate is typically described as taking place between the modernists, or Enlightenment theorists, who have long sought a definitive conception of knowledge, and the postmodernists, who for the most part reject Enlightenment notions of knowledge. The postmodernists generally contend that what we call knowledge is so complexly interwoven into culture, politics, and language that it is impossible to formulate a definitive, strongly anchored conception of knowledge.

But this debate is not always cast as a struggle between modernists and postmodernists. It is sometimes described as a tension between positivists and post-positivists, wherein those who hold out for pristine, compelling notions of the material world and the truths it contains (positivists) are contrasted to those who argue that the material world is shaped by the minds that apprehend it, and these minds will naturally form varying, but equally plausible, conceptions of this world (post-positivists). Yet another way to cast this debate is between what Jerome Bruner calls the logico-scientific mode and the narrative mode of thinking.[1] In the former, reason, logic, standard research designs, and analytical methods are employed to seek out and appraise what we know. In the latter, life experiences, in such forms as story, image, poem, and song, reveal powerful, though transitory and context-dependent, truths about our world. Other manifestations of this debate occur when we ask whether different cultures, genders, or races can lay claim to their own ways of knowing, such that they might argue for things in the world (spirits, for example) with the same certainty and assemblage of "facts" that modern empiricists adduce to explain, for example, the behavior of gases in a closed container.

For our purposes, *modern* and *postmodern* will serve as descriptive terms to refer to the main lines of the debate, picking up on aspects of culture, race, gender, and language as appropriate. Given this convenient dualism, we are then faced with the question of why this debate makes any difference to educators. One answer is that knowledge is educators' stock in trade; if they are uncertain about what it is, how can they in any reasonable sense be said to be engaged in its conveyance to or development in the young? Another difficulty centers on the classic question in curriculum: What knowledge is of most worth? That question is thorny enough without adding to it the possibility that we do not even know what knowledge is, much less what part of it is worthy.

Yet another aspect of this problem is that if educators cannot say with any clarity what is meant by knowledge, then they may be compelled to honor any and all claims to knowledge. This state of affairs has rather frightening consequences, such as someone claiming that he *knows* that one race is biologically inferior to another, or that one culture or nation-state is superior to all others, or that George Washington was the fifteenth rather than the first president of the United States, or that $1 + 1 = 11$. A great deal obviously hangs on what we mean when we employ the concept of knowledge; hence it is in the interest of educators to be quite clear about it.

Goodlad's Views on Knowledge

In his discussion of access to knowledge, John I. Goodlad states that "the school is the only institution in our society specifically charged with providing to the young a disciplined encounter with all the subject matters of the human conversation."[2] When he penned these words, the postmodern critique of the nature of knowledge in Western society was emerging in full bloom. In the light of this critique, we might wonder whether Goodlad was aware of just how much of a bull he had by the horns. A closer look at what is going on here is in order.

When Goodlad speaks of a "disciplined encounter with all the subject matters of the human conversation," he appears to be opting for what some critics would call "the Western canon": that body of knowledge and understanding "canonized" by philosophers, scientists, and theorists in Europe and America from the Renaissance through the Enlightenment and on to the present day. It consists of just what Goodlad says the human conversation consists of: "the world as a physical and biological system; evaluative and belief systems; communication systems; the social, political, and economic systems that make up the global village; and the human species itself."[3] This list, which Goodlad attributes to Kenneth Boulding, reads like an annotation on the *Propaedia*, Mortimer Adler's synoptic structuring of knowledge that constitutes the first part of the fifteenth and subsequent editions of the *Encyclopaedia Britannica*. In the *Propaedia*, Adler arranges the panoply of human understanding into ten major sections:

1. Matter and Energy
2. The Earth
3. Life on Earth
4. Human Life
5. Human Society
6. Art
7. Technology
8. Religion
9. History of Mankind
10. Branches of Knowledge

The first nine areas are the "subject matters" about which Goodlad speaks. The tenth area pertains to the notion of "disciplined encounters," for it is in area 10, branches of knowledge, that the various disciplines are contained. In that section, Adler describes five major categories of disciplined inquiry: Logic, Mathematics, Science, History and the Humanities, and Philosophy. What makes these branches of knowledge or *disciplines* different from the other nine topic areas, or subject matters, is that they contain *specified, systematic methods* for making claims about the world and about people and their ideas. These methods are believed to lead us to truth, or something as near truth as we can possibly get. Thus, what we *know* about the first nine major topic areas in the *Propaedia* is generally believed to be a result of employing the methods and theories contained in the tenth topic area, the branches of knowledge. At least that is what modernists would argue.

Finding Fault with the Canon

In essence, using the methods contained in the various branches of knowledge has the effect of "canonizing" certain conceptions of the other nine topic areas. To canonize a conception of, say, the design of our solar system is to give it authority, to call on those who see and hear this conception to regard it as the correct understanding of the design of the solar system. Hence, the various branches of knowledge, in carrying out their respective inquiries, do something more than discover or reveal heretofore hidden or unknown truths; they catapult one of a number of competing conceptions of our world into a position of ascendancy over other conceptions that might also predict or explain the phenomenon under scrutiny.

It is here that one encounters the bull that Goodlad has by the horns. In calling on teachers and schools to provide all children with a "disciplined encounter with all the subject matters of the human conversation," he appears to call for the study of conventional Enlightenment conceptions of what is known. Critics will assert that this Enlightenment "stuff" is but a particular kind of knowledge within a much wider range of possible knowledges (the mere fact that the plural form of the noun seems so strange tells us a lot about how we have traditionally thought about this concept). The critics will say that the so-called knowledge to which Goodlad refers is but a catalogue of agreements reached by, for example, white, privileged, Western, Eurocentric, hegemonic males (Whew!). What these white, European males claim to know is merely the expression of privileged discourse within a particular language community bound together by shared cultural norms.

Thus, the counterargument goes, what comes to be understood as knowledge is, to a considerable extent, the result of *who* makes the claims, *how* the claims are made, and *in what settings* the claims are made. For many postmodern critics, certain persons—white males with European ancestry, for example—hold positions of social privilege that legitimate their claims to know.

To understand this last statement, consider the notion of a *claim*. A claim is not knowledge itself but only a "knowledge candidate." For example, let us say that after considerable research, a scientist— we will call him Phelps—puts forth several claims about the structure of the atom. These claims are not yet knowledge, but rather knowledge candidates, because they lack sufficient substantiation by Phelps or by other scholars to be accepted as knowledge. The conventional story is that Phelps's claims will shift from the status of knowledge candidate to the status of knowledge itself when proved by other scientists working on the same thing as Phelps.

Not so, say the critics. Phelps has a huge advantage here, in that those who will legitimate his claims are of the same lineage as Phelps. They all speak the same language (or share the same domain of discourse), they all hold similar social positions, they all share the same mind-set with respect to the phenomenon under study. When these like-minded, like-speaking, like-cultured persons work together, they not only have the advantage of privileging their own ideas, they also function in ways that impair the opportunities for those who are not like them to gain a hearing for their knowledge claims. Women, for example, or persons of color may bring quite different mind-sets to the problems at hand, but they lack the privilege of Phelps and his cronies. Thus, the knowledge candidates proffered by those without privilege do not get a hearing.

This may seem a strange controversy in regard to the structure of the atom, and in many ways it is. While some postmodernists would cover all domains of knowledge with the shadows of subjectivity and relativity, many of them evidence concern only for putative knowledge claims in the social sciences, the humanities, and the arts. It is in these domains that the fighting becomes most aggressive, as the contesting sides argue over whether we can, in any valid and generalizable way, be sure about such things as the impact of race on human achievement, the consequence of wealth on morality, the impact of religion on goodness, or the merits of one kind of music or art in relation to another kind.

Imagine Phelps caught up in a dispute not about the structure of the atom, but about how social class and education are connected. Suppose that a fierce argument arose over whose contentions are correct. At this point, one might ask why Phelps and his cronies could not just sit down with their previously excluded antagonists to slug it out over who has the best evidence, the most elegant theories, and the tightest logic. In other words, those who had been disenfranchised would be given a seat at the table, where the various and contesting views could be expressed in an atmosphere of mutual respect. If this procedure would work, the differences between modern and postmodern views would not be nearly so great. The difficulty here is frequently referred to as the *problem of incommensurability*.

To say that this situation possesses incommensurability is to contend that you cannot bring persons of different mind-sets together to work through their differences in an effort to agree on who among them is correct. The contesting sides simply do not have enough in common to be commensurable. There are two kinds of commensurability to consider in this context. The first is physical or empirical incommensurability, which occurs when all the participants at the table are unable to find common ground on which to discuss their differences and hammer out a consensus. A typical result of empirical incommensurability is a remark like this one:

"Well, we tried to get these people together, but we simply could not get them to understand one another's positions well enough for them to move on to deliberating toward a consensus." Some post-modern critics appear to take this empirical position, asserting that we cannot cross differences in culture or language with sufficient understanding to forge a consensus on what or who is "in the know."

The other form is called moral incommensurability. It arises when, even if it were logically or empirically possible to cross the boundaries of language, culture, gender, and so forth, it would be wrong to do so. Why? Because in order to do it, you have to agree on some common frame around which all the different parties will unite. The result will always be a moral failure. This moral failure can occur in a number of different ways. The first is that the frame selected to permit dialogue across difference will invariably reflect the privilege and position of certain members of the group. As such, the dialogue will not be grounded in mutual regard and fair exchange. The second form of moral failure is even more troublesome. It asserts that the very selection of a particular frame vitiates the whole point of the activity, for it wipes out the differences that initially called for the framing in the first place. In other words, if people holding radically different views come to the table in order to deliberate about knowledge candidates, the mere act of adopting a frame that permits them to speak across their differences dissolves those differences. It is for this reason that so many of the postmodernists reject the notion of what so many of the rest of us think of as reason or rationality. When we encounter radical differences and want to resolve them, we might be heard to plea, "But why can't you just be reasonable?" or "Is it not possible for rational people to agree on such matters?" Merely by asking such questions, we press the opposition to adopt our way of thinking about such matters. That is a moral fault, according to the critic, because it eradicates difference, almost always resolving the difference in favor of those who are in positions of power and privilege.

With these tensions in mind, let us return to Goodlad's statement: "The school is the only institution in our society specifically charged with providing to the young a disciplined encounter with all the subject matters of the human conversation." Note that *human conversation* is singular here, as if there were only one ongoing conversation. Note, too, the idea of a "disciplined encounter," as if it were clear just what it means to provide the young with such a thing. As if this were not complexity enough, we must deal with such questions as: What knowledge? Whose knowledge? Whose human conversation?

It seems that Goodlad has a definite tilt toward the Enlightenment. The epistemic terrain he occupies here is similar to that occupied by such contemporary scholars as E. D. Hirsch (the author of *Cultural Literacy* and a series of books about what every child should know), Mortimer Adler (author of *The Paideia Proposal* and longtime chair of the *Encyclopaedia Britannica* editorial board), Allan Bloom (author of *The Closing of the American Mind*), and William Bennett (former head of the National Endowment for the Humanities, former secretary of education, former drug czar, and author of *The Book of Virtues*). Although the politics of these writers differ markedly, they may all be thought of as modernists. In this respect, they keep some rather remarkable company; Plato, Aquinas, Erasmus, Hume, Locke, Mill, Kant, Montaigne, and a bevy of other intellectual giants are found in this same territory. All fall into the category variously known as Western civilization, the canon, Enlightenment theory, or modernism.

All of these theorists hold that the reasoning powers of the mind are ascendant qualities of human existence and that knowledge can be discovered and refined through reason. Once refined, it perforce compels human thought, and, so compelled, the mind will ascertain truths that transcend time and place. If one accepts this view, then "providing disciplined encounters with all the subject matters of the human conversation" is a challenging but far from impossible or hopelessly confused task. Ensuring equality of access to this knowledge may be an even more formidable task than the provision of disciplined encounters, but at least we can begin this work with a fairly clear picture of what we mean by knowledge. However, if we set out to do these things in Enlightenment fashion, consider what we preclude: not only multiple knowledges constructed by such critical aspects of our being as gender, race, culture, and language, but also forms of knowledge grounded in vastly different sources of understanding, such as religious faith and lived experience.

Does this mean that the Agenda for Education in a Democracy is filled with the legacies of what are sometimes referred to as "dead, white males"? If that is not the case, then what are the epistemic grounds of the Agenda? How might we go about deciding these matters? What is a good and proper course for educators to pursue in these contested times? We shall come to grips with these questions, but not immediately. First, it is essential to gain a working familiarity with the dominant concept of knowledge in Western society. Then we will be better positioned to appreciate the critique of this account and forge our own views on the educational dimensions of this important dispute.

On the Concept of Knowledge in Western Thought

As one listens to everyday discourse about knowledge, and even to the scholarly uses of this concept, it is evident that the term *knowledge* is used in all sorts of different ways. Some of these ways are congruent with meanings for the term that have been developed in that arena where knowledge is formally studied: epistemology. Other ways of using the word are frighteningly disconnected from any of the more formal understandings of knowledge and sometimes even flat-out contradictory to these understandings. That different people use the term *knowledge* to mean different things is not in itself a tragedy. What makes multiple usages problematic is when users have little or no sense that they are deploying the term in some non-standard way, or when listeners to and readers of the term are unaware of more standard or conventional notions of knowledge and thus cannot ascertain that this or that usage deviates from or contradicts conventional usage.

It is as if there were no standard for what the measure of length known as a *meter* is, yet merchants sold cloth by the "meter," gunnery officers gave targeting instructions in "meters," and track and field events were measured in "meters." What fun it would be to claim that I won the race because I completed my definition of five hundred meters before you completed what you thought was the definition of five hundred meters. A situation of this kind seems silly in the context of meters, but such conversations occur with amazing frequency when the topic is knowledge. One is reminded here of the delightful scene in *Through the Looking Glass*, when Alice says to Humpty Dumpty, "That's a great deal to make one word mean," and Humpty Dumpty replies, "When I make a word do a lot of work like that, I always pay it extra." The word *knowledge* must be very wealthy indeed, given the amount of extra work it is called on to perform.

For example, look at the question, "What knowledge is of most worth?" When this question is addressed, most of us do not pause to ask the prior question, "What is knowledge?" Instead we attempt to answer that question within the context of subject matter areas that we presume constitute knowledge. Yet the prior question, "What is knowledge?" has become the key question in contemporary discussions about curriculum, leading to debates over multicultural education, the so-called culture wars, the fractious examination of what constitutes liberal studies, and even a large part of the argument over what constitutes political correctness. The resolution of these differences depends on bringing a measure of clarity and precision to the concept of knowledge. One of the basic ways of doing so is distinguishing between knowledge and belief.

Difference Between Knowledge and Belief

In this section, our attention is on the notion of knowledge as it developed within the modernist tradition. The task is to become as clear as possible on how the term is used within the context of the formal disciplines. Among the more helpful ways to get at the notion of knowledge is to distinguish it from belief. A claim to know something is different from having a belief in something. Consider, as an example, the proposition, "Harry's car is parked on level 1 of the Hill Street garage." If you were to probe the epistemic status of this claim, you might get one of these three different responses:

(a) I saw Harry's car parked there this morning when I parked my car, and his secretary says she still has the car keys he left with her when he arrived.

(b) Harry always parks on level 1 of the Hill Street garage.

(c) Guys like Harry prefer the first level of the Hill Street garage.

Response (a) has a higher epistemic status because it is characterized by the evidence of actually having seen Harry's car on level 1 and having the testimony of a reliable person that Harry could not have moved his car since it was observed in the garage. Claims (b) and (c) exhibit diminishing epistemic status due to the fall-off in evidentiary support and the increasing difficulty of setting out a convincing justification. However, in all three instances there is no prima facie difficulty in saying that some person *believes* that Harry's car is parked on level 1 of the Hill Street garage, whereas there is an increasingly serious problem, as one moves from (a) to (b) to (c), with saying that the person *knows* that Harry's car is parked on level 1 of the Hill Street garage.

This example illustrates the important differences between knowledge and belief. Belief is open to anyone, at any time, on just about any topic. It is subject to review, but not in the same rigorous way as knowledge. Knowledge is more constrained. It requires that conditions be met—conditions that are not required in the case of belief. To ascertain just what these conditions might be requires a distinction among the various kinds of knowledge. Two of the main categories are propositional and performance knowledge. Each kind is addressed below.

The Character of Propositional Knowledge

Propositional knowledge is the kind of knowledge most often referred to when we speak generally about something's being a case of knowledge. It is knowledge expressed in the form of propositions, or assertions about the way things are. But this way of describing propositional knowledge is too rough; we need more refinement, which will briefly take us into the domain of formal philosophy. In philosophical terms, in order for a person, S, to be said to *know* something—let us call that something *p*—it is not sufficient that *p* is true *and* that the person, S, believes *p*. It must also be the case that S has grounds for believing *p*. This view of knowledge is often called the classical view, or the "standard analysis," of knowledge.[4] It is succinctly described by the philosopher Edmund Gettier[5] in the following formulation:

S knows that *p*, if and only if

(i) *p* is true,

(ii) S believes that *p*, and

(iii) S is justified in believing that *p*.

The standard analysis establishes strict conditions for a knowledge claim. The claim must be true, it must be believed by the claimant, and the claimant must be justified in believing the claim. Thus, where *p* refers to the proposition, "The earth has a spherical shape," in order for some person S to be said to know *p*, it must be the case that (i) it is true that the earth has a spherical shape (this condition is established within the discipline that concerns itself with propositions of this type), (ii) S believes that the earth has a spherical shape, and (iii) S has justification for believing that the earth has a spherical shape.

The standard analysis is sometimes called the "justified true belief" (JTB) account of knowledge. As Gettier and others have shown, this account has some problems. Gettier's critique and the rash of follow-up analyses it spurred pertain to the meaning of *true*, in the statement, "*x* is true," and with what constitutes a proper justification for S's believing that *p*.[6] It would, however, be a serious misunderstanding of the consequences of Gettier's critique to infer that there is no longer a satisfactory or commonly accepted conception of what it means to know something in the propositional or informational sense of the term. A large percentage of contemporary epistemologists are in agreement that we can have knowledge of the world, that there are specific conditions that must be met if our claims to knowledge are to succeed, and that some form of justification is required as one among these conditions. The issue of justification, in epistemology, is over the particulars of what constitutes a defensible justification, not over whether justification is required. It will always be the case, as near as can be foretold, that some form of justification will be required if we are to know, as Lehrer puts it, "that the information one receives is correct."[7]

Criticisms of the standard account have put an end to conceptions of formal knowledge as pristine, permanent, and absolute. Again, however, it would be an error to conclude that because our knowledge is fallible, it is therefore useless to worry about what it means, or that it is simply too confusing to take seriously any epistemological account of knowledge. Fallibilism—the view that we can be wrong about what we claim to know—is a fairly well-accepted doctrine among contemporary epistemologists, although it is not regarded as devastating in its consequences for a well-wrought theory of knowledge.

Nor can we ignore the demands of justification on the grounds that we no longer hold the rock-solid, gold-plated conceptions of truth that once graced theories in epistemology. Consider Anthony Quinton's reaction to the claim that if knowledge entails truth, we can never know anything: "If I firmly believe that something is true on what I take to be sufficient grounds, I am right to say that I know it. It may be that the grounds are, in fact, insufficient and that what I claim to know is false. In that case my claim is mistaken, but it does not follow that I was wrong to make it in the sense that I had no justification for doing so."[8]

Although he occupies a position in epistemology that departs in some respects from the positions I have described in this chapter, Roderick Chisholm provides a helpful way to think about issues of justification and truth. He sets forth what he calls "The 13 Steps" for considering the epistemic status of knowledge claims:[9]

+6. Certain

+5. Obvious

+4. Evident

+3. Beyond Reasonable Doubt

+2. Epistemically in the Clear

+1. Probable

 0. Counterbalanced

−1. Probably False

−2. In the Clear to Disbelieve

−3. Reasonable to Disbelieve

−4. Evidently False

−5. Obviously False

−6. Certainly False

Although for Chisholm a proposition cannot be *known* until it attains the fourth positive step (Evident) or a higher level, other epistemologists would entertain a proposition's having epistemic merit at the level of "Beyond Reasonable Doubt." In this case, a claim is sufficiently justified to count as knowledge if it is reasonably believed by the holder, the holder having sufficient evidence to establish the claim against its competitors. This notion is parallel to the idea of "objectively reasonable belief" that Green described in his analysis of knowledge and belief in education.[10] By "objectively reasonable belief," Green means that the person has reasons for holding a particular belief that go beyond his or her own personal life experiences. These objective reasons serve as justification for holding the belief as a form of knowledge

An even softer version of propositional knowledge stipulates that what counts as knowledge in a given context is relative to what is already known in that context. If an assertion is about matters of which little is known, we may be entitled to say that we *know* that *p*, even though we have only modest justification. In other words, "It's the best we've got" at this time, and so we are entitled to claim to know it. In areas where more is known, our obligation to address this evidence and consider it in relation to our own grounds for believing the proposition is correspondingly increased. No softening of the standards may, however, go lower than Chisholm's "epistemically in the clear," by which is meant that the holder can show that there are not better grounds for rejecting the proposition than for accepting it. Clearly this is a weak standard; any claim to know that *p* on this standard is suspect and would have to be made in a context in which there was little or no evidence available to guide consideration of the proposition.

This analysis of propositional knowledge is intended to make clear that we are in possession of quite technical conceptions of what it means to know that something is the case. It should also be evident that there are vigorous disputes about the precise features of the concept of knowledge. These disputes have not seriously damaged our working concepts of propositional knowledge. Modernist philosophers believe that they have excellent arguments for maintaining a coherent, well-defined concept of knowledge. Most of these philosophers agree that the JTB concept of knowledge is overly strict (or too complex to be employed with precision), and they have remedied this deficiency by expanding the range of information or propositions that may be considered knowledge or knowledge candidates. What they have *not* done is abandon the view that knowledge must be clearly distinguished from belief, and that there must be reasonably well-defined standards for converting a knowledge candidate to knowledge itself. Furthermore, the advocates for this view hold that these standards transcend differences in context or mind-set. Indeed, their great value is precisely that they do transcend differences in language, culture, gender, and so forth, thereby enabling us as a species to share a common commitment to what is true or false, correct or incorrect, accepted or doubted.

Propositional knowledge is not the only category of knowledge. Another category, less discussed, is known as *performance knowledge*, also sometimes called *skill knowledge*. This category of knowledge is highly relevant to education, and thus worthy of our attention.

The Character of Performance Knowledge

Performance or skill knowledge pertains to knowing how to do something, in contrast to knowing that something is the case (propositional knowledge). Many of us, on hearing the notion of performance knowledge, think of the difference between *knowing that* and *knowing how*, made famous in the work of the philosopher Gilbert Ryle.[11] Of course, the distinction predates Ryle by a few thousand years, though Ryle is generally credited with reintroducing the topic into Anglo-American philosophy. In its classical Greek form, performance knowledge was called *technē* and was distinguished from *epistemē*, or knowledge about the world. *Technē* is what one has when one knows how to make something or has a skill or capacity for the exercise of some craft. Building a house, playing the lute, and translating languages are good examples of *technē*.

Everyday language acknowledges a difference between propositional and performance knowledge, as most people deal differently with a claim like, "I know that smoking is the leading cause of lung cancer," than they do with a claim like, "I know how to blow smoke rings." To establish the former claim, we say, "What evidence do you have to substantiate such a claim?" while to establish the latter, we say, "Show me." The distinction is often thought to be especially important in education, particularly in the study of teaching and the education of teachers.

In many educational psychology textbooks and courses, for example, what is presented to students is propositional knowledge—a form of knowing that something is the case. This knowledge is typically gained from research studies and other forms of disciplined study in psychology. What teacher education students often appear to want in their courses, however, is not propositional but performance knowledge—*knowing how* as opposed to *knowing that*. Students' views of their teacher education programs often improve during student teaching because they encounter a much richer orientation to performance knowledge there than in campus-based courses.

This example not only illustrates the difference between propositional and performance knowledge; it serves as an occasion for asking just how sharp a difference there is between the two. Concerned with what he regarded as fundamental errors in the Cartesian view of the relationship of mind and body, Ryle argued that *knowing how* and *knowing that* are very different forms of knowing, and that the former cannot be reduced to the latter. Ryle states, "It is therefore possible for people intelligently to perform some sorts of operations when they are not yet able to consider any propositions enjoining how they should be performed."[12] If it were in fact necessary to consider such propositions, argues Ryle, it would create a most confounding difficulty: "If for any operation to be intelligently executed, a prior theoretical operation had first to be performed and performed intelligently, it would be a logical impossibility for anyone ever to break into the circle."[13]

Ryle's adroitness in philosophical argument convinced many thinkers that *knowing how* and *knowing that* are distinct domains, independent of one another. On the other hand, there is some evidence in the philosophical literature that *knowing how* is, in an important sense, dependent on *knowing that*. For example, in his well-known work, *The Problem of Knowledge*, A. J. Ayer states that under certain conditions, "we can construe knowing how to do things as being, in its fashion, a matter of knowing facts."[14] More recently, Keith Lehrer remarked that "it is often affirmed that to know something in the other senses of 'know' [that is, competence and acquaintance] entails knowledge in the information sense of 'know.' "[15]

If there is indeed a tighter connection between *knowing how* and *knowing that* than Ryle presumed, it becomes problematic for someone to opt for a *knowing how* version of knowledge as a way of rejecting a *knowing that* version, or of saying that *knowing how* replaces *knowing that* as the primary, quintessential, or unique characterization of teacher knowledge. Consider the example of my claiming to *know how* to play bridge. In making this claim, I am also asserting that I *know that* hearts and spades take precedence over diamonds and clubs, I *know that* a one no-trump bid overrides a one spade bid, I *know that* a Blackwood convention is called for when . . . , and so forth. It may equally be true that the *knowing that/knowing how* connection also works in the other direction, such that we cannot *know that* without *knowing how*. For example, to *know that* all electrical outlets in my home supply 120 volt current, I have to *know how* to use a voltmeter. The point is that one cannot opt for performance knowledge without also understanding that one has "acquired" propositional knowledge in the bargain, and vice versa.

One should not conclude from this positing of an interrelationship between *knowing how* and *knowing that* that they are really one and the same, or that one is reducible to the other. My own sense of the matter is that while the two are distinct, they are interdependent. Departing from Ryle, however, I believe that the justification of performance knowledge is every bit as important to its epistemic status as it is in the case of propositional knowledge, and that such justification is not simply in the performance of the skill or the craft but also involves establishing the reasonableness of the performance and the evidence connecting the purpose for the activity to its eventual outcome.

Justification is a critical element in a defensible conception of knowledge, a point examined in the next section. In closing these explorations of propositional and performance knowledge, it is helpful to note that they are not the only forms of knowledge, but they are probably the most salient forms in the context of education. Knowledge by intuition, authority, and faith represent additional forms, although these are far less discussed in the scholarly literature (of Western origin) and figure much less prominently in contemporary American schooling. As such, we are on reasonably solid ground when restricting this inquiry into knowledge to propositional and performance forms.

What Do Schoolchildren Know? What *Should* They Know?

If the preceding descriptions of knowledge are applied to school settings, what might we be able to say about what schoolchildren or their teachers know? In attempting to answer, we are faced with the complexity inherent in addressing both propositional and performance knowledge. When, for example, Goodlad writes of providing to the young a disciplined encounter with all the subject matters of the human conversation, is the reference here to propositional or performance knowledge, or both? If it is the disciplines, or branches of knowledge, then the activity seems largely one of gaining access to propositional knowledge.

If educators are to provide students with propositional knowledge, the preceding analysis makes clear that they face a task of quite significant proportion. To succeed at this endeavor, students cannot simply acquire or memorize information or store data or learn facts. Instead, in order for it to be said that they *know* something, they have to meet some evidential standard, minimally that of objective reasonableness and perhaps that of clearly evident. Thus, it would not be sufficient to establish that a student had knowledge if that student merely supplied the correct answer on a test; the student must establish that she or he believes the proposition and can also provide sufficient justification for it to appear (at the very least) reasonable for others to believe that same proposition.

Now we may speak more clearly about what it means to provide access to knowledge—at least in the context of modernism and in the case of propositional knowledge. It means that students not only have information, data, or claims, but that they also believe these and have evidence for them, and indeed may even be able to establish the standing of these propositions within the disciplinary field that formulated them. If one takes this definitional standard seriously, as one clearly should in the context of standard Western scholarship, consider the scale of the enterprise of schooling. The range of the curriculum over twelve years of schooling is so extensive and so detailed that it is mind-boggling to imagine the student *knowing* all that is taught over the span of elementary and secondary schooling. How can one possibly ensure equality of access to this vast body of human understanding, if the point is to bring the student to a level of knowledge regarding it all?

Another consideration is whether "disciplined encounters with all the subject matters of the human conversation" applies to performance knowledge in the same way it so clearly applies to propositional knowledge. If the reference is to art, theater, dance, and the other performing arts, then performance knowledge is part of a disciplined encounter, even though it is often little attended to in many school settings. If, on the other hand, the reference is to such activities as carpentry, plumbing, or boat building, the answer seems far less clear. These differences between propositional and performance knowledge are sometimes framed as the distinction between academic and vocational education. In a "Commentary" essay for *Education Week*, Goodlad makes clear that he believes performance knowledge is very much a part of the subject matters of the human conversation. He contends that "as book learning moves more and more to the center of the stage, all else is obscured in the shadows at the wings."[16] It is the making of things and taking pride in the doing that Goodlad argues have been placed in the obscurity of the wings of the educational stage and should be brought into a more central place in America's schools.

This consideration of the place of performance knowledge relative to propositional knowledge concludes the exploration of Western, modernist conceptions of knowledge. Modernist conceptions of knowledge continue to play an enormous role in how educators conceive of subject matter, curriculum, and the appraisal of student learning. What is less obvious in the setting of contemporary schooling is the clear distinction between knowledge and belief, and the extensive requirements for justification that pertain to knowledge but not to belief. It is clear, however, that Goodlad's views on the nature of knowledge include a strong justificatory standard (as the call for *disciplined* encounters with the subject matters of the human conversation makes clear), and a preference for both the propositional and the performative varieties of knowledge. Yet these views appear to reflect modernist notions. Will they survive the scrutiny of critical and postmodern theory? Perhaps it is time to rethink the modernist view of knowledge.

Rethinking Modernist Conceptions of Knowledge

Recall that in the postmodernist view, knowledge is not some monolithic reconstruction of human experience, standing alone in pristine objectivity, obligating the human species to accept it on pain of being declared barbarian or irrational. It is rather a form of understanding woven into the tapestry of culture, language, time, and context. Thus, for some postmodernists (not all, for they are no more a unified and coherent body than were the existentialist thinkers of the mid-twentieth century) what is known propositionally, and perhaps even performatively, varies across language setting, cultural boundary, or gender difference. Variation of this kind might be seen as making the educational task easier or harder: easier in the sense that we may not need to attain with every learner a common standard of knowledge, harder in the sense that a thorough education may require preparing a child to cross a number of boundaries, rather than merely remaining a student of his or her own territory.

The quandaries generated by the postmodern critique are not the only problematic features of the Enlightenment view of knowledge. Contemporary cognitive scientists offer another challenge to modernism's preoccupation with the logical, rational, and justificatory characteristics of knowledge. Cognitive scientists have raised their challenges from a quite different perspective than the postmodern critics have. Rather than attacking extant conceptions of knowledge, as most postmodernists have, cognitive scientists examine the ways the mind works, then draw inferences from these discoveries to how human beings construct knowledge and give meaning to the concept itself. Among the cognitive scientists who have put forward provocative challenges, two are of interest here: Howard Gardner and Kieran Egan.

Howard Gardner is perhaps best known for his theory of multiple intelligences. MI theory, as it is sometimes called, posits seven kinds of intelligences: "the linguistic and logical-mathematical intelligences that are at such a premium in schools today; musical intelligence; spatial intelligence; bodily-kinesthetic intelligence; and two forms of personal intelligence, one directed toward other persons, one directed toward oneself."[17] As Gardner notes, schools today stress the linguistic and logical-mathematical intelligences. They thus reflect the larger commitment of contemporary Western civilization to propositional knowledge, particularly as this knowledge occurs in the disciplines and branches of knowledge.

Gardner's argument is that the schools' preoccupation with but two forms of intelligence excludes educational consideration of many of the gifts and talents of the human mind. These gifts and talents are readily evident in the other five forms of intelligence; much could be done to cultivate them if they were understood and valued in the setting of the school. Although Gardner does not examine the point in detail, there is an interesting correlation between a society's valuing of particular conceptions of knowledge and those forms of intelligence cultivated in the school setting. The schools' preoccupation with linguistic and logical-mathematical forms of intelligence reflects the premium that Western industrialized nations place on modernist conceptions of knowledge.

This preoccupation with Enlightenment knowledge is clearly reflected in Charles Van Doren's A *History of Knowledge*, wherein he contends that "of all the kinds of knowledge that the West has given to the world, the most valuable is a method of acquiring new knowledge . . . called 'scientific method.' "[18] Van Doren's praise of this form of knowledge reveals a great deal about the esteem we accord to it: "There are other kinds of knowledge besides scientific knowledge . . . but none of them, at the present time and in the foreseeable future, has the power, prestige, and value that scientific knowledge has. Science has become the most distinctive of human activities, and the indispensable tool for the survival of the billions who now inhabit the planet."[19]

The challenge that Gardner's MI theory places before us is the contemplation of forms of knowledge parallel to intelligences, such that there may be forms of knowledge corresponding to intelligences other than the linguistic and logical-mathematical. For example, can spatial or personal understanding count as knowledge, and if so, what kind of knowledge might it be? Perhaps such knowledge may be in the form of propositions or performances, but it might also be so tacit that it is difficult to state, or so intuitive that it defies scrutiny of the kind typically given to knowledge candidates in propositional form. I do not know whether such suggestions of new knowledge forms will bear fruit, but it does appear evident that Gardner's analysis forces us to "think beyond the box," leading us to ponder whether conventional, modernist accounts of knowledge exhaust the meaning of the concept as it applies to the education of the young.

Another challenge to the modernist account is provided by Kieran Egan. Egan does not set out specifically to rebut modernism, but rather to seek reconsideration of how we undertake the education of the young. It is in the course of presenting his own theory that he calls into question the monolithic conception of knowledge implied by the modernist tradition. Egan argues that phylogenetically the species has proceeded through five levels of understanding: somatic, mythic, romantic, philosophic, and ironic. Egan elaborates on these forms in this way: "Our initial understanding . . . is somatic; then we develop language and socialized identity, then writing and print, then abstract, theoretic forms of expressing general truths, and then a reflexivity that brings with it pervasive doubts about the representations of the world that can be articulated in language."[20]

Using some of the core notions of the Russian psychologist Lev Vygotsky, Egan argues that our understanding is shaped by the tools we use to gain that understanding. For example, print makes possible the shift from mythic to romantic understanding, wherein we are able to gain, through the exercise of reason and reflection, a sense of our own possibility and potential. Egan argues that we should recapitulate these phases in the evolution of the species, so that the education of the infant attends to the cultivation of somatic understanding; the education of the five- to ten-year-old child, to mythic understanding; of the ten- to fifteen-year-old youth, to philosophic understanding; and so forth. Although at first blush Egan's proposals appear odd (an appraisal of which he is fully aware), both the logic of his argument and the evidence he offers compel our careful attention to his ideas.

Egan's argument interrogates the modernist view of knowledge by raising serious questions about whether the knowledge modernists so prize is but an artifact of the philosophic mode of understanding. As such, if we take the position that the modernist conception of knowledge is the only viable one, we may preclude ourselves from cultivating some sense of knowing in the somatic, mythic, and ironic domains of understanding (the romantic mode is excluded because, for the point I am making here, there are such close connections between it and the philosophic mode). Egan suggests precisely this possibility when he describes the benefits to be gained from using the five forms of understanding he describes: "Academic disciplines and their knowledge are not being dispensed with; rather, the traditionalist curriculum—made up of attempts to answer what is the most privileged knowledge for best forming the rational mind and criteria for education derived from some image of an ideal epistemological condition or an ideally educated person—will disappear. The new [kinds of understanding] justify a richer curriculum that will require more knowledge and more varied forms of knowledge."[21]

Both Egan and Gardner urge us to look beyond conventional understandings of the properties of knowledge. They do this as theoreticians, claiming that there is more that we know than is revealed by the traditional branches of knowledge, and as educators, claiming that we fail to educate children when we limit our conception of knowledge to modernist notions. When joined to the critiques of modernist notions by postmodernists, we are faced with a number of severe challenges if we are not exceedingly careful how we interpret the call to provide all children a disciplined encounter with all the subject matters of the human conversation.

Knowledge and the Human Conversation

Thus far we have explored how the concept of knowledge is related to notions of disciplined encounters and subject matters, but little has been said of the third element, the human conversation. In turning to this third key idea in the second part of the mission statement of the Agenda for Education in a Democracy, it would be helpful to note where this idea comes from and how it was initially framed. It comes from Michael Oakeshott, a philosopher and political theorist. In September 1974, on the occasion of the centennial of Colorado College, Oakeshott delivered the Abbott Memorial Lecture, which was later published as an essay entitled "A Place of Learning."[22] In this essay, Oakeshott goes to considerable length to expand our thinking on the idea of a culture. "A culture," he contends, "is not a miscellany of beliefs, perceptions, ideas, sentiments and engagements," but is instead "a variety of distinct languages of understanding."[23] Liberal learning, he argues, calls on us to become acquainted with these languages, to distinguish among them, and to recognize them as modes for understanding ourselves and others. The voices of these languages can be joined in a conversation, "an endless unrehearsed intellectual adventure in which, in imagination, we enter into a variety of modes of understanding the world and ourselves and are not disconcerted by the differences or dismayed by the inconclusiveness of it all."[24]

The human conversation is thus one of multiple languages, each expressing a mode of understanding the world, without dismay at the differences these languages reveal. At first blush, it appears that Oakeshott would have no difficulties with the postmodern critique or the cognitive structures proposed by Howard Gardner or Kieran Egan, for these might be understood as different languages or modes of understanding. On the other hand, one wonders what enables a listener educated in one language to grasp the meanings of a speaker of a different language. On closer reading of Oakeshott, one gains the sense that the multiple languages to which he refers are the languages of the poet, the artist, the physicist, the philosopher, and other representatives of the branches of knowledge and subject matters Adler describes in the *Propaedia*.

What we typically call "languages" is not what Oakeshott means in this case. The reference is not to Russian, French, or German, but to the discourses characteristic of the disciplines. Oakeshott refers, for example, to "a language such as that of a philosophical or historical understanding,"[25] indicating that his notion of the languages of understanding is what we think of as the different disciplines. (Recall Adler's division of the branches of knowledge into the five domains of logic, mathematics, science, history and humanities, and philosophy.) On this reading, Oakeshott is as much a modernist, a devotee of Western civilization, as so many of the white, European males referred to earlier in this chapter. Read in this way, the notion of a human conversation becomes not an invitation to alternative ways of knowing the world but a limit on how and what we may be said to know.

If we are to create a space in our educational thinking for the postmodernist critique or for the expansive ideas of a Gardner or an Egan, we must relinquish the highly privileged position that the traditional disciplines and branches of knowledge hold in our culture and schools. How we do that while still sharing standards enabling us to reach a measure of agreement on what is true, what is known, what is accurate or correct is the problem of these times. It is not an easy problem to address, but to fail to do so places us in a most awkward position.

A conception of knowledge as something that is transcendent and immutable, "out there" beyond the knower, typically leads to conceiving of teaching as an activity of imparting knowledge—of moving it from some place out there to some place in here, where "here" is a location inside the head of the student. In this view, teaching is a kind of trucking operation, and knowledge is the freight that is being hauled. It is hauled from textbooks, worksheets, web pages, films, and reference works to the interior of the learner's mind. By this scheme, there is almost no interaction between the knower and the known. Rather, the idea is for the learner to receive and store the freight as carefully and as faithfully as possible. The learner's interests and motives, talents and abilities, count for little in this process; adults with certain credentials have already decided what knowledge is worth knowing, as well as when and where this knowledge will be transported to the learner. Gardner and Egan caution that this transportation metaphor may be a legacy of modernist epistemology; the postmodernists would say that it should come as no surprise that so corrupt a metaphor follows from so erroneous a conception of knowledge.

Indeed, Goodlad does have a bull by the horns when he contends that a central purpose of schooling is to provide all children with a disciplined encounter with all the subject matters of the human conversation, as in so stating he appears to fall squarely within the modernist camp. Yet he would certainly find it repugnant to think of himself in league with the current raft of politically conservative educational theorists, and the "trucking knowledge" metaphor is alien to virtually all he has written on the subject.[26] This critical element in the Agenda's mission harbors a great deal of complexity and is subject to major disputes over its value. On the other hand, it also harbors a fascinating challenge. That challenge is to honor the extraordinary contributions and exceptional worth of modernist conceptions of knowledge while refraining from framing the entirety of educational discourse and practice in such terms. The challenge is to think carefully about how to open the human conversation to voices that we at first do not understand, or that we understand but initially want to resist or demean. The challenge is not simply to acquire, in Oakeshott's words, the languages of the modes of understanding, but also to understand the borders and boundaries of these languages, so that we may have a sense of what it would mean to cross these borders, venturing into new places that conventional Western thought does not encourage us to enter.

Reason, in the sense recently argued for by Thomas Nagel, enables us to converse across the borders of subject matters, disciplines, and communities of thought and practice different from our own.[27] Without reason, it is difficult to ascertain how there can be any sort of conversation, much less multiple conversations, conversations that cross borders and occur on previously unexplored territory. When, however, reason is restricted to some traditional sense of the disciplines, or when it is argued that it can be cultivated only by mastering some common curriculum selected by the curricular priesthood, then we are confined to a modernist version of knowledge. Reason can indeed be cultivated and expanded through the study of the disciplines, but it may also be corrupted or extinguished by these very same disciplines; much depends on how they are studied and who guides us in this study. The disciplines are not the only way to cultivate reason, although they do contain the historical record of our efforts to become more and more reasonable, and as such they can be very effective ways to cultivate reason. However, being well parented and well friended is another way to cultivate reason. Being well reared in a church, temple, or synagogue may be yet another way. Being curious and open and willing to speak to and learn from those who are different may be still another way.

The modernists may have slipped one over on us by encouraging us to think that reason is accessible only through their carefully constructed depositories of knowledge. There can be little doubt that these depositories are a fine source, but they are not the sole source. As a way of keeping our minds open to alternative and perhaps superior possibilities, we should understand what we know and what we believe as part of a context, a community. It is a community that most of us entered without reflection, and occupy unaware that it is but a context and not the universe consisting of all there is. The human conversation is more than a way into this context. Just as important, it is also a way out of it.

Given Goodlad's many commentaries on the human conversation, it is evident that he would agree. In this agreement, the bull becomes a great deal tamer, and thereby more easily led to new and different ground. This new ground is neither modernist nor postmodernist, but rather the ground between. It acknowledges the problems of canonical knowledge but does not discard standards for knowing merely because they carry the risk of canonizing one view over another. This ground between includes propositional and performance knowledge, while adhering to both the necessity and the possibility of justifying any form of knowledge claim. This ground between values human reason and holds it as a common and unifying capacity of the human species. It does not privilege some knowledge over other knowledge, but recognizes diversity in knowledge and in knowing, while maintaining the need for criteria to distinguish between knowledge and belief. This ground between views Western thought with a reverent but skeptical eye, contending that the immutable certainties once promised by Western philosophers are no more than the alchemist's dream of changing lead to gold, but this loss of pristine immutability does not warrant wholesale relativity and subjectivity. This ground between acknowledges the contributions of both modern and postmodern, but takes a position outside both. The ground between is where Goodlad has led the bull and where one is most likely to locate the defense of the second part of the mission statement of the Agenda for Education in a Democracy.

Notes

1. Jerome S. Bruner, *Actual Minds, Possible Worlds* (Cambridge, Mass.: Harvard University Press, 1986).

2. John I. Goodlad, *Teachers for Our Nation's Schools* (San Francisco: Jossey-Bass, 1990), p. 49.

3. Goodlad, *Teachers for Our Nation's Schools*, p. 49.

4. See R. K. Shope, *The Analysis of Knowing: A Decade of Research* (Princeton, N.J.: Princeton University Press, 1986).

5. Edmund Gettier, Jr., "Is Justified True Belief Knowledge?" *Analysis* 23 (1963): 121–123.

6. See, for example, Roderick Chisholm, *Theory of Knowledge*, 3rd ed. (Englewood Cliffs, N.J.: Prentice Hall, 1989); Keith Lehrer, *Theory of Knowledge* (Boulder, Colo.: Westview Press, 1990); Keith Lehrer, *Metamind* (New York: Oxford University Press, 1990); and Shope, *Analysis of Knowing*.

7. Lehrer, *Metamind*, p. 253.

8. Anthony Quinton, "Knowledge and Belief," in Paul Edwards (ed.), *The Encyclopedia of Philosophy* (New York: Macmillan, 1967), vol. 4, pp. 345–352.

9. Chisholm, *Theory of Knowledge*, p. 16.

10. Thomas F. Green, *The Activities of Teaching* (New York: McGraw-Hill, 1991).

11. Gilbert Ryle, *The Concept of Mind* (New York: Barnes & Noble, 1949).

12. Ryle, *Concept of Mind*, p. 30.

13. Ryle, *Concept of Mind*, p. 30.

14. A. J. Ayer, *The Problem of Knowledge* (Harmondsworth, U.K.: Penguin Books, 1956), pp. 13–14.

15. Lehrer, *Theory of Knowledge*, p. 4.

16. John I. Goodlad, "Beyond Half an Education," *Education Week*, February 19, 1992, pp. 44, 34.

17. Howard Gardner, *Frames of Mind*, 10th anniversary ed. (New York: Basic Books, 1993), p. xi.

18. Charles Van Doren, *A History of Knowledge* (New York: Ballantine Books, 1992), p. 184.

19. Van Doren, *History of Knowledge*, p. xxiv.

20. Kieran Egan, *The Educated Mind* (Chicago: University of Chicago Press, 1997), p. 171.

21. Egan, *Educated Mind*, p. 25.

22. Michael Oakeshott, "A Place of Learning," in Timothy Fuller (ed.), *The Voice of Liberal Learning* (New Haven, Conn.: Yale University Press, 1989), pp. 17–42.

23. Oakeshott, "Place of Learning," p. 38.

24. Oakeshott, "Place of Learning," p. 39.

25. Oakeshott, "Place of Learning," p. 38.

26. See his response to my tongue-in-cheek suggestions about the epistemological company he sometimes appears to keep in Gary D Fenstermacher, *On Knowledge and Its Relation to the Human Conversation*, Work in Progress Series no. 6 (Seattle: Institute for Educational Inquiry, 1997).

27. Thomas Nagel, *The Last Word* (New York: Oxford University Press, 1997).

5

Access to Knowledge

Mona H. Bailey

*Increasingly, the issue will be whether students, as a
consequence of the schools they happen to attend and
the classes to which they are assigned, have equality of
access to knowledge.*[1]

John I. Goodlad

The message that there is a moral imperative to provide all students equal access to knowledge in our schools is directed particularly to the constituent settings of the National Network for Educational Renewal (NNER), where educators are engaged in the work of renewing schools while simultaneously renewing the programs that prepare teachers to teach in those schools. It is directed as well to educational institutions outside the NNER that are interested in or working toward renewal. Leaders of these renewal efforts are encouraged to engage in critical inquiry into their practices and to participate in ongoing conversations that will ensure access to knowledge for all children and youths.

Nevertheless, barriers persist in many, if not most, of the schools and school districts today—barriers that diminish access to knowledge for large percentages of poor, minority, and non-English-speaking students—even while the reform of P–12 schools is a national, state, and local priority. Six cohorts of Leadership Associates have addressed this priority during their participation in the Leadership Program of the Institute for Educational Inquiry (IEI), and the work in progress in the NNER settings to achieve equal access to knowledge for all students is hopeful.

In the current wave of reform, the moral dimensions of schooling have faded into the background. Today's reform of P–12 schools and the attendant calls for greater accountability for student achievement are being fueled by economic issues, in particular, by concerns about the global and national competitiveness of the American economy. These concerns are compounded by the increasingly high numbers of adults whose low skills undermine their ability to earn the wages necessary to support themselves. This growing population unfortunately faces a corresponding lack of jobs for people with low skills.

But our system of compulsory schooling must do more than educate children and youths for economic self-sufficiency; it must also educate them in the more profound directions of personal development, freedom, and civic responsibility. As Gary Fenstermacher puts it in Chapter One of this book, schooling must advance not only economic opportunity for the individual but also democratic community. If we see the answer to the question of what schools are for, as educator John Goodlad does in *The Moral Dimensions of Teaching*, "as responsibility for critical enculturation into a political democracy, the cultivation of character and decency, and the preparation for full participation in a democracy,"[2] then teaching and those who teach must be grounded in these moral capacities.

Embedded in the IEI's six-year-old Leadership Program are activities, readings, and experiences to help Leadership Associates gain a fuller understanding of the moral dimensions of teaching, including those pertaining to educators' responsibility to provide all young people access to knowledge. Leadership Associates and their setting colleagues engage in conversations, reflection, and inquiry about all of the postulates John Goodlad (see Appendix A) has advanced and the evidence, or lack of evidence, of these postulates in their settings. Leaders and Leadership Associates must themselves become fully knowledgeable of, and fully committed to, these moral dimensions in order to engage in meaningful and lasting renewal in their settings.

Access to a High-Quality Education

A closer look at the moral dimensions of providing access to knowledge requires a repositioning of our thinking about access. For much of this century, the challenge for minority students in the United States was to gain access to free, public, and compulsory schools. Having now gained this access through the actions of the courts, today's students are faced with a new challenge: to gain access to what goes on inside the schools. John Ogbu reminds us that segregation in American schools has now substantially disappeared, but nevertheless observes: "Minorities and whites may be in the same schools but do not necessarily receive the same education or learn similar rules of behavior for achievement."[3] John Goodlad, in his book, *A Place Called School*, put the situation this way: "The central problem for today and tomorrow is no longer access to school. It is access to knowledge for all. The dual challenge is that of assuring both equity and quality in school programs."[4]

School districts spend vast amounts of money to redistribute students from their segregated neighborhoods, only to sort and resegregate them inside the schools into tracks of low ability and high ability. Segregation is illegal but still alive and well today in the schools of this nation in the form of tracking students into advanced placement, high honors, honors, regular, remedial, and gifted classes. Consider an inner-city high school serving approximately fifteen hundred students from throughout a major U.S. city. This high school enrolls many of the district's students who are certified as gifted and have attended both the elementary and middle school gifted programs. More than half (55 percent) of the school's students are white, with the largest percentage of the minority population being African American. This school also continues, year after year, to have one of the largest contingents of merit scholars in the state. But almost all of the merit scholars are white or Asian. The school's curriculum consists of advanced placement classes in English, social studies and mathematics; honors classes in the same subjects; and regular and low-ability classes in all of these subjects as well. Mostly minorities are in regular and low-ability classes, and mostly white students are in honors and advanced placement subjects and classes. And very few minorities are in advanced classes in algebra, trigonometry, math analysis, and calculus.

Many school districts enroll, and will continue to enroll, large numbers of bilingual students and students with limited English proficiency. Some of these young people adapt to their new school environments and are academically successful. Studies show, however, that many of these students are placed in programs that assume low levels of achievement and focus on remedial education. Latino children in particular often begin school behind their non-Latino white peers, and the variance widens as many of these children progress through school. Dropout rates for Latino students, while declining, remain extremely high: U.S. Department of Education statistics report that 29 percent of sixteen- to twenty-four-year-old Latinos are dropouts, whereas 13 percent of African Americans and 7 percent of non-Hispanic whites of that age group are so classified.[5]

The reality is that for students who are poor, members of a minority group (particularly African American, Hispanic, or Native American), from single-parent families, or non-English speakers, the chances are disproportionately high that they will acquire knowledge in a remedial program, a low group or track, a vocational program rather than a college-preparatory program, and/or a program taught by a teacher who is not well prepared. All of these situations characterize what Martin Haberman calls "the pedagogy of poverty."[6] A significant number of American students who have limited access to both quality and equity in their education are concentrated in urban school districts. Haberman, who has studied many urban classrooms, observes that they share a common form of teaching. A basic menu, found at all levels and subjects, includes such acts as giving information, asking questions, giving directions, making assignments, monitoring seat work, giving tests, reviewing tests, assigning and reviewing homework, marking papers, giving grades, and settling disputes. These acts, taken together to the exclusion of such acts as problem solving, inquiry, reflection, and cooperative learning, make up the pedagogy of poverty. "Unfortunately," observes Haberman, "the pedagogy of poverty does not work. Youngsters achieve neither the minimum levels of life skills nor what they are capable of learning."[7]

Many poor children who are academically behind their age-level peers in the basic-skills subjects receive much of their instruction in remedial programs that provide few opportunities to learn higher-order thinking skills. Often the more challenging and advanced curriculum and programs are not options for them until they have "caught up" or are performing at least at grade level. A recent study of academic instruction for disadvantaged students, however, refutes the idea "that, for most of the children of poverty, academically challenging work in mathematics should be postponed until they are 'ready'—that is, until they have acquired full mastery of basic skills" and argues for "instruction that emphasizes meaning and understanding" for all students. Although children of poverty "are often lacking in certain basic skills," the study observes, "they can acquire these skills at the same time that they gain advanced skills (which provide a broader, more meaningful context for learning 'the basics')."[8]

In a briefing paper to the College Board's National Task Force on Minority High Achievement, L. Scott Miller describes the changing demographics in this country. Bureau of the Census projections suggest that African Americans, Hispanics, and Native Americans may collectively constitute 42 percent of the under-eighteen population by the year 2030.[9] This projection is highly significant to educators, given that these particular minority groups are much more likely to grow up in disadvantaged circumstances, in poverty, and/or with poorly educated parents. These are the children and youths most at risk in today's schools—those for whom access to equity and quality programs that include higher-level knowledge and skills is yet to be realized.

As moral stewards charged with ensuring access to knowledge for all students, we must ask an essential question: Is it primarily different language, different culture, or different social class that determines which groups of children will have access to higher levels of knowledge? These inequities in different students' prospects for access to knowledge and school success pose a grave danger to the well-being of our society.

Approaching the diversity of students as a national asset rather than as a problem and renewing all of our educational programs to prepare all students for full citizenship in an increasingly diverse society present not only a moral challenge but an imperative to change practices that deny access. The moral predicament facing everyone engaged in educational renewal work is the maldistribution of opportunities to gain access to even the most generally useful knowledge in most schools, with poor and minority students on the short end of the distribution.

Barriers to Equal Access

Equal access to knowledge has been constrained by societal attitudes and conditions in the schools that act as barriers. These barriers that limit access have received a great deal of attention from the research community. But although research findings show that underachieving students by and large do not benefit from approaches currently in place in many schools, these approaches, practices, and policies are slow to die.

Four of the most persistent of these ill-fated school conditions that limit access to knowledge, and must therefore be confronted in educational renewal work, are racism, misguided curricular practices, low teacher quality, and ill-considered policies concerning standards and accountability.

Racism

John Ogbu argues that there are racial barriers that must be understood and then overcome to ensure that minority students will have
equitable opportunities to gain access to knowledge. Ogbu posits that
in the case of African American students, racial barriers come from
both social and educational systems; that is, the treatment of African
Americans both within the larger society and within schools ad-
versely affects the quantity and quality of their educational experiences. This treatment has given rise to a pattern of coping responses
and perceptions by African American students. "Why try?" some
ask. Success in school will not guarantee them a share in society's
reward system. They will still be less likely than their white classmates to secure decent jobs or housing. School officials, Ogbu contends, have been aware of the realities of the labor market and hence
have channeled African American students into educational tracks
that prepare them for jobs below the ceiling, the place they custom-
arily and commonly have held in the employment structure.[10]

Not many educators recognize that their own prejudicial thoughts
about race determine their expectations for their students and moti-
vate their behaviors toward them. James Banks, bell hooks, Cornel
West, Vivian Paley, and many others have written eloquently about
the ways in which educators and noneducators alike can come to
understand racial and cultural barriers and how those barriers can
affect their own practices.[11] Having deepened their understanding of
themselves, teachers can learn to overcome past practices and establish classrooms and schools that nurture the learning of all students.

Curricular Practices and Policies

Tracking has been and continues to be a widespread curricular practice throughout all levels of schooling, although student results clearly
show that the effects of tracking run counter to what teachers, administrators, and parents want: helping all children to learn. Since the
1980s, when her study of tracking in schools resulted in her book
Keeping Track,[12] Jeannie Oakes has eloquently and passionately argued

for detracking schools, and she poignantly observes: "One finding about [tracking] placements is undisputed: Disproportionate percentages of poor and minority youngsters (principally black and Hispanic) are placed in tracks for low-ability or noncollege-bound students; further, minority students are consistently underrepresented in programs for the gifted and talented."[13]

Students placed in different levels within tracked structures have access to considerably different types of knowledge and intellectual skills. Those in high-ability groups, for example, are likely to experience high-quality course content, as well as a pedagogy that allows them to develop critical-thinking and problem-solving skills. In other words, they experience the repertoire that prepares them for college and then leadership positions in society. Young people placed in low-ability groups, on the other hand, are taught different content and are not expected to learn the same skills. In a low-ability English class, students are typically taught basic reading skills by means of workbooks or kit activities and are given easy stories to read. The learning tasks likely include memorizing and repeating answers to teachers. These students are not generally provided access to the knowledge that would allow them to move into higher classes, let alone be successful if they got there.[14]

Tracking has troublesome consequences. And when it interacts with the conditions and events that make up the schooling context, the result is even more troublesome.[15] This interrelationship can be seen not only in the organization of curriculum and instruction but also in the experiences and accomplishments of students. School policies, while varying from district to district, play a role in determining the extent, specificity, and flexibility of the tracking structure. A high school serving a high percentage of impoverished minority and immigrant students, for example, is likely to emphasize a general or vocational program and unlikely to offer advanced mathematics, sciences, and foreign languages, as would a school emphasizing a college preparatory program. Something is very wrong with the picture of fourteen keyboarding classes in a school with only one chemistry class. Teacher assignment policies, which result in poor students' having fewer of the best teachers, also affect the quality of instruction and the curriculum offered. All of these policies, including textbook adoption policies, act together to influence students' access to knowledge at both the school and classroom levels.

Teacher Quality

Many people today are raising the question: Are teachers also tracked? The research of Jeannie Oakes, Donna Davis, Merrilee K. Findley, and James E. Rosenbaum regarding teacher quality consistently shows that they are, with those teachers "judged to be the most competent and experienced assigned to the top tracks."[16] Linda Darling-Hammond and Joslyn Green assert that "the students in greatest need of the best teaching are the least likely to get it." They further note that the distribution of good teachers has a serious impact on student learning: "Perhaps the single greatest source of educational inequity is this disparity in the availability and distribution of highly qualified teachers."[17]

The quality of those who teach is more acutely important today than ever. The National Commission on Teaching & America's Future made this point in no uncertain terms in its 1996 report, *What Matters Most*. The commission's first premise declared: "What teachers know and can do is the most important influence on what students learn."[18] Teacher effectiveness, in turn, depends on both knowledge and pedagogy. "To be effective," the report continued, "teachers must know their subject matter so thoroughly that they can present it in a challenging, clear, and compelling way." Yet 27 percent of newly hired teachers in the United States in 1990–1991 had either no teaching license or only a temporary, provisional, or emergency license. Twenty-three percent of high school teachers lacked even a minor in their teaching specializations, and 50 percent of those who taught a second subject had less than a minor in that field. Barely half of mathematics teachers in public high schools (53 percent) both held a state license and had completed a college major in mathematics.[19] However the statistics are analyzed, an alarming number of teachers are inadequately prepared to teach.

The practice of hiring underprepared and ill-prepared teachers has pernicious implications for the goal of providing all students access to knowledge. We know from the work of Linda Darling-Hammond and Eileen Sclan that novice teachers holding some form of alternative certification tend to secure positions in schools with large numbers of students from low-income families and/or students of color.[20] One would expect to find, therefore, that poor and minority students are less likely to be taught by qualified teachers than are advantaged students. Statistics support this conclusion. For example, *Education Watch: The 1996 Education Trust State and National Data Book*, reported that in 1990–1991 only 42 percent of the math classes in high schools with more than 50 percent minority enrollments were taught by teachers who had majored in mathematics. By contrast, in high schools with less than 15 percent minority students, 69 percent of the math classes were taught by math majors.[21] Pamela Grossman and Frank Murray have found a direct connection between teacher competence and teacher bias. Teachers lacking formal teacher preparation are likely to hold minimal expectations for young people of color or from low-income families. Such teachers also tend to harbor misconceptions about the nature of learning and effective teaching.[22]

The issue of teacher quality also suggests that we need to look at how teachers are prepared. Many investigators have come to the conclusion that teachers tend to teach as they have been taught. Today's classrooms, however, require teachers who can offer a rich curriculum to a diverse student body. "The education of teachers," John Goodlad asserts, "must be driven by a clear and careful conception of the educating we expect our schools to do, the conditions most conducive to this educating (as well as the conditions that get in the way), and the kinds of expectations that teachers must be prepared to meet."[23] Currently there is a mismatch between teachers and their students, particularly in urban classrooms. More than 80 percent of teachers in urban schools are white, suburban, middle class, and English-only speaking, while their students are principally nonwhite, poor, and with limited English proficiency.

School districts are attempting in significant ways to upgrade and enhance teacher quality by providing many more—albeit not enough—inservice professional development opportunities. Goodlad, however, rightly observes that this will not cure the nation's teacher quality challenge because, as he puts it, "Many thousands of teachers are insufficiently prepared in the subjects they teach to take advantage more than cosmetically of the subject-oriented inservice workshops and institutes currently available to them."[24]

Standards and Accountability

The route to improving schools in almost all states and many school districts has led to the adoption of standards spelling out what students must know and be able to do. Large-scale assessments are and will continue to be conducted by states and districts to measure student performance on these new standards in all the content areas. But a warning must be sounded. Standards will prove to be yet another misguided effort unless there are concurrent drives to improve teacher quality and eliminate entrenched curricular practices that result in educational inequities for minority and poor students. Let us be sure that the playing field is leveled in terms of access to knowledge and the skills for acquiring and applying knowledge before we implement large-scale assessments. Let us ensure also that we base our accountability at least partly on alternative assessments, such as student portfolios or exhibitions of achievement as described by Theodore Sizer in *Horace's School*.[25] Raising the bar for everyone is necessary and good. Let us not quarrel with that. However, let us ensure that poor Latino, Native American, African American, and immigrant students have the opportunities and the supports necessary to achieve high standards.

Other conditions that undermine access to knowledge and must be considered along with major curricular and teacher-quality issues include grading students on conduct rather than academic performance, using biased textbooks and curriculum, treating minority children differently in the classroom and in disciplinary situations, and failing to build understanding of cultural and language differences or to create programs to deal with problems arising from those differences. If we do not deal with these barriers completely as part of the renewal process, schools will continue to relegate some students to separate and unequal futures in our democratic society.

Removing the Barriers

Within the NNER, there is now a core of Leadership Associates whose knowledge and understanding of the moral dimensions of access to knowledge have been deepened. These Associates have already begun, with others in their settings, to replicate the IEI's Leadership Program. Their respective agendas seek to renew teacher preparation programs and schools simultaneously. Reformulating policies, curricula, and teacher training and placement practices to provide all students quality access to knowledge must be high on their renewal agendas—a daunting challenge requiring bold and urgent action.

In addition to Leadership Associates, other members of the NNER settings' partnerships—teachers, principals, superintendents and other districtwide leaders, and university faculties—have critical roles to play in removing these barriers and replacing them with practices, programs, and policies that serve all students equitably. Robert Sinclair and Ward Ghory remind us that in the effective school in a democracy, principals, teachers, parents, and students have special roles to play and specific responsibilities to uphold in the process of reducing marginality and increasing learning for all students.[26] Students on the margins who are experiencing limited access to knowledge present a crucial challenge to educators. "Simply put," Sinclair and Ghory advise, "if American public schools are to become even more effective, it is necessary to reach and teach those young people who are not realizing their potential."[27]

Policies set at the district level that lead to inequities in access to knowledge need to be rescinded and replaced with policies ensuring equity and quality for all students. Beyond policies, responsible district administrators and their university partners should provide support and resources for teachers and other professionals to develop new skills and knowledge and to have professional opportunities to collaborate about what and how students learn.

At the school level, the principal has the responsibility to articulate the school's mission of quality education for all students and to encourage teachers and other staff to believe not only in the capabilities of their learners but also in their own abilities to create vigorous ways for all students to learn. As the key figure in establishing the conditions for teachers to work together to address the needs of their students, the principal must provide to teachers opportunities for reflection and discourse with their colleagues.

The teachers' role is critical. Teachers must take responsibility to prepare themselves to the highest professional standards so that they can use the best current knowledge about learners and learning. Sinclair and Ghory posit that "educators have an obligation to help students become more powerful learners by teaching them the identifiable learning skills related to success within prevailing classroom conditions."[28] As moral stewards, teachers need to be acutely aware that casual and misguided decisions with regard to tracking and grouping students, apportioning the domains of knowledge in the curriculum, allocating daily and weekly instructional time, and other practices can distribute knowledge unfairly and inequitably. Walter Feinberg charges teachers with yet another important role: helping to constitute a public. This role involves teachers' using "their collective ability to identify conditions that inhibit children from developing the skills needed to become participants in a self-forming public"—and rectifying those conditions.[29]

Teacher educators from colleges of education, colleges of arts and sciences, and the P–12 schools must combine their efforts to provide renewing and vibrant programs that offer a wide array of courses, conversations, and practical experiences in exemplary classrooms. John Goodlad's nineteen postulates set forth the necessary conditions for the education of educators in a social and political democracy (see Appendix A).

Parents must accept the responsibility to work with teachers and the school in collaborative and productive ways for the benefit of their children. This also means reinforcing at home strategies that enable school success. For two decades, James Comer has championed the development of school communities in which parents join with educators and other service professionals to bring about wholesome and nurturing practices that ensure access to knowledge for all children.[30]

Ultimately, of course, students must play a key role in developing attitudes and performance behaviors that lead to school success. But students need help from the adults in the learning environment to learn these behaviors, which are not naturally or instinctively acquired.

Two Renewing Partner Schools

Focusing on learners who are not successful can be the best rallying point for building collaboration among all the partners to create schools that carry out the moral mission of public education. Promising and rewarding work toward this end is at various stages throughout the NNER. The following sections describe the hard work and earnest efforts under way at two of the network partner schools that are at different stages of renewal.

Bailey Gatzert Elementary School, Seattle, Washington

Serving just under five hundred prekindergarten through fifth-grade students, Bailey Gatzert is an elementary school in the Seattle School District.[31] In addition to the neighborhood children, the school serves pupils bused from both ends of the city. The school is one of several centers for homeless elementary students; those who attend Bailey Gatzert maintain their relationship with it through a district practice of transporting them to the school from wherever their current "residence" is situated. Slightly more than 85 percent of Gatzert students are minority, with African American students representing the largest group. More than 85 percent participate in the free and reduced-cost lunch program. More than a quarter of the students, speaking collectively sixteen different languages and dialects, are enrolled in bilingual programs. The number of special education students doubled in one year from thirty-five to seventy.

Until recently, access to knowledge for Gatzert students was illusory, as is evidenced by the school's academic standing for 1992–1993. That year, Gatzert ranked at the bottom of all elementary schools in Seattle for reading, language arts, and mathematics.

A dedicated principal–instructional leader, newly assigned to Gatzert, took on the challenge of restructuring this underachieving elementary school in 1993–1994 by recruiting new faculty and challenging faculty who chose to remain. Guided by a shared mission to develop an educational program that was instructionally and developmentally appropriate for each student and an educational climate in which all children would learn, the staff commenced a journey to accomplish a number of objectives:

- Realign the curriculum

- Move from basal-driven instruction to thematic integrated units that infuse multiculturally relevant information into students' daily learning

- Emphasize learning processes and an attitude of lifelong learning

- Work cooperatively and collaboratively to develop a program that builds on student strengths and experiences

- Integrate technology in the day-to-day curriculum offerings

- Work with families to meet the academic, social, and emotional needs of all children

The journey thus far has resulted in a school program that promotes accelerated academics and a curriculum that is integrated and thematic. The school includes a full-day kindergarten, smaller classes, and an extended school day and a Saturday Academy to meet the needs of the students and families. Reading is emphasized and is supported by a large and active library program. Each student has twenty minutes of sustained silent reading in class each day, and students are encouraged to participate in a variety of reading incentive programs, including the Accelerated Reader Program. Teachers read aloud to students each day and then discuss the story elements to gauge comprehension. Students are scheduled to work in the computer lab every other day on reading, math skills, and word processing.

Gatzert takes seriously the belief that it takes a whole village to educate children. Support staff, including an intervention specialist, a counselor, a family support worker, and a case manager from a community service center, all work together to meet the challenging needs of students and their families. Parent volunteers are augmented by community volunteers to help during and after school. High school and university students tutor Gatzert students. Big Sisters offers an in-school program, and the YMCA provides child care. Parents and guardians participate in unique activities that give them opportunities to learn about wellness, nutrition, parenting skills, and effective ways to access community services.

Since Gatzert's journey of renewal commenced in 1993–1994, significant academic achievement gains have been made. Students who experience more than two years of education at Gatzert are making meaningful academic progress in reading, language, and mathematics. Academic achievement and the involvement of parents and the community are the cornerstones of this diverse school. Although this journey toward equity and excellence is less than five years old at the time of this writing, the picture today is one of a school climbing the ladder of success.

Bel Air High School, El Paso, Texas

A school of two thousand students, mostly Hispanic, with the remaining students being African American and white, Bel Air High School in Ysleta School District was at the bottom.[32] As the dean of instruction observed, "*Failure* was the common word."

In the mid-1990s, Bel Air reconstituted itself to turn its failures around. The process started with faculty and staff being required to apply for their positions and make a firm commitment to working toward success for all students. The dean later said that they were looking for risk takers—teachers who see all students as being potentially successful and employ a variety of instructional practices in order to reach everyone. Professional development for the rehired and the newly hired was key to building teachers' confidence and skills. Staff now participate in ongoing professional development, spending three days in August followed by a team-building activity every Wednesday during the school year.

At the outset, structural barriers that had impeded access to knowledge were dismantled. For example, the barrier of departmental isolation was broken down. Today different departments work together for a common cause: student achievement. Strategic goals and plans were developed to meet state and local accountability requirements. Parents and community members were invited to give their support to the changes taking place at the high school.

Major changes to the academic program and the schedule resulted in increased learning opportunities for students. A block schedule, consisting of ninety-minute instructional sessions, was instituted. All freshmen were placed in a math program that integrates algebra and geometry, features hands-on activities, and uses integrated technology. This program provides the foundation for students to take more advanced math courses later. All sophomore students are blocked for the year in English, reading, and writing.

Four centers have been established to support students' learning: library, math, learning assistance, and health. Each of these centers is showing an increase in student and teacher usage. In the library center, for example, book circulation increased from 6,100 in the 1995–1996 academic year to nearly 9,500 in 1996–1997. The library served 616 classes in 1996–1997, up from 433 in 1995–1996. These program and schedule changes have had beneficial results: increased attendance rates, a decrease in the number of failures, gains in student test scores, and a lower dropout rate.

Putting the Ideal into Practice

Bailey Gatzert Elementary School and Bel Air High School, as well as many others, offer hope that the ideal can be successfully put into practice in the real world of schools. Our collective and highest priority—to educate all children commonly and successfully—*can* be attained. To achieve this end, now and into the future, we must be prepared to provide poor children and their schools equal access to competent teachers. This, in turn, requires that teacher educators help to improve the capacity of all teachers by increasing their knowledge and their ability to use that knowledge. At the same time, society must make a commitment to providing the resources necessary to ensure high-quality, balanced, and rigorous curricula and programs for all students.

In their book *Kids and School Reform,* Patricia A. Wasley, Robert L. Hampel, and Richard W. Clark observe that schoolteachers and administrators must examine their beliefs in order to serve all students well. Renewal efforts that authentically connect with students, these authors argue, combine high expectations with a caring pedagogy, vary routines by using a broad repertoire of teaching strategies, insist on rigorous student performance during the times that innovative practices are being employed, and personalize learning for students by reducing the number of students in classrooms, houses, or units to offer myriad opportunities for them to participate in the human conversation.[33]

If we can achieve access to knowledge for all students in schools of the NNER, we have a great chance of succeeding, if we have the will, in every school throughout the nation. Sinclair and Ghory offer a challenge that should guide our collective work in fulfilling the moral imperative of ensuring equal access to knowledge for all children and youths: "The last and first priority for each single school, as it mirrors the democratic society it serves, is to take the lead in providing equal opportunity for learning so that all young people may realize the promise of their potential."[34]

Notes

1. John I. Goodlad, *A Place Called School: Prospects for the Future* (New York: McGraw-Hill, 1984), p. 131.

2. John I. Goodlad, "The Occupation of Teaching in Schools," in John I. Goodlad, Roger Soder, and Kenneth A. Sirotnik (eds.), *The Moral Dimensions of Teaching* (San Francisco: Jossey-Bass, 1990), p. 28.

3. John U. Ogbu, "Overcoming Racial Barriers to Equal Access," in John I. Goodlad and Pamela Keating (eds.), *Access to Knowledge: The Continuing Agenda for Our Nation's Schools,* rev. ed. (New York: College Entrance Examination Board, 1994 [orig. 1990]), p. 75.

4. Goodlad, *A Place Called School,* p. 140.

5. These statistics are for the year 1996 for "status dropouts": "persons who are not enrolled in school and who are not high school graduates." (Persons who have received a general equivalency diploma are classified as graduates.) U.S. Department of Education, National Center for Education Statistics, "Dropout Rates in the United States," *Digest of Education Statistics* (September 1997), available at http://nces.ed.gov/pubs/digest97/d97t103.html (accessed May 5, 1998).

6. Martin Haberman, "The Pedagogy of Poverty Versus Good Teaching," *Phi Delta Kappan* 73 (December 1991): 290–294.

7. Haberman, "Pedagogy of Poverty," p. 291.

8. Michael S. Knapp, Patricia M. Shields, and Brenda J. Turnbull, *Academic Challenge for the Children of Poverty*, Summary Report (Washington, D.C.: U.S. Department of Education, 1992), p. i.

9. L. Scott Miller, Briefing paper for May 9, 1997, meeting of the National Task Force on Minority High Achievement, p. 4.

10. Ogbu, "Overcoming Racial Barriers."

11. James A. Banks, "Multicultural Education: Developments, Dimensions, and Challenges," *Phi Delta Kappan* 75 (September 1993): 22–28; bell hooks, *Teaching to Transgress* (New York: Routledge, 1994); Cornel West, *Race Matters* (Boston: Beacon Press, 1993); and Vivian G. Paley, *White Teacher* (Cambridge, Mass.: Harvard University Press, 1989).

12. Jeannie Oakes, *Keeping Track: How Schools Structure Inequality* (New Haven, Conn.: Yale University Press, 1985).

13. Jeannie Oakes, "Tracking in Secondary Schools: A Contextual Perspective," *Educational Psychologist* 22 (Spring 1987): 136.

14. Recognition of this problem inspired Henry M. Levin to found the Accelerated Schools Project. For the philosophy behind Accelerated Schools, see his Prologue to Wendy S. Hopfenberg, Henry M. Levin, and Associates, *The Accelerated Schools Resource Guide* (San Francisco: Jossey-Bass, 1993), pp. xi–xvi. See also the videotape *Accelerated Schools Project: Don't Remediate—Accelerate* (Seattle: Institute for Educational Inquiry, 1998).

15. Jeannie Oakes and Martin Lipton, "Tracking and Ability Grouping: A Structural Barrier to Access and Achievement," in Goodlad and Keating (eds.) *Access to Knowledge*, pp. 187–204.

16. Linda Darling-Hammond with Joslyn Green, "Teacher Quality and Equality," in Goodlad and Keating (eds.), *Access to Knowledge*, p. 245.

17. Darling-Hammond with Green, "Teacher Quality and Equality," p. 239.

18. National Commission on Teaching & America's Future, *What Matters Most: Teaching for America's Future* (New York: National Commission on Teaching & America's Future, 1996), p. 6.

19. National Commission on Teaching & America's Future, *What Matters Most*, p. 15.

20. Linda Darling-Hammond and Eileen Sclan, "Who Teaches and Why: Dilemmas of Building a Profession for Twenty-first Century Schools," in John Sikula, Thomas Buttery, and Edith Guyton (eds.), *Handbook of Research on Teacher Education*, 2nd ed. (New York: Macmillan, 1996), pp. 67–101.

21. Education Trust, *Education Watch: The 1996 Education Trust State and National Data Book* (Washington, D.C.: Education Trust), p. 8.

22. Pamela L. Grossman, *The Making of a Teacher: Teacher Knowledge and Teacher Education* (New York: Teachers College Press, 1990); and Frank B. Murray, "Beyond Natural Teaching: The Case for Professional Education," in Frank B. Murray (ed.), *The Teacher Educator's Handbook: Building a Knowledge Base for the Preparation of Teachers* (San Francisco: Jossey-Bass, 1996), pp. 3–13.

23. Goodlad, *Teachers for Our Nation's Schools*, pp. 3–4.

24. John I. Goodlad, "Beyond McSchool: A Challenge to Educational Leadership" (paper presented to the National Academy of Sciences symposium, "Reflecting on Sputnik: Linking the Past, Present, and Future of Educational Reform," Washington, D.C., October 1997). Available at http://www2.nas.edu/center/goodlad.htm (accessed May 7, 1998).

25. See examples of exhibitions in Theodore R. Sizer, *Horace's School: Redesigning the American High School* (Boston: Houghton Mifflin, 1992), pp. 23, 48, 65, 79, 98, 118, 133.

26. Robert L. Sinclair and Ward J. Ghory, "Last Things First: Realizing Equality by Improving Conditions for Marginal Students," in Goodlad and Keating (eds.), *Access to Knowledge*, pp. 125–144.

27. Sinclair and Ghory, "Last Things First," p. 137.

28. Sinclair and Ghory, "Last Things First," p. 139.

29. Walter Feinberg, "The Moral Responsibility of Public Schools," in Goodlad, Soder, and Sirotnik (eds.), *Moral Dimensions of Teaching*, p. 183.

30. James Comer, *School Power: Implications of an Intervention Project* (New York: Macmillan, 1980).

31. Profile information on Bailey Gatzert Elementary School was provided by Pat Sander, principal.

32. Profile information on Bel Air High School was provided by Susana Gonzalez, dean of instruction.

33. Patricia A. Wasley, Robert L. Hampel, and Richard W. Clark, *Kids and School Reform* (San Francisco: Jossey-Bass, 1997), pp. 69–96.

34. Sinclair and Ghory, "Last Things First," p. 142.

6

Voicing Democracy in an Imperfect World: Toward a Public Pedagogy of Nurture

Donna H. Kerr

I sometimes find myself yawning at particular academic discourses that I well understand are utterly important, and it worries me. It is the teacher in me who yawns. The discussions in question regard the kinds of knowledge, beliefs, values, and the like that are arguably essential to the functioning of a democracy. I have even contributed to this literature. Moreover, I still read with appreciation works that address anew what would ideally constitute education in a democracy and the related values inherent in liberal education and "cultivating humanity." My problem comes when I am teaching and am confronted with clearly undemocratic tendencies—sometimes in my students, sometimes in myself. As I interact with students, these works of philosophers (including myself), curriculum theorists, political and social theorists, historians, and others strike me as distractingly, disappointingly beside the point. They do not seem to help me know what to do, how to be with my students and myself, or more generally, how to cultivate living in democratic ways. In this chapter I explore why coming face to face with students seems to disconnect me from the scholarly discourse on democracy and education and, further, come to imagine how democracy might be voiced in how we are with one another in our ordinary lives, including our lives in the classroom. I am here picking up on Gary Fenstermacher's suggestion in Chapter One that we need to attend to "the voice of democracy." I find the expression apt, for it reminds us that democracy can be realized only at the level of the individual human voice. To begin, let us eavesdrop on the voice of sixth-grader Maxine in an episode from Hong Kingston's *The Woman Warrior: Memoirs of a Girlhood Among Ghosts*.[1]

Born to Chinese parents in California, Maxine does not talk during her whole first year of school. It simply does not occur to her to talk, and she even enjoys her silence, until she finds out that all the while she was flunking kindergarten. Subsequently, Maxine struggles with the conflicting personas that the American and Chinese cultures accept and reward. The subdued, passive, subservient, group-oriented persona expected especially of girls in the Chinese part of her world clashes with and impedes her efforts to develop the independent, self-confident character celebrated in American culture. Only with great difficulty does Maxine develop even a weak, hesitant, raspy American voice that she takes into the sixth grade, when the episode we consider here takes place.

Horsing around after American school and before it is time to leave for Chinese school, Maxine darts into the girls' lavatory, where a Chinese American classmate follows in pursuit—a classmate who still does not talk in school. Unexpectedly for both girls, Maxine turns on her silent playmate and announces: "You're going to talk. . . . I am going to make you talk, you sissy-girl." The silent girl embodies everything Maxine has come to loathe in herself: her own weakness, fragility, hesitance, difficulty in putting herself forward. In this moment of being alone with the "dumb" girl, the intense pain of Maxine's inner struggle translates into a violent confrontation. The only way that she can feel better now is for the other girl to talk. Maxine is desperate; she *must* make her talk.

As Maxine's repeated demands are met with continued silence, she becomes violent, squeezing the other girl's cheeks and time and again pulling her hair. Maxine finds everything about her disgusting: her bodily fragility, her haircut, her posture, her gestures, her clothing. She especially hates this girl's passivity in letting Maxine pick on her without uttering a single word. Verbal abuse, physical abuse, provocations, bribes—all are to no avail. Maxine, unable to escape her own rage that escalates with her abject failure to evoke a "voice," finally herself starts to cry. Eventually the silent girl's older sister comes into the lavatory and thus provides a way out. Too late for Chinese school, they all walk home together. In the wake of this incident, Maxine spends the next eighteen months in bed with a mysterious illness.

What if you or I as a teacher were to walk into this scene of hatred and violence—into this quintessentially undemocratic exchange? What would either of us do? What should a teacher do? Yes, prejudicial attitudes against "Chinese" children and their families doubtless contributed to Maxine's self-loathing. We have social theory to help us say that. But what are you or I to *do*? Should we shout, "Stop pinching her!" much as Maxine shouted, "Talk!" and rush to comfort the silent girl? And then what? To try to get another angle of vision, let us revisit this encounter as a case of undemocratic pedagogy with Maxine as the "teacher," the one trying to "teach" the silent girl to talk. Indeed, this is the role that Maxine assigns herself, if in a somewhat apologetic manner.

As a teacher, Maxine sets about to bring the silent girl to have a voice of her own, to force a subjectivity. Maxine's own voice is so fragile that she cannot tolerate the other girl's silence. Many teachers remember at least one time when they "forced" students in similarly painful ways from which they could not extricate themselves until the bell rang. The expressions of hatred and violence in this "exchange" between Maxine, the teacher, and her "student" intensify through a repeating cycle in which Maxine demands that the silent girl be otherwise, that she utter something. When the silent girl does not even try, Maxine reiterates her demands and physically tries to force an effort. As the violence ratchets upward, Maxine becomes frightened by "its" destruction, which she blames on the silent girl, who, Maxine claims, could stop the violence if only she would carry out Maxine's demands.

The teaching session begins with a statement of its goal or purpose in the form of the exhortation, "Talk!" Frightened by her own destructive power (the silent girl's skin might come off in her hand), Maxine calls for her student to be strong, to resist, to just say "No." Well, if she cannot do that, could she just acknowledge that she exists? Maxine exhorts her to say her name. There being no cooperation, our teacher punishes her student by pulling her hair, following which she tries to provoke her into cooperating by claiming that she, the teacher, "knows" that her student can speak in Chinese *and* English, because she heard her do so once when she walked past her house. Again noncooperation is met with punishment, more hair pulling. The adult narrator tells us that Maxine sees her student as so weak and disgusting that she now tries to get the silent girl just to acknowledge her pain: "Say 'Ow.'" In response to continued passivity, Maxine again administers punishment and bids her student to acknowledge her desire: "Say 'Stop.'" There again being no response and the "student" being reduced to a passive, weak, snot-producing baby-like thing, teacher Maxine declares, "You're such a nothing." Maybe the silent girl wants her mama: "Cry, 'Mama.'"

With still no response, Maxine could pull all of her hair out and make her bald. "O.K. O.K. Don't talk. Just scream." Our teacher's rage now becomes too much for herself to bear, so she begins to plead that her student merely say "a" or "the." "Please." And when not even that works, and she has exhausted her exhortations and punishments, Maxine is terrified by the reduction of her student to a nothing. Our young teacher blurts out through her own tears, "You think someone is going to take care of you all your stupid life?" and justifies her own actions by saying, "I'm doing this for your own good."

Clearly, Maxine's teaching example succeeds neither for her student, who remains silent and now also doubtless hurts from the abuse, nor for the "teacher," who subsequently takes her own "stupid life" out of the world for eighteen months. How might we be with one another so as to allay such hatred and violence in our interactions and to promote each other's voices and more democratic ways of being with one another? These are not hypothetical questions. As a teacher, what am I to nurture? Kindness? Respect? Maybe even a sense of what it might be to take pleasure in another's company? As a teacher interested in promoting democratic, moral ways of relating to one another, where might I turn for help?

Here I think of those academic discourses that say much that seems reasonable, wise, and true. Consider the following statement: "If one comes to see one's adversaries as not impossibly alien and other, but as sharing certain general human goals and purposes, if one understands that they are not monsters but people who share with us certain general goals and purposes, then understanding will lead toward a diminution of anger and the beginning of rational exchange."[2] This is from Martha Nussbaum's illuminating discussion of the Stoic idea of citizenship as developed in the *Meditations* of Marcus Aurelius. Surely this statement is true and therefore pertinent to cultivating ourselves and others as citizens of a democratic world. And yet even as I nod assent, I sense that I thereby understand Maxine and my own task of nurture no better. For Maxine, the problem seems to be not one of difference but of sameness. The silent girl looks like Maxine. She acts like Maxine. Therein is the source of Maxine's rage. She appears to violate the silent girl, *not* because she is *different* from Maxine, but precisely because she is in some important ways the *same*. Maxine does not even "see" the silent girl; she sees only her own weakness against which she struggles so hard to eke out a pitiable voice.

We come closer to finding something pertinent in Nussbaum's discussion of "the narrative imagination" as "essential preparation for moral interaction."[3] Nussbaum writes that as children ascribe to themselves and recognize in themselves attitudes such as hope and fear, and traits such as courage, self-restraint, dignity, perseverance, and fairness, "they become capable of compassion." Again, I follow and agree. But then there is a turn that sets me adrift. "Compassion involves the recognition that another person, in some ways similar to oneself, has suffered pains or misfortune in a way for which that person is not, or not fully, to blame."[4] In trying to make sense of what is going on for Maxine, I think I am misled by Nussbaum's emphasis on *the other*. What if we were to rewrite the sentence by reversing the order, thus relocating the focus to one's attitude toward and understanding of *oneself?* The new claim would read: Compassion involves the recognition that one has, as have others, suffered some significant pain or misfortune in a way for which one is not, or not fully, to blame. Something about this change in emphasis seems pertinent. Maybe that is what would be necessary for Maxine to feel compassion for the silent girl. Could it be that the democratic turn comes in recognizing *oneself* as an *other*, in some form of self-understanding? Maxine's violence seems born of hating aspects of herself that she sees in the silent girl, rather than of hating aspects of the silent girl that she subsequently injects into herself. What is wanted for compassion, it seems, is still that Maxine see a connection between herself and the silent girl, but one that has a crucially different structure. Herein is the topic for the balance of this chapter.

Elsewhere, Nussbaum seems to acknowledge the extrarational structure of the psyche through her treatment of the work of Marcus Aurelius: "Even if we never fully understand the action, the very activity of asking the question and trying to depict the person's psychology to ourselves in the manner of a good novelist is the antidote to self-centered rage."[5] Yet again the emphasis appears to be misplaced if we seek to make sense of Maxine's rage, which appears to be not self-centered but "self-unaware" or even "self-missing"; the emphasis seems to obscure nurture's need to help Maxine come to herself.

As teachers, we need to know what is going on with Maxine— to understand her, the rage behind her violence. As theorists of democracy and education, we need to see that our discussions often are in a fundamental way misleading or at least irrelevant to teaching, an activity that we presume to be pertinent to the cultivation of democracy. Carol Gould's *Rethinking Democracy* is the work in democratic theory that comes perhaps closest to appreciating that we collectively need to turn serious attention to the formation of the self if we are to have hope to extend and deepen the prospects for democracy. In a chapter entitled "The Democratic Personality: Self Development, Character, and Political Participation," Gould argues that although democracy's nemesis, the authoritarian personality, has been the focus of sustained and serious attention of social democratic theorists in this century (witness the studies of Theodor Adorno, Max Horkheimer, and Hannah Arendt, for example), "there has not been comparable attention paid to what we may call the democratic personality, or to the social and political environment that fosters it."[6] More specifically, Gould is interested in "the personality or character that is appropriate to participation in democratic institutions" and how "such democratic forms of political and economic life contribute to the development of individual character."[7] She argues that a "self-active[,] engaged individual, whose participation in democratic life is an expression of his or her freedom" and "the disposition to reciprocity" are fundamental aspects of a democratic personality.[8] Gould understands the relevance of certain psychic dispositions to democracy and what they formally entail, thus helping us see that the nurture of these dispositions is work for the public domain.[9] But we must look beyond Gould to answer the questions for teaching with democracy as an aim: How is the democratic, as opposed to the authoritarian, personality formed, and how specifically might teachers promote that formation?

Here I pause to recap my argument to this point and to respond to a possible criticism. Using Nussbaum's *Cultivating Humanity* as an example, I have claimed that democratic theory in the social, political, epistemological, and ethical registers has not provided the guidance the teacher needs to nurture democracy. Some may argue that the case of Maxine, which I use to illustrate the failure of these discourses to attend to *nurturing* democracy, is but a minor anomaly that is marginal to our interest in democracy. Here I can only acknowledge

my implicit claim that self-hatred as a source of prejudice and violence is fairly common, though with a wide range of forms and
intensities. There are certainly many other published cases to which
one could turn. For example, Raphael Campo presents a particularly illuminating account of self-loathing in *The Poetry of Healing:
A Doctor's Education in Empathy, Identity, and Desire*.[10] In addition, I
acknowledge that to proceed, one must trust that my highly selec-
tive treatment of texts in democratic theory is not misleading.

The Undemocratic Tendencies of the Psyche

I imagine that what I am about to say will strike some as very annoying, for sometimes I am myself thus annoyed. To look at the formation of the self, the psyche, is to get a glimpse of ourselves. I am
reminded of the Templar's agony in Gotthold Ephraim Lessing's
eighteenth-century German Enlightenment play *Nathan the Wise*.[11]
The Templar wants Nathan to become his father by giving him his
daughter Recha in marriage. It being the case that Recha is Nathan's
adoptive daughter and, unbeknownst to the Templar, the Templar's
biological sister, Nathan does not assent. By finding out something
about himself, that he is Recha's brother, he comes face to face with
the fact that he cannot have that which he wants so badly. We
sometimes are no more cheered when we peer into our own psyches.
We thereby are likely to get annoying news. This is an unavoidable
risk in taking nurture public.

Elisabeth Young-Bruehl picks up the psychological aspect of
democratic theory where Carol Gould leaves off. In *The Anatomy
of Prejudices*, Young-Bruehl argues that we have been hindered in
coming to understand prejudice (hence, I would add, the prospects
for democracy) partly by our leaning uncritically on Adorno's work
on the authoritarian personality, which casts the prejudiced personality as "rigid, ideologically conservative, conventional, superfi-
cial, and disconnected from feeling."[12] Adorno's *The Authoritarian
Personality* and other major studies of prejudice—for example,

Gordon Allport's *The Nature of Prejudice* and Gunnar Myrdal's *The American Dilemma*—assume that prejudice is of a kind.[13] Young-Bruehl calls us to consider what *This Bridge Called My Back: Writings of Radical Women of Color* adumbrates: prejudice is not of one kind, but at least three.[14] She employs Freudian theory to argue that each kind of prejudice is a product of a distinctive formation of the psyche. In this view, three distinct and different character traits—obsessional, hysterical, and narcissistic—"are formed in reaction to the types of conflicts that can lead to pathologies, if uncontained."[15] In Young-Bruehl's argument, these character traits account for anti-Semitism, racism, and sexism, and, expressing different psychic structures, they are not of a single kind. (Homophobia, she argues, is especially complex, for all three types fund it.) It follows, then, that to devise social policies and educational programs to reduce one type of prejudice would not at all necessarily be to address another type. Correlatively, social movements that encourage all three types of prejudice, as did the Ku Klux Klan in the 1920s, tend to be powerfully destructive of the prospects for democracy.[16]

Before summarizing each of these character types, let us consider more closely what is being claimed and what is at stake for educating ourselves for democracy. Young-Bruehl is proposing that it is the nature of the human psyche that we are formed into certain character patterns in reaction to particular conflicts. In each case the formation may take a "relatively normal" route or, if "uncontained," a pathological one. In the case of Maxine, which I do not attempt to categorize here, if the rage directed at the silent girl were to reflect the forming of a particular character type and if it were not "contained" in its development, then Maxine could become incapable of developing an acceptably democratic character, a fact that would play itself out in severe forms of prejudice and violence, well out of reach, one imagines, of the moral or narrative imagination. If it is true that we are unavoidably prone to such intrasubjective formations that structure how we are with one another, then social theories claiming that the self is but a social construct and plastic to the core appear naive at best. Young-Bruehl focuses on how the particular formations of the psyche, once they have "congealed," leave us with selves that are not totally plastic—ways of being with which we have to deal commonly for a lifetime.

Young-Bruehl may or may not "get everything right" (for example, just how many structurally different prejudices and character types there are and whether particular prejudices correspond to particular character formations generally or can be played out multiply and variously in individuals). The important point is to allow for the possibility that a theory of formation of the psyche may contribute to our understanding of the nurture of democratic "virtues" that Gould, Nussbaum, and other theorists place at the core of democracy's prospects. If we are truly interested in nurturing democratic dispositions, beliefs, and values, where else, after all, can we turn but to theories regarding how our psyches function?

First, a word about my synopsis of Young-Bruehl's character types. Without my reviewing the theory of their etiology, here follows a brief (hence, inevitably flawed) description of the constellation of habits and beliefs typifying the three distinct character formations, with attention to how each structures the self or psyche in social life. These types, Young-Bruehl argues, "congeal only in late adolescence," though hints of them appear earlier.[17] Any person may have overlapping character traits—indeed, only rarely do pure forms appear—although a single trait seems to predominate as the central organizer of psychic life, except in "multiple personalities." Moreover, none of us is a "developmental paragon, the perfectly normal person."[18] Not only do we live in an imperfect world in which our psyches are imperfectly formed, but also those formations feed back into our social world in the form of prejudice and violence.

It is not my wish to convey a gloomy picture of our prospects for democracy, but clearly the additional complexity may strike one as bad news. Instead, in presenting by means of Young-Bruehl's work a glimpse of our undemocratic tendencies, I mean to advance my overall argument that as theorists of democracy, we need to take the psyche seriously. Otherwise we will have nothing pertinent to say to ourselves as teachers or to ourselves as persons living our lives among others.

The Obsessional Character

Obsessional characters are dominated by defenses mobilized around anal desires or fantasies—defenses to protect obsessionals against their own "dirtiness" and related desire.[19] The self is fortified or protected by rigid habits serving to distance one from the dirtiness and loss of control by "projecting" or displacing the "polluting" thoughts or desires onto others, whom one is at pain to label clearly (for example, with the Star of David or with a pink triangle).[20] Sometimes the displacement takes the form of "marginal ceremonies," such as repetitive handwashing or checking multiple times to see if the door is locked. The psyche's defensive task of protecting the self from the dirty and uncontrollable takes various forms; strict conformance to dress codes (even a preference for wearing uniforms), holding tightly to routines, and the like function to reassure obsessionals of their "superiority." In more developed cases of this trait, obsessionals "need" to keep track of the others onto whom they have located their own "unbearable" dirtiness and related desires. In such instances, the obsessional moves from simply labeling others as inferior to controlling their behavior and, at the worst extreme, to annihilating the "recipients" of their projections and then trying to erase any traces that the annihilated ever existed.[21]

Here comes some news that we as academics may not want to hear: sometimes obsessionals keep large, messy, disturbing issues under control or at bay by focusing on small legal or technical issues or "by becoming engrossed in semantic disputes and logic chopping, . . . commentaries upon commentaries, citations upon citations, in arcane or very academic language."[22] Lest we think that we as teachers escape the obsessional formation, consider the following:

> Obsessionals are often attracted to . . . institutions . . .
> where they can treat people like scum, dirt to be cleaned
> up, or like uncivilized children. . . . [Consider] both the
> obsessional routines of schools and a "captive audience
> of students. . . . [Obsessionals'] pleasure often focuses on
> humiliations they are able to bring about in the domain
> of their anal fixations. They relish making their victims
> feel shame over their bodily needs by regulating their
> toilet use with passes and schedules, depriving them of
> any provisions for their modesty, getting them to dirty
> themselves, engaging in all kinds of what the Italian
> chronicler of Auschwitz, Primo Levi, called "excremen-
> tal coercions."[23]

This psychic displacement of that which is uncomfortable in oneself onto others blocks introspection—introspection that, I might add, educational transformation may require. Obsessionals direct their attention to the need to control certain others and, at the same time, tend to believe that their own feelings, which they cannot articulate, are under others' control.[24] The obsessionals' desire both to be in control and not to be controlled by others may express itself as "the snobbery of self-declared social reformers, peo-ple who think that they, and they alone, can make the world as it (morally) ought to be."[25] Whether in its milder, if insidious forms (such as labeling some as from "the other side of the track," as was common practice in the small town where I was born) or in its severest form (calling for the annihilation of some), the obsessional formation of the psyche is part of the human condition in an imper-fect world. It clearly fails on Gould's democratic criterion of reci-procity. Moreover, talk of the importance of tolerance for others or reciprocity—part of the formal requirements of democracy—does not address the obsessional's threat to democracy, the incapacity to tolerate certain feelings within his or her own self.

The Hysterical Character

Hysterical characters are dominated by "the power of their oral and genital desires in [and] over them, defying their defensive efforts at repression."[26] Their sexual feelings and related desires are projected onto others, so that they are left with bodies with lives of their own.[27] Their emotional lives, for whatever reason too strong to contain in themselves, are cast out onto others. They are "emotionally hungry"—a hunger fed "by eating, by assimilating or taking in or engaging everything and everyone greedily, by enjoying endless conversations for their atmosphere of conviviality and intimacy, or by being without boundaries, merged in ways that echo their childhood mergers with their mothers." Tellingly, they commonly "launch relationships with great emotional display, energy, theatricality. Disappointments always come, leaving them enraged and despairing."[28]

Unlike obsessionally based prejudice, hysterical prejudice has a self-contradictory feature: the hating of the other, onto which one's own desire is projected, represses the love felt, the displaced desire. Hence, the hysteric both *hates* the other, whom he or she "needs" to find succor or to feel sexually alive, and *loves* the same other who makes him or her feel good. The result, once again not democratic, is prejudice against persons whom one, in turn, needs. The "upstanding citizen" visits a brothel and then "forgets" that he does so. "The central chapters of *The Autobiography of Malcolm X* form a casebook about white visitors to Black Harlem who actually visit their own fantasies."[29] Unlike the obsessional's prejudice, the hysteric's prejudice requires that the recipients of his projections "merely" be "kept in their place" and nearby, perhaps most conveniently in the household. (Some may be reminded here of the boss at work who insists on treating his or her employees as "family.") That is, only by playing out a game of dominance and submission can the hysteric feel "fed." The intrapsychic master is starving, and succor and fulfillment of desire are relegated to an intrapsychic servants' quarters.

Thus, the outward strength of an individual's social prejudice derives from this inner formation that leaves the self starving with an insatiable hunger. According to this theory, were "the burden of desire and self-reproach" to be removed by a reunification of the "unacceptable" projected part of the self with that which is "owned," the psychic engine of certain common undemocratic ways of being with others would be stilled.[30]

For a picture of the full complexity of how the hysterical trait presents itself, one would need to understand differences between its oral and phallic forms and the different ways it plays out for males and females. Suffice it here to attend to shared features. Those onto whom the "frightening" feelings linked to one's own desire are projected—desire without which one cannot feel fully alive—must be regarded as part of a "lower" life that is somehow without minds (for example, children and adults cast as "lower" by virtue of class or race). Just who is cast in the recipient role does not seem to matter to the hysteric. For example, "Upon moving into a region with a common prejudice, [hysterics] will take on the prejudice even if it was not part of their upbringing." That is, hysterics "rely heavily on projection for defending themselves against their [own] libidinal and aggressive impulses—they unconsciously make over or transfer to others their impulses," to which they subsequently can have access only by controlling the other.[31]

The Narcissistic Character

Young-Bruehl notes that "narcissism is difficult to discuss in terms of characterology because [it] is part of every character type, pure or mixed."[32] To some extent, everyone loves himself or herself. If we did not, we would all in some way destroy ourselves. And everyone begins life in a womb in a state in which almost all needs are fulfilled. "After this fusion has been disrupted, the child and later the adult seek to recover its nirvanic pleasures, its feeling of 'there is no other' (no disappointment, no outside, no difference, no rivalry)."[33] If this psychic structuring is uncontained, the narcissist experiences

others as part of himself or herself. That is, others must be controlled and managed as instruments for the narcissist's purposes,
rather like one's own limbs. Roughly sketched, narcissists are "ambi-
tious and oriented toward a future when longed-for goals will be
achieved." This can be expressed either by leading (that is, by building confidence in one's own achievements via the attainment of
power) or by following, by "submitting to another's power" and
"enjoying reflected glory."[34] Narcissists may depend heavily on
another's applause and so need to maintain a fan club, stay aloof,
and even appear arrogant to avoid disappointment; they may be
thrown into depression by the rejection of their efforts or projects.

Narcissistic prejudice involves using others for maintaining one's
own illusion of being the only subject. If all of the recruited fan
club—the groupies, sycophants, and other hangers-on—were to
"resign" or suddenly show themselves to be independent and with
superior minds, the system would collapse.[35] Involving a fundamental "imbalance of respect" (my term), narcissism is incapable of
reciprocity and, as such, is "democratically" undemocratic, for it re-
gards relations with most others (no labels needed), including those
the narcissist respects, as sources of "enabling" criticism. With relationships reduced to instrumentalities rather than being allowed to
flourish as the pleasure of reciprocal company, the leader can experience profound loneliness, even in the presence of attentive others (read: instruments). Functioning on a "theory" that only through
one's own actions can one feel really alive, the leader narcissist takes
the initiative in love and wants to be loved for his or her loving.
This being a nigh-onto-impossible feat, they may have to transform
the very need to be loved—a passive need—into activity, such as
"expressing themselves either directly or in a sublimated mode like
intellectual activity."[36] Hence, the narcissists' partners are exploited
as material for their own creations. When narcissism functions at
the full extent of its madness, the narcissist either tries to control
others (the leader narcissist) or to submit to the idealized other. The
ominous others, the ones against whom narcissists are prejudiced,

are not those they dominate, but those whom they perceive to be out of their control, such as those who seem smarter and unsympathetic, and any others whose presence begins to shake the foundations of their "theory" that they are each the only subject around. Thus, narcissism breathes undemocratic life into society both in the form of instrumental domination and as prejudice against those who threaten the "only me here" fantasy.

Narcissism's being something that in some measure we almost all experience, it is hardly surprising that many others across various discourses have made similar or related observations. (When trying to understand the human condition, I am impressed by ideas that seem to recur across intellectual traditions.) For example, in casting the democratic character as one that includes *both* a disposition to initiative-taking agency *and* an inclination toward reciprocity, which entails an honoring of others as subjects, philosopher Carol Gould seems to be assuming a backdrop of narcissistic tendencies in her argument that calls for cultivating a certain disposition (the initiative-taking that follower narcissists lack) and restraining another (the tendency of narcissists not to see others as independent subjects, but to treat them as tools for their own purposes), which is inimical to reciprocity.

Feminist psychoanalyst Jessica Benjamin, situated more in the tradition of Winnicott than Freud, argues that perhaps the "most fateful" human paradox is generated by the fact that "the other subject is outside our control and yet we need him." Here the democratic character, which unavoidably harbors narcissistic tendencies (though to differing degrees from person to person), faces the task of "disentangling" ties to others "to make of them not shackles but also circuits of recognition."[37]

Similarly, in *The Double Flame*, Mexican novelist Octavio Paz, essaying to understand the connection between eroticism and love, observes that "love has been and still is the great act of subversion in the West. . . . It does not deny the Other or reduce the Other to a shadow but is instead the negation of one's own sovereignty."[38] Love (perhaps also democracy?) is possible only through recognizing not only that the other has an existence independent of one-self, but that "recognition aspires to reciprocity but is independent of it." Importantly, love "is a wager no one is certain of winning because its outcome depends on the freedom of the Other."[39] Hence, we might reason, the democratic character is one that is capable of *being vulnerable*, of *tolerating uncertainty*, of *risking the self* with others. In the context of the West, where narcissistic tendencies seem to flourish—abetted in recent centuries by liberal individualism and economies that encourage instrumental regard of the other—might not these be democratic virtues for public nurture?

For yet one more illustration, I turn to Mikhail Bakhtin in *Problems of Dostoevsky's Poetics*, in which he calls us to see the creation of "the great dialogue" that constitutes Dostoevsky's novels.[40] I suspect that academics in the West find Bakhtin's notion of dialogue so intriguing precisely because it suggests a kind of place for the West to "work through" its dominant narcissism. In Dostoevsky's novels, characters enter only by becoming a part of a "dialogue." To do that, they need to maintain a *dual attitude*. As an example, Bakhtin considers *Crime and Punishment*: "The entire orientation of Stavrogin in this dialogue is determined by his dual attitude toward the 'other person': by the impossibility of managing without his judgment and forgiveness, and at the same time by a hostility toward him and resistance to his judgment and forgiveness."[41] Characters in Dostoevsky's novels develop through their struggling with themselves in the dialogue, that is, *in public*. The struggle and growth cannot be an individual, isolated, private affair, walled off. Instead, Dostoevsky gives his novels' characters the public space needed to work through their tensions and so develop, rather than leaving them with only the possibility of acting out their static selves, as is the case with the epic character.[42] Recall Maxine. She had a place only to act out her madness, an experience so arresting that she put herself away for a year and a half.

Just what sort of place would allow Maxine to work through the process of finding a strong, "initiative-taking" voice of her own? Could we design such pedagogically accessible places? Perhaps in this effort we would need to rethink the advisability of a notion of political correctness that drives our undemocratic tendencies into the dark, where they cannot be engaged. Clearly some notion of "democratic adequacy" would still be pertinent, but not one that would hide the evidence of prejudices from public view. But we are getting ahead of ourselves. As democratic theorists, we first need to enrich our conception of what we humans are like, how we come to act the ways we do.

Enriching How We Think About Human Action

In *The Mind and Its Depths*, Richard Wollheim helps me understand the yawns I confessed at the outset of this chapter: "Virtually all those who are not either ignorant of Freud or totally sceptical of his findings believe that he altered, radically altered, our conception of the mind. He effected a change in what we think we are like, and it was a big change. Astonishingly enough, it is philosophers who have been the slowest of all people to recognize this fact. They have been slowest to recognize that this fact has anything to do with them."[43]

As a teacher interested in nurturing democratic ways of being with one another, I could see the need for a richer conception of what we are like, one more akin to ways of understanding the psyche that have already found their way into fiction, into how we commonly understand ourselves and others, and even into some of the self-help literature to which we as teachers sometimes turn when academic discourses fail us. I have, thus, felt the need for a more psyche-wise conception of human action and behavior in my own work as a philosopher. I needed a way to read anew John Goodlad's Postulate Sixteen (see Appendix A). That is, I needed to allow myself to observe that my theoretical understandings have been too anemic for addressing the demands of nurture facing me as a teacher, parent, friend, and person sometimes bemused by my own ways of being with others.

Wollheim argues specifically that psychoanalytic theory deepens, elaborates, and contextualizes our ordinary psychological explanation of human action. Following Wollheim's lead, I wish to argue that this theoretical enrichment can keep the teacher profitably awake—awake to the possibilities and prospects of nurturing democratic aspects of ourselves. On this more complex landscape of what human experience entails, we can search for clues about how to nurture Maxine and ourselves.

Here is Wollheim's argument in brief. To begin, "ordinary psychological explanation" (philosophers will recognize that Wollheim draws on the now-classic work of Donald Davidson) accounts for an *action* by appealing to the agent's appropriately related *desire* and *belief*. If the agent has a desire and a belief that together rationalize an action, he has a *reason* for doing it. Further, the reason must be *causally efficacious*—the reason that he did it.[44] The formula is, then, that a human action is explicable by appeal to the belief and desire (together, the reason) that caused it. Psychoanalytic theory, Wollheim points out, helps us see, first, that desires and beliefs do not have to be conscious to cause action (witness Maxine's hurting the silent girl); second, that unconscious beliefs and desires, rather than the reasons the agent offers as rationalization, may be the cause of an action or, in other instances that things we do may be not actions but only activities, behavior explicable only by reference to "mechanisms of defense, so-called because we use them to fend off unwanted desires, but which also have constitutive roles to play in the build-up of our personalities"—such as projection and projective identification;[45] and, third, that human behavior can be explained by reference to "certain psychological constellations as successively salient" in a developmental narrative. "What makes these labels explanatory is the understanding that they stand for particular desires, particular chains of association, particular mechanisms of defense, specific phantasies, associated with the developmental phase that the label picks out."[46]

If as theorists of democracy we were to enrich our concept of ourselves as humans in this way, we would understand why some of our seemingly innocuous statements might in fact stand as barriers to nurturing democracy. Consider the earlier claim that if we understood that others are not monsters but that they share certain general goals and purposes with us, then we would be less angry and so able to begin a rational exchange, which, by implication, will surely make things better. This is a causal claim about how to reduce anger. To the contrary, think of even the mildly obsessional whose anger can be quelled only by labeling "those dirty Jews." Consider even the mild hysteric who can be fed only by calling on someone cast as lower for the fulfillment of desire. Historically, not even religious exhortations of an angry God, much less rational lectures, seem to erode this way of being that, as Young-Bruehl suggests, may undergird much of racism. (Moreover, deconstructing "race" will not make this source of undemocracy and madness disappear.) Think of the narcissist who relentlessly and in some sense unavoidably tries to control others as instruments for his or her own use. A Kantian sermon on the Categorical Imperative imploring us to treat others as ends, not means, cannot persuade the narcissist to give up using others as tools. Perhaps it is time for the philosopher in me to stop uttering things about democracy as if all pertinent desires and beliefs were consciously held, as if all pertinent human activity consisted of human action (in other words, that it is caused by beliefs and desires that one holds as reasons), and as if the human requirements of democracy and education were describable by psyche-naive philosophy.

Toward a Public Pedagogy of Nurture

They would be truly unusual persons (not quite alive?) who did not recognize one or more of Young-Bruehl's character types in themselves. Perhaps seeing ourselves as thus participating in the "madnesses" of the human condition is all we need to feel a compassion for Maxine, whose rage not only terrifies the silent girl but also leads Maxine to withdraw to her bed, where she regresses to the baby-like dependence to which she had reduced the silent girl, onto whom she had projected her own feelings of weakness. Maybe it is that we do not have to share goals and purposes in order to feel compassion. Maybe we have "only" to see ourselves as prone to unconscious values and beliefs and mechanisms of defense—to see ourselves with human psyches.

If we were to think of the formation of our psyches as not a highly private affair to be tightly guarded within the family (the conservative agenda?), but as something that arises from experiences we cannot author, then perhaps we could cut ourselves the slack to begin to admit our "madnesses" to ourselves. We might then see that Maxine's self-loathing is not something to be solved (the liberal agenda) but rather something needing to be aired in a place where it can resolve itself into a strong voice so that there remains no psychic need to project "bad" parts of the self onto others and then have to hate what one sees in the other.

Having gone this distance, I have to admit that I do not know what could constitute a public pedagogy of nurture. I do know that it is not contained in the recent mandates for educational reform and that until democratic theory catches up with the last hundred years of descriptions and explanations of the psyche, as Wollheim urges, we teachers are pretty much on our own to figure out what nurturing democratic dispositions involves. On the terrain we have traversed in this chapter, however, we can find some strong clues. By way of conclusion and commencement, I list the salient findings" here:

- God, as played by George Burns in the film *Oh, God!* was right. There are some design flaws in creation, and the oversized avocado pit is not the only one. We humans are prone unconsciously to project out onto others things that seem too frightening to hold within. This design flaw accounts for much that is undemocratic in ourselves and our students. Just as there is no point in preaching to avocados about the virtue of smaller pits, there is no point in preaching ideal democratic behavior. It will not change anything. The better move would be to become more aware of and acknowledge openly our madnesses, so as to help our students and ourselves try to learn to become self-responsible, rather than sliding unaware into activities and actions of hatred and control of others.[47]

• We ought to take care not to reduce our interest in Maxine to her torturing of the silent girl (one imagines various punishments that some might want to mete out), but to try to figure out ways to help her find it bearable to see the weakness as being in herself and to lean on others to help her to develop a voice, something no one can do alone. Moreover, we need to be prepared to provide that support— something that happens not by having Maxine fail kindergarten, but by becoming curious about what being silent means to Maxine.

• To develop a democratic character one needs to be a subject, to have a voice of one's own. Expecting "academic excellences" of our young in a reform movement based on a "bill of competencies" is reasonable partial educational fare, inasmuch as it provides some of the means for forming and pursuing one's goals and purposes. However, such a conception of education, if treated as sufficient unto itself, fails to understand that the development of a self is logically prior to imagining "goals and purposes." If we mark as failures students who seem not to be developing, for whatever reason, robust voices, our action is unspeakably evil.

• Unless we are aware of the "madnesses" of our own psychic life, we cannot distinguish, on the one hand, our pedagogic "guidance" as an acting-out that responds to "noise" within ourselves from, on the other hand, efforts that are self-responsible and responsive to our students, to borrow Buber's couplet for the education of character.[48]

• Those of us who are in positions of authority over and responsibility for young people—or in positions of authority over anyone— need especially to look into ourselves when we experience anger, feel a strong urge to set others right, feel hatred, or experience tension when others do not carry out our plans. Chances are that whatever "help" or "care" we might be offering is not innocent, but plays out our own madness. Such "help" disregards and mistreats others.

- Introspection of the sort that would enable us to know ourselves is exceedingly difficult, because the very part that needs our attention we tend to dump onto others and then gripe about "them," make policies to control "them," and sincerely believe that the only route to our feeling better is "their" either correcting themselves or even ceasing to exist.

- For the mild obsessionals and hysterics among us, democratic virtues of the psyche include tolerating feelings within the self (feelings of aggression, of "badness," of libidinal desires, and the like), rather than projecting these "scary" things out onto others to be hated, and learning meta-talk about those uncomfortable feelings. (I fancy a view of wildly successful parenting and teaching as one from which we would all emerge perhaps a bit worn at the edges but better acquainted with our psyches and engaged in working through our "madnesses" rather than converting them to harmful activity.)

- For narcissists, democratic virtues include the abilities to be vulnerable, to tolerate uncertainty in relations with others, and to risk selves with others. Schooling reformed around "competencies" may hamper acquisition of these virtues, for it may well serve to fuel the view that all else in the world, including education, is only an instrumental extension of the self. Hence, the exclusive focus on competency reform may well undermine democratic life, the very thing it is rationalized as fostering.

- And finally, I allow a point deriving from something I mentioned only parenthetically. Effective "democratic education" for the narcissist would surely entail a revision in the concept of the ideal mother, so as to valorize as the nurturer a desiring self who takes pleasure in relationships of mutuality, rather than valorizing a "selfless nurturer"—the oxymoron that feeds narcissism's growth. This revision could also help remove teaching from the intrapsychic servants' quarters, where teachers are cast as "lowly" and controlled by perpetual reform efforts.

In parting, I offer my only hunch about how to nurture democratic dispositions: we do it as second nature once we learn how to navigate our way responsibly around our own psyches. I say these things boldly to my teacher self *and* to my sometimes Enlightenment-blinded theorist self, whom I need to give permission to take Maxine's story into account.

Notes

1. Maxine Hong Kingston, *The Woman Warrior: Memoirs of a Girlhood Among Ghosts* (New York: Vintage International, 1975). The story of Maxine and the silent girl may be found on pp. 175–181. Conversations with Brigitte Prutti, professor of Germanics at the University of Washington, have much enriched my understanding of this story.

2. Martha C. Nussbaum, *Cultivating Humanity: A Classical Defense of Reform in Liberal Education* (Cambridge, Mass.: Harvard University Press, 1997), p. 65.

3. Nussbaum, *Cultivating Humanity*, p. 90.

4. Nussbaum, *Cultivating Humanity*, pp. 90–91.

5. Nussbaum, *Cultivating Humanity*, p. 97.

6. Carol C. Gould, *Rethinking Democracy: Freedom and Social Cooperation in Politics, Economy, and Society* (Cambridge: Cambridge University Press, 1988), p. 283.

7. Gould, *Rethinking Democracy*, p. 284.

8. Gould, *Rethinking Democracy*, p. 306.

9. Others have observed by different routes that nurture has not been a part of public Western history. Jessica Benjamin, for example, attributes the "social banishment of nurture and intersubjective relatedness to the private world of women and children" to "a tendency to elevate the desexualized mother whose hallmark is not desire but nurture." See *The Bonds of Love: Psychoanalysis, Feminism, and the Problem of Domination* (New York: Pantheon, 1988), pp. 185 and 91, respectively.

10. Raphael Campo, *The Poetry of Healing: A Doctor's Education in Empathy, Identity, and Desire* (New York: Norton, 1997).

11. Gotthold Ephraim Lessing, *Nathan der Weise*, ed. Christoph E. Schweitzer (Boston: Suhrkamp/Insel, 1984 [orig. 1779]); also *Nathan the Wise, Minna von Barnhelm, and Other Plays and Writings*, ed. Peter Demetz (New York: Continuum, 1991).

12. Elisabeth Young-Bruehl, *The Anatomy of Prejudices* (Cambridge, Mass.: Harvard University Press, 1996), pp. 7–15.

13. Theodor Adorno et al., *The Authoritarian Personality* (New York: Harper, 1950); Gordon Allport, *The Nature of Prejudice* (Reading, Mass.: Addison-Wesley, 1954); and Gunnar Myrdal, *The American Dilemma: The Negro Problem and Modern Democracy*, 2 vols. (New York: Random House, 1972 [orig. 1944]).

14. Cherríe Moraga and Gloria Anzaldúa (eds.), *This Bridge Called My Back: Writings by Radical Women of Color* (New York: Kitchen Table Press, 1983 [orig. Persephone Press, 1981]).

15. Young-Bruehl, *Anatomy of Prejudices*, p. 202.

16. Young-Bruehl, *Anatomy of Prejudices*, p. 245.

17. Young-Bruehl, *Anatomy of Prejudices*, p. 20.

18. Young-Bruehl, *Anatomy of Prejudices*, p. 209.

19. Young-Bruehl, *Anatomy of Prejudices*, p. 207.

20. Young-Bruehl, *Anatomy of Prejudices*, pp. 214, 218.

21. Young-Bruehl, *Anatomy of Prejudices*, pp. 217–218.

22. Young-Bruehl, *Anatomy of Prejudices*, p. 211.

23. Young-Bruehl, *Anatomy of Prejudices*, pp. 213–214.

24. Young-Bruehl, *Anatomy of Prejudices*, p. 215.

25. Young-Bruehl, *Anatomy of Prejudices*, p. 219.

26. Young-Bruehl, *Anatomy of Prejudices*, p. 207.

27. Young-Bruehl, *Anatomy of Prejudices*, pp. 219–220.

28. Young-Bruehl, *Anatomy of Prejudices*, p. 220.

29. Young-Bruehl, *Anatomy of Prejudices*, p. 222.

30. Young-Bruehl, *Anatomy of Prejudices*, p. 223.

31. Young-Bruehl, *Anatomy of Prejudices*, p. 229.

32. Young-Bruehl, *Anatomy of Prejudices*, p. 230.

33. Young-Bruehl, *Anatomy of Prejudices*, p. 231.

34. Young-Bruehl, *Anatomy of Prejudices*, p. 232.

35. Young-Bruehl, *Anatomy of Prejudices*, p. 233.

36. Young-Bruehl, *Anatomy of Prejudices*, p. 233.

37. Benjamin, *Bonds of Love*, p. 221.

38. Octavio Paz, *The Double Flame: Love and Eroticism*, trans. Helen Lane (New York: Harcourt Brace, 1995 [orig. in Spanish, 1993]), pp. 150–151.

39. Paz, *Double Flame*, p. 151.

40. Mikhail Bakhtin, *Problems of Dostoevsky's Poetics*, ed. and trans. Caryl Emerson (Minneapolis: University of Minnesota Press, 1984 [orig. 1973]).

41. Bakhtin, *Problems of Dostoevsky's Poetics*, p. 262.

42. Here I am applying a distinction from psychoanalytic theory to cast in another light Bakhtin's Dostoevsky. The clearest statement of the originally Freudian distinction between "acting out" and "working through"—a couplet especially pertinent to gaining an understanding of human transformation—that I have found to date is made by Jean Laplanche and L.-B. Pontalis in *The Language of Psycho-analysis* (New York: Norton, 1973 [orig. 1967]), as quoted by Dominick LaCapra in his *Representing the Holocaust: History, Theory, Trauma* (Ithaca, N.Y.: Cornell University Press, 1994), pp. 208–209. "Acting out" is defined as "action in which the subject, in the grip of his unconscious wishes and phantasies, relives these in the present with a sensation of immediacy which is heightened by his refusal to recognize their source and their repetitive character" (p. 4). "Working through" is, in contrast, "a sort of psychical work which allows the subject to accept certain repressed elements and to free himself from the grip of the mechanisms of repetition" (p. 488).

43. Richard Wollheim, *The Mind and Its Depths* (Cambridge, Mass.: Harvard University Press, 1993), p. 91. In chap. 6, "Desire, Belief, and Professor Grünbaum's Freud," Wollheim argues that the now widely cited work of Adolf Grünbaum, *The Foundations of Psychoanalysis: A Philosophical Critique* (Berkeley: University of California Press, 1984), is centrally flawed. For one historian's careful, lucid review of the central criticisms of Freud's work, including the Grünbaum criticism, see Paul Robinson's *Freud and His Critics* (Berkeley: University of California Press, 1993).

44. Wollheim, *Mind and Its Depths*, pp. 93–94. As Wollheim notes, Donald Davidson's account appears in his *Essays in Action and Events* (New York: Oxford University Press, 1980), esp. essays 1 and 5.

45. Wollheim, *Mind and Its Depths*, pp. 94–99. The quotation is from p. 99.

46. Wollheim, *Mind and Its Depths*, p. 102.

47. Through a discussion of this point with Allison Kerr, I have come to appreciate more fully the possibility that the only route to becoming aware of our own madnesses may be observing them first at a safe distance, that is, in others.

48. Martin Buber, "The Education of Character" in *Between Man and Man* (New York: Macmillan, 1965), esp. p. 11.

Serving as Moral Stewards of the Schools

Wilma F. Smith

Carol was exhilarated as she began her first teaching job. She envisioned herself embarking on a solo voyage across the ocean. At age twenty, she was certain that she was prepared to take on her class of thirty-two fourth graders. Carol had performed admirably during her three-month student teaching assignment during the quarter prior to her graduation. She had been fortunate to work with a master teacher who expected the most from her students and was delighted to share her considerable repertoire of teaching strategies and her philosophy of teaching. As she moved her boxes of files and materials into her own classroom, Carol still could scarcely believe that she was on her own. She had charged through her undergraduate work in ten straight quarters, completing requirements for three minors: geography, music, and education. Carol had been anxious to get through all of the general education requirements and methods classes so that she could do her "practice teaching." She had crammed in course overloads and taken correspondence courses on the side, all to get through college and launch her teaching career.

Carol's college advisers dealt with her as an individual. They checked off requirements and approved her registration during the brief rest stops on her race through a collage of required and elective courses. Carol sailed through some perfunctory observations in a scatter of classrooms, completed her quarter of practice teaching, and received her certificate on a Friday in March 1957. The following Monday, she embarked on her maiden voyage as an elementary teacher.

Carol's first year went by in a whirl: eleven subjects to teach to thirty-two nine-year-olds, playground duty, bus duty, lesson planning, weekly faculty meetings after school. She ran the school library, her assigned contribution to the good of the school. Carol taught in virtual isolation from the other teachers in her school. Even during her first year of teaching, no one served as her mentor or confidant. She had no time for preparation during the school day and no opportunity to engage in professional development activities, except the once-a-year one-day institute for all the teachers in the region. If Carol had heard John Goodlad speak at such an institute on the topic of the teacher's role as a steward of the school, she would have been astounded. "If all our institutions are the bones of our civilization," he might have said, "they must be well nourished and carefully nurtured. If schools are part of this skeletal structure, as we so often claim, they must not be neglected or they will decay. Teachers are their primary stewards. Their preparation programs must alert them to this responsibility and begin to prepare them to assume it."[1] Certainly Carol could have related to the concept of being a steward of her fourth-grade classroom, but beyond that classroom door she could see herself working as a steward only of the library collection.

Unfortunately, many of the programs that prepare teachers today still perpetuate that solo voyage paradigm of individual teachers in individual classrooms. Individual student teachers are assigned to individual cooperating teachers and are supervised by an individual professor. Yet it stands to reason that if we expect teachers to develop a comprehensive grasp of the "values, knowledge, and skills to be brought to bear in the ongoing renewal of the schools in which [they] will spend their professional careers,"[2] their general and professional education programs must prepare them quite differently. Specifically, teacher candidates must have the opportunity to complete their field experiences in renewing schools where teachers, principals, students, and parents work together in a spirit of stewardship.

Stewardship of the whole school rarely has been perceived as the classroom teacher's role. In fact, most teachers have not held leadership roles in school renewal and change. Instead, most teachers go to work every day to teach groups of twenty to thirty students of approximately the same age. They are isolated from regular contact with other adults during the day in self-contained classrooms and are evaluated on their performance as individuals standing alone, "delivering" a curriculum that is prescribed elsewhere in the school district or state education office. Most principals also function as stand-alone leaders, held accountable individually for the performance of the students in their schools. Carol's first school was fashioned after this traditional pattern. She worked very hard, loved her students, and received outstanding performance evaluations, but she was not a steward of her school.

Not until twenty years after her first year of teaching did Carol come to know what it meant for teachers to work together as stewards of a school. She was hired in a different district as the principal of a nongraded elementary school where teachers and students were organized into five clusters, each with four teachers and one hundred students aged five to eleven years. The teachers worked together in teams, pairing up to teach various content themes to students who were arranged into primary or intermediate groups. Once a week the school's site council met to consider schoolwide issues concerning the curriculum, student characteristics and needs, instructional strategies, assessments of progress, school climate, parent relations, and the like. In her first months at this school, the teachers took Carol aside and enculturated her into "the way our school does its business." They insisted that she read several books, including *The Nongraded Elementary School,* by John Goodlad and Robert Anderson, which was the model for the school's organization.[3] During her four years as principal, she learned what it meant to collaborate for the good of the whole school. It became clear to Carol that "the most compelling moral imperatives for teachers pertain to their necessary vigilance in ensuring that their school fulfills its designated functions well and equitably and to the nature of the unique relationship between the teacher and the taught."[4]

Carol retired after thirty-three years in public education, joyfully watching her son, Tony, enter the teaching profession. He made his decision to teach after he had experienced an excellent liberal education, lived in Russia during the fall of communism, and returned home to work as a teaching assistant with young people whose first language was not English. At about that time, the College of Education at the University of Washington, a member of the National Network for Educational Renewal (NNER), radically redesigned its program for elementary teacher preparation. Tony applied and was selected to be a member of the first cohort of thirty graduate students.

His preparation for teaching was staggeringly different from Carol's. He had already completed a rich liberal education, lived abroad, and thought deeply about working with children who were viewed as being at risk in school because their English proficiency was limited. He had seen good and bad teaching practices in three different schools in a variety of classrooms. And now he was privileged to be part of a teacher preparation program in which he would have the opportunity to learn alongside twenty-nine other students with faculty who would soon become his colleagues. Theory and practice were connected from the outset, as educational foundations courses required the students to observe in a number of schools and to wrestle with the issues of stewardship set out in Goodlad's Postulate Twelve: "Programs for the education of educators must involve future teachers in the issues and dilemmas that emerge out of the never-ending tension between the rights and interests of individual parents and interest groups and the role of schools in transcending parochialism and advancing community in a democratic society." (The postulates are set out in Appendix A.) Students were intrigued, puzzled, and sometimes upset by this tension, and they engaged in dialogue among themselves, with their professors, and with the teachers in the schools. They wrote in reflective journals, read and interpreted scholarly works, and conversed by e-mail with educational leaders across the country.

When Tony began his first year of teaching a multiage classroom of seven- to nine-year-olds, he was fortunate to enter a school culture where the norm was clearly stewardship of the school for everyone: the principal, teachers, support staff, parents, and community members. The issues that Carol was discussing with teachers some twenty years into her teaching career were woven into the everyday conversations of the educators in Tony's school. The teachers seemed to accept that the tension Goodlad describes in Postulate Twelve is "not something that affects only administrators. As moral stewards of the schools, they are inescapably a part of it."[5] School organization, grouping of students, curriculum, teaching practices, student behavior, time schedules, teacher leadership, and assessment became the warp and woof of the teachers' work together. *Inclusiveness* was the operative word as these educators tackled the tough problems surrounding their students' lives in and out of the school. All of the children had to be included in the school community. All of the educators had to be included in planning for schoolwide renewal. And all of the parents and guardians had to be included in the life of the school. In practice, this meant no pull-out programs. Students were kept together for two years. Teachers worked in grade-level and vertical teams. Time schedules were altered to permit in-depth planning, professional development, and conferences with parents. These teachers were truly serving as stewards of their school.

Stewardship is central to the life of the college and school faculties who work together in the approximately five hundred partner schools of the NNER. Partner schools are major players in the simultaneous renewal of schooling and the education of educators. Sometimes called "professional development schools," they share a commitment to Goodlad's nineteen postulates, especially Postulate Fifteen, which speaks most directly to their role in simultaneous renewal: "Programs for the education of educators must assure for each candidate the availability of a wide array of laboratory settings for simulation, observation, hands-on experiences, and exemplary schools for internships and residencies; they must admit no more students to their programs than can be assured these quality experiences."

In addition to the postulates, partner schools embrace common values that reflect their commitment to stewardship:

- Partner schools of the NNER ensure that all learners have equitable access to knowledge.

- Partner schools recognize and honor diversity, commit to multicultural curricula and culturally responsive practice, prepare individuals for active participation in a democratic society, and promote social justice.

- Partner schools contribute to the growth of students as citizens in a democratic society, contributors to a healthy economy, and fully human individuals versed in the arts and ideas that help them take advantage of their talents. In short, they are schools prepared to enculturate learners for participation in a democratic society.

- Partner schools enable educators to make educational decisions with students and other stakeholders.

- Partners create educative communities that seek to develop a more just and sustainable society.[6]

Acting on their shared beliefs about moral stewardship, the NNER partner schools seek to accomplish four purposes: to educate children and youths, prepare educators, provide professional development, and conduct inquiry.

Defining Stewardship

Webster's Seventh New Collegiate Dictionary defines a steward as one who actively directs affairs to safeguard and improve something precious and, in the process, earns a sense of fulfillment and distinction. If teachers as stewards are actively directing affairs, as the definition insists, they certainly are not passive, compliant workers who merely follow others' dictates; rather, they are true leaders of renewal, taking initiative for needed change and actively engaged in making important decisions together. As moral stewards, they safeguard and improve what is precious in their schools.[7] Throughout the NNER, school and university partners in simultaneous renewal focus their collaborative work on six interrelated aspects of stewardship: commitment to a shared mission, development of democratic community, dedication to whole-school renewal, engagement in critical inquiry, participation in professional development, and preparation of future educators.

Commitment to a Shared Mission

The mission of schooling in a democracy, according to John Goodlad, "comes down to two related kinds of enculturation; no other institution is so charged. The first is for political and social responsibility as a citizen. The second is for maximum individual development, for full participation in the human conversation."[8]

The four-part mission of teacher education described in Chapter One is geared to the mission of schooling and grounded on the moral dimensions of teaching in a social and political democracy. The four components of this mission are enculturating the young in a democracy, ensuring access to knowledge for all children and youths, engaging in a nurturing pedagogy, and serving as stewards of the schools. Stewardship requires that the educator attend to all four. "The fulfillment of educational mission," says Goodlad, "depends primarily on the ability of teachers to cultivate this democratic setting (moral stewardship) and to create learning opportunities that embrace all of their students (caring pedagogy)."[9]

Peter Senge, describing the work of the leader of a learning organization, likens it to that of a designer, a teacher, and a *steward*. The leader becomes a steward of the organization's vision, which is grounded on "a sense of purpose or destiny" to bring learning and change into society as a whole.[10] "In a learning organization," Senge asserts, "leaders may start by pursuing their own vision, but as they learn to listen carefully to others' visions they begin to see that their own personal vision is part of something larger. This does not diminish any leader's sense of responsibility for the vision—if anything it deepens it."[11]

As they work together as stewards of their schools, teachers and their principals realize and refine their personal visions, developing what Roland Barth describes as "a kind of moral imagination that gives them the ability to see schools not as they are, but as they would like them to become."[12] Barth believes that schools are most effectively improved by the teachers, principals, and students who live within them. He states emphatically, "The excitement of working in schools, the satisfactions, the rewards come from studying a difficult situation and then generating one's own plan for improving things. Why should educators be placed—or place themselves—in the position of only implementing the grand ideas of others, ideas with which they may not agree?"[13]

Michael Fullan asserts that "moral purpose," coupled with change agentry, is the key to continuously renewing the school. He stresses that the moral purpose of each individual teacher is the starting point for developing a shared vision of the school. However, teachers rarely have the opportunity to discuss their own visions, much less work through one that is shared by their colleagues. Given the time to communicate and collaborate, teachers will find that they can translate their own moral purposes into social agendas for organizational change.[14]

At Shepard Accelerated School in St. Louis, a partner school in the NNER's Metropolitan St. Louis Consortium for Educational Renewal, the entire staff, together with a cohort of student teachers from Harris-Stowe State College, participates in biweekly conversations about their school mission.[15] They discuss various aspects of their collective work, seeking to do "whatever it takes" to help all of their students succeed. Former principal Savannah Young, a Leadership Associate from Cohort III, adopted the idea of conversation as a vehicle for school renewal. Teachers from half of the faculty cover the classes of the other teachers every other week to provide the two-hour time block for these critical conversations. Initially these conversations were viewed as "just one more of our principal's new ideas that she brought back from some conference." However, the teachers have come to value their dialogue and to take initiative in suggesting topics and readings. They say that their commitment to the school mission has deepened as a result of these conversations. They feel more connected to their teaching peers and are more enthusiastic about their work with their own students, as well as the preservice teachers.

Benedict College, a member of the South Carolina Network for Educational Renewal of the NNER, conducts an induction ceremony for juniors who have been admitted into the education program. In the audience are over a dozen PreMATE clubs, composed of high school students who have indicated their interest in becoming teachers. PreMATE is a part of Benedict's Minority Access to Teacher Education (MATE) Program, designed to attract academically gifted high school and college students from across the state into teaching. The induction ceremony features a recitation of the Benedict College Student Educator's Pledge, the pinning of inductees by education faculty advisers, speeches from several newly inducted student educators about their dedication to teaching, and reports from each PreMATE Club.[16] This moving celebration inspires students as well as teachers from high schools and the college, and

it brings into sharp focus their collective commitment to the mission of teaching.

The teachers and graduate students at Dole Intermediate School,
together with their colleagues from the College of Education at the
University of Hawaii, work together in teams to advance the school's
mission to provide access to knowledge for all children in their community. When a recent state budget shortfall took away their support for team preparation time, these dedicated faculty members
elected to find time outside the school day to continue their work in
developing cross-disciplinary units and engaging the middle school
students in the process of inquiry. "This work is too important to let
our teamwork go," the teachers assert. This collaboration results in
a synergy of renewed dedication to the school's mission to make sure
that all children succeed.

Development of Democratic Community

For the teacher, being a moral steward of the school encompasses
much more than teaching the students in the classroom. Stewardship is inescapably intertwined with the development of democratic
community. Schools that conscientiously work toward the common
good are never free of the tension that exists between creating a
public and responding to the individual needs and rights of students.
Amy Gutmann characterizes this tension between our values of
individual freedom and civic virtue as both difficult and challenging. Gutmann posits that a democratic theory of education refuses
to dissolve these tensions and insists on finding a principled way of
living with them.[17]

Mark Gerzon urges educators to incorporate conflict into the
curriculum to give students a genuine experience of democracy in
action:

> An integral part of education is learning that democra-
> tic communities are strong enough to contain their deep-
> est differences. If we avoid discussing these differences

in schools, out of the misguided notion that we are protecting children from being wounded in the culture wars,
we are imparting values by default. We are telling young
people that we don't trust them to deal with the diversity present in their own communities. We are also
telling them that we adults do not know how to deal
with conflict ourselves.[18]

The ongoing conflict between two legitimate purposes—individual rights and the common good—is an issue that schools must
always face. "How and where are the two reconciled?" asks Bruce
Thomas. The best way, he concludes, is "to honestly and persever-
ingly grapple with and define purposes and then openly search for
the means of reconciling the conflicts."[19] Teachers must be nurtured
as they wrestle with these moral dilemmas of teaching. "If the individual is to act in morally meaningful ways," Thomas argues, "the
little sovereignties we call institutions must constitute a context
that nurtures and rewards such action. . . . If little sovereignties such
as schools and school systems are to nurture and reward democratic
individuality, they must themselves be disciplined by democratic ideas
and the methods that flow from them."[20]

A just and caring school community environment is safe and
orderly. Teachers nurture their students while holding high expectations for their learning. Meaningful routines that provide necessary
practice for success are coupled with teaching strategies that actively
engage the students in their work. Teachers introduce innovative
practices while continuing to insist on rigorous standards of performance. Teachers get to know their students well because they interact with fewer students per day and provide a variety of structured
opportunities for civil discourse to build democratic character.[21]

The education of democratic character, according to Donna
Kerr, is education for "a community of persons who neither feel a
need to control others nor require the direction of others to feel
whole. It is," Kerr concludes, "genuine education for a community

made up of *democratic relationships*."[22] These relationships, Linda Darling-Hammond adds, require "not only experiences that develop serious thinking but also access to social understanding, developed by personal participation in a democratic community and direct experience of multiple perspectives. To accomplish this, schools must enact democracy rather than merely preach about it."[23]

Kailua High School on the windward coast of Oahu, Hawaii, is a member of the Hawaii School University Partnership of the NNER. Here, the students themselves led two community forums to explore ways in which their school might strengthen its programs for all students. Teachers and principal served as recorders and observers while the student leaders engaged citizens in spirited discussions about a wide range of issues of concern to them. Other activities at Kailua High School involve graduate students from the University of Hawaii, who explore critical schooling issues through conducting semester-long inquiry projects. Over the past five years, the entire community has become engaged in discussing and managing conflict, developing creative solutions to problems, and building tolerance and respect for divergent views. Principal Mary Murakami, a Leadership Associate from Cohort III, is passionately committed to the ideal of "democracy as education." Her openness to self-renewal and her commitment to the young people and adults make her a dynamic model of a moral steward of the school.

The development of democratic community has been a prolonged effort at Ysleta Elementary School, a partner of the University of Texas at El Paso and an affiliate of the Alliance Schools Initiative. Authentic public engagement is achieved at Ysleta by bringing parents and community members into the ongoing life of the school in meaningful ways. The parents, for many years estranged from the classroom environment, now initiate their own action plans and collaborate with the educators to bring about true educational renewal. Principal Dolores DeAvila, a Leadership Associate from Cohort IV, sees the engagement of families and community as the very heart of school renewal. She has worked with university faculty to develop a required course for preservice teachers that prepares them to connect with the families of the students they will be teaching during their internships. At Ysleta, conflict is viewed as content for dialogue and debate, with the goal of teaching students that, as Benjamin Barber states, "democracy is a polity of strangers and a polity of antagonists and a polity of people who don't get along, and maybe even don't share fundamental values, but still have to live together and have to find a way other than the gun or the fist to solve and resolve or live with their differences."[24]

The Wakefield Community School in rural Nebraska is a partner with Wayne State College in the Nebraska Network for Educational Renewal of the NNER. The Wakefield School is also affiliated with the School at the Center Project of the Annenberg Rural Challenge. The principal and teachers are dedicated to making this K–12 school the center of their community, and they engage in a variety of year-long activities to connect their students with the community, and vice versa. Principal Jeanne Surface, a Leadership Associate from Cohort V, served as a co-organizer of the Nebraska Network for Educational Renewal's Leadership Institute in 1997. The participants spent a two-day session considering the meaning of stewardship in their school-university partnerships. They engaged in spirited discussions with Paul Theobald, a Leadership Associate from Cohort II and author of *Teaching the Commons*,[25] about ways in which the rural schools can become key players in revitalizing their communities. Such schools are involved in joint planning and action, many using technology to improve communication among participants geographically distant from one another. They engage in curriculum development in the humanities, mathematics, and the sciences. And they become catalysts for discussions of critical rural issues such as community housing, small business development, and learning opportunities that encourage young people to build careers in their local communities.

Dedication to Whole-School Renewal

Stewards of the schools are purposefully engaged in the renewal process. Steward teachers believe that there is more to teaching than working in their own classrooms, and they derive respect and fulfillment from taking on leadership roles for the renewal of their schools. They understand and respect the points of view of other teachers and administrators, and they enjoy orchestrating interactions with other adults as well as with children. Roland Barth observes that "opportunities to engage in school leadership are attractive for . . . teachers because they offer possibilities for improving teaching conditions; they replace the solitary authority of the principal with a collective authority; they provide a constructive format in which adults can interact . . . ; they help transform schools into contexts for adults' as well as children's learning; and participation in leadership builds community."[26]

Many educators agree that the school is the unit of change. James Comer says, "No matter what form the school development effort takes—no matter how large or the level of staff training—the plan should focus on the whole school, and the process should involve all levels of staff."[27] Schools must become self-renewing, cultivating the capacity for solving their own problems and meeting the needs of the unique set of young people within their boundaries.

Whole-school renewal is not easy. John Goodlad, for example, cautions that "schools will have great difficulty . . . in becoming self-renewing without support from their states and local districts and especially from their surrounding constituencies.[28] Theodore Sizer agrees: "Flexible and appropriate school and system structures are important. A steady and supportive district and state are important. Without them, dedicated teachers cannot turn their commitments into action. But the game of serious education ultimately rests with powerful teachers, supportive parents, and determined students. Finding the way to gather these people together is the heart of the matter, the ultimate systemic reform."[29]

Pearl Ridge Elementary School in Aiea, Hawaii, is a member of the Hawaii School University Partnership of the NNER. Principal Raymond Sugai, a Leadership Associate from Cohort IV, is a consistently energetic, positive, and collaborative leader of the school. Everyone in Pearl Ridge—students, teachers, aides, preservice teachers, parents, and grandparents—seems to be exuberant and enthusiastic about collaborating. Joe Zilliox, liaison faculty member from the University of Hawaii at Manoa and a Leadership Associate from Cohort V, meets his eighteen preservice teachers at Pearl Ridge to observe their teaching and to conduct college classes at the school. A principal intern is completing her work in the university's educational leadership program. The school is fairly bursting with parents, grandparents, and volunteers. Mentor teachers and preservice teachers work together, sharing ideas and learning from one another. Instructional groupings throughout the school promote cooperative learning designed to develop teamwork, independence, and social and academic skills. A positive, purposeful, and dynamic climate pervades the entire school. Expectations are high for everyone. The preservice teachers are definitely becoming more aware of their role as members of the profession writ large. Many of them put in 240 or more hours of fieldwork before they even enter student teaching. Surely all of the participants in renewal at Pearl Ridge are moral stewards of their school.

Madeira Junior/Senior High School is a partner of the Institute for Educational Renewal at Miami University of Ohio. During the past few years, a number of fruitful partnership activities have expanded and deepened the collaboration for school renewal. Cohorts of student interns are assigned to teams of master teachers. Madeira staff conduct weekly seminars for interns and participate in on-site classes to improve their ability to mentor the interns. Doctoral students collaborate with Madeira staff to address problems of leadership, school change, instruction, and curriculum. Miami University liaison Bernard Badiali, a Leadership Associate from Cohort V, believes that schools are at their best when they are sites of struggle with ideas and concepts. Further, he senses that educational renewal "begins with coming to terms about the purpose public schools should serve in society."[30] Truly, it takes a whole school, a whole university, a whole community to bring about school renewal that is centered on preparing our young people to live in a democracy.

Engagement in Critical Inquiry

Stewards of renewing schools constantly examine their practices for alignment with their mission. They keep abreast of educational research, work diligently to improve their teaching strategies, attend to students' interests and needs, and ascertain how well their students are using their minds. Kenneth Sirotnik insists that

> school improvement must take place in schools by and for the people in them; description, judgment, decision making, and action taking regarding improvement efforts require informed inquiry and critical thinking; this *evaluative* process includes multiple perspectives on what constitutes appropriate knowledge and information; and this process is not a one-shot deal but an ongoing part of the daily worklife of professionals involved in their own school improvement efforts.[31]

Busy school people do not find it easy to question the "regularities" (the day-to-day routines and schedules that organize school life) in their daily individual work, much less the collective work of their school. Seymour Sarason's comprehensive inquiries into the role of school culture in change describe the difficulty of altering one's own thinking about the way things are done. "To do so deliberately for the serious purpose of discovering new questions and problems is even more difficult," Sarason writes, "because one tends not to want to believe that one's investigative territory can be mapped rather differently and that new 'lands' can be discovered by others whose perspective is different."[32] Then, if one does attempt to take on another perspective, new questions arise about what to look at, how to look at it, and what other questions must now be asked about it.

This collective questioning about the efficacy of teaching and learning is central to renewal. Paul Heckman describes a partnership within which teachers are nurtured to examine classroom conditions and solve schoolwide problems together. Each school develops a process of inquiry with the following characteristics. First, teachers gather together and describe what they do. Next, they discuss why they engage in these practices, which promotes further inquiry and a search for additional information and new knowledge. With other teachers, they then compare the new knowledge with their existing practices and, if needed, seek to change their own practices.[33]

Sometimes inquiry can be nurtured through an honest admission by a principal or teacher that he or she cannot solve a problem alone. If the culture of the school nurtures this problem-sharing approach, the individual can shed the burden of having to know how to do everything. Sharon Quint describes how principal Carole Williams of Seattle's B. F. Day Elementary School established the groundwork for teachers to help one another: "If teachers can openly discuss those things they are unhappy with, they can begin to discuss how they would like things to be. It is at this point that staff development meetings can offer avenues of new thought regarding students, parents, and the role of schooling."[34]

The University of Connecticut's teacher education program features a fifth year in which students inquire into the conditions of teaching and learning in the partner schools affiliated with the university. Kay Norlander-Case and Timothy Reagan, faculty members at the University of Connecticut and Leadership Associates from Cohort II, have designed seminars to teach the skills of reflection and critical inquiry. Students immerse themselves in the life of a school and collaborate with teachers and college faculty to inquire deeply into issues and problems of teaching and learning.

The five school-university partnerships of the South Carolina Network for Educational Renewal of the NNER seek to promote tripartite inquiry into teaching and learning.[35] A schoolteacher, an education professor, and an arts and sciences professor inquire into some aspect of teaching and learning from three different perspectives. These projects have been highly motivating and inspiring for the participants, and they have resulted in a strengthening of teaching practices at both the P–12 and college levels. Many of the projects have also involved college and school students, and some have spilled over into the community. Projects have included inquiry into teaching foreign languages in elementary schools, interdisciplinary teaching in mathematics and science in secondary schools, integrating technology into the curriculum, teaching literacy in elementary and secondary schools, matching teaching styles to learning styles, and developing dance education. The members of the tripartite teams readily share the intellectual excitement that these inquiry projects have generated.

The University of South Carolina and its partner, Richland County School District Two, have taken collaborative inquiry a large step further. In the fall of 1997, after three years of independent and collaborative study, research, and planning, this partnership of the NNER opened a small elementary school of choice called the Center for Inquiry. The theory underlying this school is that ongoing inquiry into best practices will drive renewal. Indeed, the culture of inquiry permeates the school, from the principal's office to the playground. Parents and other visitors are given articles about inquiry to read prior to making a visit to the center. They complete a response log, which asks them to list three things learned from the articles, three things they expect to see during their upcoming visit to the center, and any "burning questions" they would like to have answered about curriculum and learning at the center. One of the more remarkable aspects of the Center for Inquiry is the equal sharing of responsibilities and resources by the district and the College of Education. Formal agreements between the university and the district shaped the mission, curriculum, staffing, and student enrollment in the center. For example, the student body is deliberately diversified as to race, gender, socioeconomic status, and academic achievement, making it truly heterogeneous in nature. On a visit to the classrooms, one notices that the children, too, are enthusiastic about inquiry. They take the initiative to ask questions of the teachers, of each other, and of visitors who are fortunate enough to spend some time with them.

Participation in Professional Development

The ongoing professional growth of teachers, administrators, and professors is central to the renewal of schools. Professional development activities should be embedded in the culture and connected to the process of critical inquiry. According to Bruce Joyce, Richard Hersh, and Michael McKibbin, "If the education profession is to flourish and if schools are to be a vital force in society, it is necessary to rebuild the school into a lifelong learning laboratory not only for children but for the teachers as well." They describe three purposes of staff development: "to enrich the lives of teachers and administrators so that they continuously expand their general education, their emotional range, and their understanding of children"; "to generate continuous efforts to improve schools"; and "to create conditions which enable professional skill development to be continuous."[36]

Certain conditions must be in place if professional development activities are to fulfill these three purposes. The school culture must provide trust and support, encourage and nurture risk taking, ensure collaborative inquiry into teaching and learning, embrace cooperative decision making, and provide specific avenues for instruction and training.

Many of the NNER settings join college and university faculty partners in professional development. Barbara Gottesman, former director of the South Carolina setting, advocates peer coaching as a model for teachers and professors to renew their skills and knowledge, strengthen their practice, and broaden their repertoire of instructional methods.[37] In the process of peer coaching, hierarchical roles are set aside as three educators coach one another, following prescribed patterns of interaction: one person teaches a lesson segment, another observes and gives specific feedback, and a third observes the coach-teacher interaction and gives evaluative feedback on the process. The sets of three might include a teacher, a student teacher, and a college supervisor, or perhaps a principal, a college professor of science, and a teacher.

When all parties work together to improve teaching and learning, the school becomes a self-renewing entity as it "recreates itself into a healthy learning community where working together, studying together, and growing together has been planned into the system as a way of life . . . synonymous with lifelong learning."[38]

The collegial relationships required for working, studying, and growing together are not easily built. Even if all the parties come to the tripartite faculty relationship (classroom teacher, education professor, arts and sciences professor) with attitudes of parity and respect, the development of authentic colleagueship is a complex process.[39] All three partners must be able to view themselves as both teacher educators and school teachers. At some point, their effective professional development will need to include training that helps them perform their expanded roles. How will they develop trust and rapport with one another? In what ways can each person bring expertise to bear on their collaborative work? How and where will the colleagues find the necessary resources? How might the partners extend their collaborative inquiry and professional development to others throughout the school and college?

Harold Wilson Middle School, a partner school in the New Jersey Network for Educational Renewal/Montclair State University setting, has served as a center for teachers' professional development. Former principal Lourdes Z. Mitchel, a Leadership Associate from Cohort III, together with her colleagues from Montclair State

University, designed the partnership with professional development at the heart of their collaboration. There was a unity of purpose in the partners' commitment to active, theory-into-practice inquiry. This partner school was grounded on four assumptions: that the overlapping missions of schools and colleges should become shared missions in the setting of the partner school; that preparatory programs and continuing development opportunities for teachers should be knowledge based; that reflective, critical thinking is important to the learning of teachers and students; and that those responsible for the professional development of teachers should be prepared to model what they recommend.[40]

Over four years at Harold Wilson Middle School, eight-week blocks of time were provided for professional development activities such as self-assessment, seminars and demonstrations, and follow-up coaching in the classrooms of the participating teachers. Middle school teachers across the district cycled through the professional development sequence as Harold Wilson teachers taught their students. Today this partner school serves as an inservice site for staff developers from all the schools in the district, continuing to link theoretical insight with the wisdom of practice.

Winthrop University, a member of the South Carolina Network for Educational Renewal, established the Center for Pedagogy, which has evolved into a dynamic entity for simultaneous renewal. Ten college faculty members are assigned to work one full day a week in the partner schools. As a result of this significant commitment, professional development activities have blossomed. A summer institute for over forty faculty members from the partner schools, the college of education, and the college of arts and sciences resulted in a heightened interest in interdisciplinary inquiry and collaboration. Twenty school improvement projects have been completed by school-college faculty teams. In the spring, a conference for partner school teachers and principals featured dialogue around the theme, "What does it mean to be a teacher in a democracy?"

Teacher Preparation

A key function of NNER partner schools is the preparation of future educators. John Goodlad describes partner schools as "integral components of the three-way partnership among teachers joined with professors in education and the arts and sciences for the education of educators."[41] A number of NNER settings are developing centers of pedagogy, broad umbrella units that bring together partner schools and all the other parties responsible for the education of educators.

JoAnn Canales, a Leadership Associate from Cohort III, is concerned about preparing teachers to be moral stewards of urban schools with ethnically and socioeconomically diverse student bodies. In her study of 106 teacher candidates, she found a need for focused discussions and specific courses about reality-based issues that preservice teachers will encounter, as well as structured opportunities for teacher candidates to work with children of various cultural and ethnic backgrounds. She concluded that if teachers are to be prepared to undertake the role of moral stewards in urban schools, programs must be developed that both select teacher candidates who have a sincere interest in working with inner-city youths and require extended time in urban partner schools. Such programs must also provide three key elements: practical curricula that address the needs of diverse learners, opportunities for teacher candidates to reflect on their own beliefs and feelings about working with individuals who are different from them, and an array of field experiences, including working with the partner school's community and having support during the first year of teaching.[42]

Westridge Elementary School, a member of the Brigham Young University–Public School Partnership of the NNER, is a renewing partner school in which preservice teachers are assigned in cohorts of over twenty for their first field experiences. Seminars are cotaught by an education professor, the principal, and a teacher facilitator, who integrate the work of the cohort into the ongoing life of the school. Westridge is a year-round school: the academic year is arranged in quarters of study with two-week intersessions. During these intersessions, a number of college students have an opportunity to work with school faculty to conduct special enrichment and remedial programs. The student teachers are an integral part of the school and are regarded as junior faculty. The principal notes that teachers have become increasingly involved in discussions on the subject of what constitutes good instruction. The preservice emphasis has provided meaningful, personal inservice experiences for the Westridge teachers, as well as rich learning opportunities for the college students.

The Metropolitan St. Louis Consortium for Educational Renewal launched its Center for Inquiry and Renewal in 1996.[43] This center was designed to be a collaborative model of both preservice education and professional development for experienced educators. One of its major activities was the establishment of an early childhood teacher education cohort comprising students from Maryville University and Harris-Stowe State College. Two faculty members (one from each institution) and two schoolteachers (from partner elementary schools) worked together over the summer to plan the first year's course for the cohort. This quartet served as an instruction team throughout the academic year, providing seminars and rich field experiences for the students, and they continued to mentor the students as they progressed through their second year in the program.

Feedback from the first cohort indicates that these teacher education students changed dramatically in the way they think about children, teaching in a democracy, racial and cultural differences, and schooling in general. At a recent consortium conference, the members of this cohort talked about what they had learned from each other and from their experiences with regard to their guiding question: "What does it mean to be a morally responsible teacher in a diverse, democratic society?" Surely these students are beginning to understand the teacher's role as a moral steward of a school.

Stewardship of Democratic Schools

All of this discussion about stewardship of the schools is predicated on the theory that a school itself is a democratic place where teachers, students, administrators, preservice teachers, and college professors build symbiotic partnerships with each other and with the school community. Rarely can schools renew themselves on their own. Although the school is the unit for renewal and change, it is part of an ecology that affects its ability to transform its practices and sustain desired innovations. Time and again, those who write about the effectiveness of educational reform exhort policymakers, administrators, and communities to play their critical roles in supporting enduring school renewal.

Stewardship is a new way of looking at policy, leadership, and governance. As Peter Block points out,

> Stewardship is the umbrella idea which promises the means of achieving fundamental change in the way we govern our institutions. Stewardship is to hold something in trust for another. Historically, stewardship was a means to protect a kingdom while those rightfully in charge were away, or, more often, to govern for the sake of an underage king. The underage king for us is the next generation. We choose service over self-interest most powerfully when we build the capacity of the next generation to govern themselves.
>
> Stewardship is . . . the willingness to be accountable for the well-being of the larger organization by operating in service, rather than in control, of those around us. Stated simply, it is accountability without control or compliance.[44]

Genuine collaboration is complex and difficult. Even with the best of intentions, efforts to work together can run out of steam, encounter crises, or fade when leaders leave. As Seymour Sarason points out, the regularities of the schoolhouse have to be changed in order for people to experience deep-down renewal.[45] Those regularities derive from the school culture, where rules of behavior are not always explicit. However, these rules and regularities essentially define the way the parties collaborate.

Clearly, the structure of the school is central to encouraging collaboration. New structures must be created to give stability and ongoing support to the efforts being made by school and university people to bring about lasting change and create a culture of inquiry and renewal. Such a culture is based on trust, which sustains and nurtures democratic relationships. These relationships are strengthened when the parties share commitment to a common purpose, enjoy equal status, carry out clear roles in decision making, maintain honest and open communication, and share responsibility and accountability for their work. As school and university faculties work together, they find it necessary to construct carefully a new language of collaboration. This language is created as the parties develop new rules and regularities that help them to be more conscious about how they choose to talk, when and where they choose to talk, what they choose to talk about, and who is invited into the conversation.[46]

Reprise

Returning to Carol and her lack of preparation to serve as a steward of her school, we now can see that her perspective on her role would have been widened immeasurably if she had been privileged to attend college in one of the settings of the NNER. Carol's preservice program would have prepared her for stewardship by consistently making the connections between theory and practice as she observed, taught, and reflected on her work during a full year's internship in a partner school. She and her classmates in the cohort would have struggled alongside their master teachers and professors with those issues and dilemmas emerging out of the ongoing tensions between the rights and interests of individuals and the development of democratic community. Carol, like the preservice students in the St. Louis setting, would have explored the guiding question, "What does it mean to be a morally responsible teacher in a diverse and democratic society?"

If Carol had been fortunate enough to find a teaching position in one of the NNER partner schools, she would have become a member of a culture in which the norm was clearly stewardship of the school for everyone: principal, teachers, support staff, parents, and community members. School organization, grouping of students, curriculum, teaching practices, student behavior, time schedules, teacher leadership, and assessment would be topics for inquiry, dialogue, discussion, and decision making. Schedules would permit in-depth planning, professional development, and conferring with parents. Carol, together with her colleagues from the school and the partner university, would truly enact the moral dimensions of the mission of teaching: enculturating the young in a democracy, ensuring equal access to knowledge for all students, engaging in a nurturing pedagogy, and serving as moral stewards of the schools.

Stewards actively direct affairs to safeguard and improve something precious, and in the process, they earn a sense of fulfillment and distinction. The sense of fulfillment that comes from being moral stewards of the schools grows from educators' knowing that they have had a part in enabling young people to create a better tomorrow for our democracy as they participate fully in the human conversation.

Notes

1. John I. Goodlad, *Teachers for Our Nation's Schools* (San Francisco: Jossey-Bass, 1990), p. 52.

2. Goodlad, *Teachers for Our Nation's Schools*, p. 52.

3. John I. Goodlad and Robert H. Anderson, *The Nongraded Elementary School*, rev. ed. (New York: Harcourt Brace Jovanovich, 1963

[orig. 1959]). This book continues to be timely and has been re-issued with a new introduction by the authors (New York: Teachers College Press, 1987).

4. Goodlad, *Teachers for Our Nation's Schools*, p. 53.

5. John I. Goodlad, *Educational Renewal: Better Teachers, Better Schools* (San Francisco: Jossey-Bass, 1994), p. 86.

6. Richard W. Clark, Donna M. Hughes, and Representatives from the National Network for Educational Renewal, "Partner Schools: Definitions and Expectations" (Seattle: Center for Educational Renewal, University of Washington, 1995 [orig. 1993]), p. 1. The full document is reprinted, with slight modifications, as Appendix B.

7. Paul Theobald has delineated what stewards do, grouping these actions into four categories: orchestrating continuing reflection on a shared sense of the purpose of schooling, providing a context for learning through developing community, focusing everyone's attention on what values are held in common, and skillfully providing equal learning opportunities for all of their students. "Stewardship of Schools," presentation to the Nebraska Network for Educational Renewal Leadership Institute, Lincoln, September 23, 1997.

8. John I. Goodlad, "Democracy, Education, and Community," in Roger Soder (ed.), *Democracy, Education, and the Schools* (San Francisco: Jossey-Bass, 1996), p. 112.

9. Goodlad, "Democracy, Education, and Community," p. 113.

10. Peter M. Senge, *The Fifth Discipline: The Art and Practice of the Learning Organization* (New York: Doubleday, 1990), p. 346.

11. Senge, *Fifth Discipline*, p. 352.

12. Roland S. Barth, *Improving Schools from Within: Teachers, Parents, and Principals Can Make the Difference* (San Francisco: Jossey-Bass, 1990), p. 147.

13. Barth, *Improving Schools from Within*, p. 150.

14. Michael Fullan, *Change Forces: Probing the Depths of Educational Reform* (Bristol, Pa.: Falmer Press, 1993), pp. 8–18. Fullan's book is predicated on the assertion that moral purpose and change agentry

must go hand in hand if educators are to bring about durable school renewal. Without moral purpose, change efforts are aimless and fragmented. Without skillful change agent strategies, moral purpose becomes mere rhetoric, and reforms lose their meaning.

15. Shepard is also a member of the Accelerated Schools Project, which "calls for the transformation of schools that serve at-risk children to accelerate their education by using the enrichment approach usually reserved for gifted and talented students." Henry M. Levin, "Accelerated Schools After Eight Years," in Leona Schauble and Robert Glaser (eds.), *Innovations in Learning: New Environments for Education* (Mahwah, N.J.: Erlbaum, 1996), p. 329.

16. The Benedict College Student Educator's Pledge: "I believe that I am becoming the nation's most valuable resource, for through my hands will pass the nation's posterity. Becoming a teacher will enable me to perpetuate the efforts and dreams of my visionary ancestors. As a quality teacher, I will instill in young minds pride in self and legacy, dignity of self and of work, willingness to serve, and knowledge that nurtures wisdom. I will make a noble contribution to society. I believe that I, a quality teacher, will be an architect of America's future. I believe and hereby pledge myself to continuously pursue the training that will make me a quality teacher, so help me God." Education Majors' Achievement Recognition Ceremony, Benedict College, April 29, 1993.

17. Amy Gutmann, "Democratic Education in Difficult Times," *Teachers College Record* 92 (Fall 1990): 8.

18. Mark Gerzon, "Teaching Democracy by Doing It!" *Educational Leadership* 54 (February 1997): 11.

19. Bruce R. Thomas, "The School as a Moral Learning Community," in Goodlad, Soder, and Sirotnik (eds.), *Moral Dimensions of Teaching*, pp. 280–281.

20. Thomas, "School as a Moral Learning Community," p. 283.

21. Four connected pairs seem to enable students to benefit from school renewal efforts in high schools affiliated with the Coalition of Essential Schools: repertoire and routine, caring and expectations,

innovation and rigor, and small scale and civil discourse. For full descriptions, see Patricia A. Wasley, Robert L. Hampel, and Richard W. Clark, *Kids and School Reform* (San Francisco: Jossey-Bass, 1997).

22. Donna H. Kerr, "Toward a Democratic Rhetoric of Schooling," in John I. Goodlad and Timothy J. McMannon (eds.), *The Public Purpose of Education and Schooling* (San Francisco: Jossey-Bass, 1997), p. 80.

23. Linda Darling-Hammond, "Education, Equity, and the Right to Learn," in Goodlad and McMannon (eds.), *Public Purpose of Education and Schooling*, p. 47.

24. Benjamin R. Barber's comments appear in "Education for Civility and Civitas: Panel Discussion," in Goodlad and McMannon (eds.), *Public Purpose of Education and Schooling*, p. 129.

25. Paul Theobald, *Teaching the Commons: Place, Pride, and the Renewal of Community* (Boulder, Colo.: Westview Press, 1997).

26. Barth, *Improving Schools from Within*, pp. 132–133.

27. James P. Comer, *School Power: Implications of an Intervention Project* (New York: Macmillan, 1980), p. 238.

28. John I. Goodlad, *A Place Called School: Prospects for the Future* (New York: McGraw-Hill, 1984), pp. 31–32.

29. Theodore R. Sizer, *Horace's Hope: What Works for the American High School* (Boston: Houghton Mifflin, 1996), p. 106.

30. D. J. Hammond, Bob Larbes, and Bernard J. Badiali, "Experiencing the Promise of Simultaneous Renewal: A Portrait of Madeira Junior/Senior High School" in *Portraits of Twelve High School Partner Schools in the National Network for Educational Renewal*, Reflections on Practice Series no. 3 (Seattle: Center for Educational Renewal, University of Washington, 1997), p. Madeira–10.

31. Kenneth A. Sirotnik, "Evaluation in the Ecology of Schooling: The Process of School Renewal," in John I. Goodlad (ed.), *The Ecology of School Renewal* (Chicago: University of Chicago Press, 1987), p. 41. Critical inquiry is described as a dialectic around sets of questions such as: What goes on in the name of X? How did it

come to be that way? Whose interests are (and are not) being served by the way things are? What information and knowledge do we have—or need to get—that bear upon the issues? Is this the way we want it? What are we going to do about all this (p. 42)?

32. Seymour B. Sarason, *Revisiting "The Culture of the School and the Problem of Change"* (New York: Teachers College Press, 1996), pp. 119–120.

33. Paul Heckman, "Understanding School Culture," in Goodlad (ed.), *Ecology of School Renewal*, pp. 71–72.

34. Sharon Quint, *Schooling Homeless Children: A Working Model for America's Public Schools* (New York: Teachers College Press, 1994), p. 121. This is the moving story of Benjamin Franklin Day Elementary School in Seattle and its principal, Carole Williams, who radically redefined her work and reinvigorated her staff and community to transform children's lives. Overcoming their own fears and prejudices, Williams and her staff expanded the school's social role and established new coalitions to serve the needs of homeless children.

35. The following colleges and universities, together with their partner school districts and schools, comprise the five partnerships: Benedict College, Columbia College, Furman University, the University of South Carolina, and Winthrop University.

36. Bruce R. Joyce, Richard H. Hersh, and Michael McKibbin, *The Structure of School Improvement* (New York: Longman, 1983), pp. 149–150.

37. Barbara L. Gottesman and James O. Jennings, *Peer Coaching for Educators* (Lancaster, Pa.: Technomic, 1994).

38. Bruce Joyce, James Wolf, and Emily Calhoun, *The Self-Renewing School* (Alexandria, Va.: Association for Supervision and Curriculum Development, 1993), p. 23.

39. For an extensive treatment of the teacher-leader side of this collegial partnership, see Ann Lieberman (ed.), *Building a Professional Culture in Schools* (New York: Teachers College Press, 1988).

40. For information about professional development schools in the New Jersey Network for Educational Renewal, see Robert A. Pines,

Lourdes Z. Mitchel, and Nicholas Michelli, "Promoting Professional Development," in Russell T. Osguthorpe, R. Carl Harris, Melanie Fox Harris, and Sharon Black (eds.), *Partner Schools: Centers for Educational Renewal* (San Francisco: Jossey-Bass, 1995), pp. 73–97.

41. Goodlad, *Educational Renewal*, p. 109.

42. JoAnn Canales, "Creating Moral Stewards for Urban Schools" (paper presented at the American Association of Colleges for Teacher Education Conference, Washington, D.C., February 1995). Canales's presentation was a follow-up to her inquiry project as a Leadership Associate from Cohort III.

43. The Metropolitan St. Louis Consortium for Educational Renewal is a member of the NNER and encompasses Maryville University, Harris-Stowe State College, and several partner schools in St. Louis and its suburbs.

44. Peter Block, *Stewardship: Choosing Service over Self-Interest* (San Francisco: Berrett-Koehler, 1993), p. xx.

45. Seymour B. Sarason, *The Predictable Failure of Educational Reform: Can We Change Course Before It's Too Late?* (San Francisco: Jossey-Bass, 1990).

46. Wilma F. Smith, Barbara Gottesman, and Phyllis Edmundson, *Constructing a Language of Collaboration*, Reflections on Practice Series no. 2 (Seattle: Center for Educational Renewal, University of Washington, 1997).

Part III

Developing Leadership

Case Studies

8

The Hawaii School University Partnership

Antonette Port

I n Hawaii, the concept of partnership is well established in a number of areas, including business, education, government, and local communities. Working together is very much a part of the local culture, which itself reflects the contribution of a number of ethnic groups, especially those of Asian-Pacific and indigenous Hawaiian origin.

For many years, the Hawaii State Department of Education (DOE) and the College of Education (COE) at the University of Hawaii at Manoa have shared responsibility for the professional development of both preservice and inservice teachers. More recently, the Kamehameha Schools joined them in the development of teachers for children of Hawaiian ancestry. In 1986, the three institutions formalized their partnership by establishing the Hawaii School University Partnership (HSUP) and joining the National Network for Educational Renewal (NNER). The mission of the Hawaii Partnership reiterated the mission of the NNER: the simultaneous renewal of teacher education and schooling.

The University of Hawaii at Manoa is the major institution of higher education in the state, and its College of Education provides over 40 percent of the teachers hired by the DOE. The DOE functions as a large, centralized school system, with one state superintendent of schools and one board of education determining educational policies for 250 schools. There are seven semiautonomous districts, with the district superintendents functioning under the general direction of the state superintendent as part of his leadership team. Within this context, the HSUP collaborates at all levels with the University of Hawaii, as well as the DOE and its districts and schools.

Developing Leadership in the HSUP

The HSUP carefully planned the development of its potential leaders through its nominations to the Leadership Program of the Institute for Educational Inquiry (IEI). Over five years, a cadre of Hawaii Leadership Associates was developed, with representatives coming from all levels of the DOE, COE, and the colleges of arts and sciences. The newly appointed director of the HSUP and the director of the newly developed Master of Education in Teaching program, for example, were nominated and accepted for Cohort I (1992–1993). This action not only served as a strong staff development opportunity for the two individuals but also helped to develop a common philosophical base for renewal conversations between the two institutions. Two more nominations were made and accepted for Cohort II (1993–1994): the assistant superintendent for personnel in the DOE and the associate dean of academic affairs for the four colleges of arts and sciences. In 1994–1995 (Cohort III), the district superintendent for the Honolulu District and the principal of a secondary partner school were added to the leadership team. They were followed in Cohort IV by the principal of an elementary partner school. By 1996–1997 (Cohort V), the chair of the newly restructured elementary cohort program and the chair of the Department of Teacher Education and Curriculum Studies in the COE were selected to balance out representation with COE emerging leaders. The coordinator of the new Middle Level Master of Education program participated as a member of Cohort VI. This cadre of ten from state, district, and school levels within the DOE, the COE, and the colleges of arts and sciences provided the core from which the local leadership associates program was initiated.

Each IEI Associate undertakes a year-long inquiry project. The inquiry project undertaken by the district superintendent of Honolulu in Cohort III played a key role in initiating the Hawaii Leadership Associates Program in 1995. He felt that he had benefited professionally from the selected readings, participation in the conversations, and his associations with others in the NNER, and he wanted his district principals to have similar opportunities.

The HSUP had been planning to establish a local leadership associates program to begin in 1996. However, because this district superintendent was so committed and eager to begin immediately, and because he was also willing to put district staff development funds into the budget to assist with the cost of implementation, the partnership agreed to begin a local leadership associates program in the fall of 1995.

At the same time, the IEI invited NNER sites to participate in a week-long facilitator session designed to assist them in planning their own local leadership programs.[1] The HSUP took this opportunity to send the two members of Cohort III to the session. They returned to Hawaii with a draft plan and much enthusiasm. The entire team (which at that time consisted of six IEI graduate Leadership Associates, including me) met several times to formulate the Hawaii Leadership Associates Program and to implement it in December 1995.

We recognized the need to bring others into the conversation as the circle of involvement in the Hawaii partnership widened. In addition, we were becoming acutely aware that providing a fuller understanding of the underlying philosophical and moral grounding of the Agenda for Education in a Democracy would be an important and daunting challenge.

Our previous educational experiences with staff development and our own collective wisdom had convinced us that annual or semiannual forums, discrete workshops, or college courses, no matter how well planned and executed, were not likely to accomplish our purpose. What was needed, we believed, was sustained dialogue across role groups to break down the barriers of position and allow us to learn from each other. As a team, we also believed that we needed to focus on each participant's development as a change agent within his or her own particular sphere of responsibility.[2] The major purpose of the Hawaii Leadership Associates Program became to engage professional educators in conversations and reflective activities that would increase their understanding of the moral dimensions of education[3] and how these dimensions might be integrated into efforts to renew teacher education and schooling.

The Hawaii Leadership Associates Program

The Hawaii Leadership Associates Program mirrors the IEI Leadership Associates Program in purpose, design, and anticipated outcomes.[4] It was our intent to replicate, as much as possible, the program that we had experienced and found so beneficial to our own development. We were unable to deliver a twenty-day program locally and settled for four intensive two-day sessions during the workweek. The expected outcomes for the participants of the program are as follows:

- To establish collegial connections and collaborate with teachers, school principals, arts and sciences faculty, and education faculty toward the renewal of schools and the education of educators

- To view educational change, including curricular and program renewal, as a constant and to become effective change advocates within their institutions

- To expand their understanding of the public missions of education: preparing citizens for a democratic society; nurturing the intellectual, social, and emotional growth of students; providing equal educational oppor-

tunity for all students; and assuming responsibility for
the quality of our schools

- To conduct inquiry into educational issues related to
  their personal involvement in teacher education and
  school renewal

Twenty to twenty-five participants are selected each year from
faculty of the University of Hawaii and teachers and principals in
the partner schools, schools that are considering becoming partner
schools, and the Kamehameha Schools. Application packets describing the program, its purposes and themes, criteria for selection,
and session dates and topics are widely distributed toward the end
of each spring semester. Applicants submit a résumé and complete a
brief statement indicating how participation in the associates program will benefit them and what they feel they can contribute to
the program. The application deadline is the end of August, and
the first session is usually scheduled for late October or early November. Applicants must make a commitment to participate in all
sessions and activities, if selected. Applicants are expected to

- Demonstrate a commitment to the responsibilities of
  educating the young for citizenship in a democracy

- Serve in an institutional leadership role or have the
  potential for assuming a leadership role in that setting

- Demonstrate dedication to the vision of simultaneous
  renewal of the schools and the education of educators

- Recognize the nature and challenges inherent in bringing about institutional change and be willing to become agents for change

- Engage in critical inquiry, reflection, and dialogue with
  other educators

- Dedicate energy to personal learning, mastery of new skills, and application of knowledge

- Believe in the necessity for collaboration among institutional leaders, staff, and the school community

There is a conscious attempt to select applicants for each cohort who represent the diversity in the partnership: teachers, principals, state DOE personnel, COE faculty, and arts and sciences faculty. Cohort I in 1995, for example, consisted of twenty-one participants: eight from the schools (principals, vice principals, and teachers), one from the state office, five arts and sciences faculty, and seven COE faculty. Of Cohort II's twenty-one associates, nine were school-level participants, one was a district specialist, four were arts and sciences faculty, and seven were members of the COE faculty.

The leadership associates come together at a hotel four times during the academic year—one that is centrally located but away from their work sites in order to reduce the number of distractions, create an "immersion" effect, and strengthen the image of professional development. Participants engage in seminars, conversations, and reflective activities. Each session is designed around specific themes:

Session 1: Moral Dimensions of Teaching in a Democracy

Session 2: Access to Knowledge, Pedagogical Nurturing

Session 3: Stewardship of Schools

Session 4: Creating Educative Communities

The Hawaii leadership associates view videotapes and read books or articles on topics related to the themes. They also engage in discussions that stimulate reflection, and share their reflections and experiences with other associates. Each designs an inquiry project.

Sessions are structured to begin at 8:00 A.M. with a continental breakfast and an icebreaker type of activity—for example, music, movement, singing, and paired introductions. Next comes a one-and-one-half to two-hour conversation on the readings related to the theme for that session. There is a midmorning break, another conversation block, lunch, and then more conversation in the afternoon. Associates usually work in groups of four or five, and they spend a good deal of time learning from each other. Graduates of the IEI Leadership Associates Program participate in all of the activities as members of small groups. There are no presentations or lectures as such. Facilitators make brief introductory comments about a topic, link and review concepts, and present background information, but their comments are usually brief, and in no sense are they didactic teaching. There are simulations and activities to create awareness of collaboration across all levels, followed by questioning to elicit reflection on these activities. At the end of each two-day session, associates are asked to do a "quick-write" in which they evaluate the session and make suggestions for the next one. Participants are invited to join in the planning process with the IEI graduate Associates and are asked to recommend books or articles related to the program's themes.

Readings

The readings for the Hawaii Leadership Associates Program were carefully selected from among those the members of the planning team had encountered during their IEI program sessions related to the moral dimensions of the four major parts of the mission of teaching in a democracy.[5] We valued the experiences and discussions our readings had generated, and knew that these readings should provide the basis for the conversations and reflections of our local leadership associates. Our major challenge was to narrow down the readings from those appropriate for a twenty-day program to those that would fit into an eight-day program. Moreover, it was not long before the readings we selected were augmented by new titles discovered by the associates in Cohorts I and II. And as a result of our encouraging the Hawaii leadership associates to suggest other titles related to the major themes, we now include articles published by local professionals on diversity, equity, bridging home and school cultures, and the history of education in Hawaii.

Conversations

The conversations have become the core of our program. The concept of conversation is introduced immediately as a way of talking about the thoughts, questions, and insights generated by the readings. Conversation is not a debate or a tool for persuasion; it is an opportunity to respond honestly to the readings, share that response with others, and share in others' responses. Participants may differ without disagreeing or being disagreeable. Deliberately establishing small groups of four or five that cut across levels of position and institution assists immensely in breaking down the barriers of position. We provide a safe environment where classroom teachers and principals comfortably engage in conversations with university professors and state and district specialists on issues that are serious and sometimes sensitive in nature. The conversations generate a level of openness and trust that provides opportunities for further collaboration on issues beyond the scope of the program.

Activities and Discussions

The activities and the discussions that follow them are intended to create an understanding of a specific concept and how that concept might be applied. For example, one of our early activities stresses collaboration. A member of the planning team introduced an activity called "Collaborative Squares." The activity requires participants to fit various shapes and sizes of cardboard together to form a square without speaking or taking pieces from one another. The only way the puzzle can be solved is by individuals' observing each other's attempts and giving up pieces in order to share in the solution. The debriefing that follows highlights the participants' insights into what constitutes true collaboration and how their insights could be applied to their current work in the partnership.

Inquiry Project

Discussion of the inquiry project begins in session 1, when participants are introduced to its purposes and underlying intent. Leadership associates are presented with some ideas for inquiry projects, and members of previous cohorts are invited back to present their projects to the new cohort. Following the presentations, graduate associates facilitate small-group brainstorming sessions to help participants explore possible inquiry project topics. By the second session, participants are expected to submit a topic or a brief description of what they plan to do. Sessions 2 and 3 include a small-group discussion on the progress of the inquiry projects with opportunities for participants to assist one another. Associates present their inquiry projects at the fourth and final session. In some cases, participants have collaborated with each other or with school faculty. And some university faculty have presented their inquiry projects at local and national meetings. Following is a sampling of inquiry project topics from Cohorts I and II:

- "A Study of Parental Expectations and Perceptions of a Public High School and a Private Middle School," a collaboration between the vice principal of a public high school and a vice principal of a private middle school whose institutions have similar student populations

- "Looking at Recruitment and Admission of Underrepresented Students: Increasing Gender and Ethnic Diversity in Pre-service and In-service Teachers," a collaboration between an academic adviser of student services for the colleges of arts and sciences and a COE faculty member

- "The Nature and Quality of In-service Training for Teachers of Students of Limited English Proficiency in Hawaii"

- "Art Education and the Educating of Teachers at the University of Hawaii," which describes, assesses, and evaluates the University of Hawaii Art Education curricular structure in terms of its mission statement and the understanding of visual culture it engenders

- "Reengineering and Renewal of State Offices in Support of School Renewal," an inquiry into an ongoing project at the state Office of Personnel Services

Evaluation

Our evaluations initially took the form of self-assessments for both the planning group and the participants. We were developing and adapting the program and learning throughout the entire year what worked in our setting. At the end of the first three sessions during that first year, we administered quick-writes. Participants were given about ten to fifteen minutes to reflect on the session and to write briefly on what they felt worked or did not work for them. Sometimes they were asked to connect what had transpired during the two-day session to their own work. The quick-writes and the reflections requested of the participants at the end of each session provided the planning team with immediate feedback. This feedback was analyzed at the first planning meeting following a session, and the information was used to plan for the upcoming session. Thus, these activities served as self-assessment for both the participants and the planners. At the end of session 4 of Cohort I, we held a lengthy, large-group "town meeting" in which participants were asked to reflect on the program and make suggestions for future cohorts. The planning team took copious notes, engaged in their own reflection, and made several revisions based on this feedback.

For Cohort II, the quick-writes and the reflections continued. However, instead of the town meeting at the final session, participants were asked to complete a program evaluation form consisting of five open-ended questions:

1. In what ways has the Hawaii Leadership Associates Program enhanced your own learning and professional growth?
2. How has the Leadership Associates Program supported your understanding and your ability to advance the work of simultaneous renewal in your work site?
3. Please comment on these program activities with regard to their helpfulness to you and let us know how each might be enhanced in value for the next cohort:

   3.1 Readings
   3.2 Conversations/Small-Group Discussions
   3.3 School Visits
   3.4 Inquiry Project
   3.5 Informal Networking
   3.6 Open-Space Discussions

4. What suggestions would you make regarding the structuring of time (for example, number of sessions, length of sessions, daily schedule, sites)?
5. Do you have any additional suggestions for improvement or general comments?

This evaluation provided more focused feedback on the structure and design of the program: how participants felt about it and what they perceived its impact on them to be. Generally they told us that what had contributed to their own learning and professional growth were the readings and the discussions based on them, that the conversations were valuable in helping them to see the bigger picture, that they learned to clarify their own thinking through discussions with others from different levels, that the mix of participants across role groups was a unique and positive learning experience for them, and that they believed that their networking would continue. They also told us that they wanted more time for conversations but that the "open-space" activity, in which individuals could propose a topic for discussion and others had the opportunity to "sign up," had not worked for them. They were critical of some of the readings and identified the readings and activities that were most useful.

The planning team analyzed, reflected on, and used this information in preparing for Cohort III, but still needed to know in what ways, if any, the program had really made a difference. We asked each participant to complete an action plan for the coming year to indicate how he or she would apply the knowledge, ideas, and personal contacts gained in the Hawaii Leadership Associates Program. From the replies of the fourteen of the twenty-one participants who responded, it was clear that these individuals had thought seriously about what they were taking back to their work sites from participating in the program. Several indicated that they would continue to work on or expand their inquiry projects. Some indicated that the program had affirmed their work and their efforts in educational renewal and strengthened their commitment to continue. Of special significance was the fact that none of them made weak, appeasing statements.

Lessons Learned

One of the first lessons we learned from Cohort I of the Hawaii Leadership Associates Program was not to overstructure. We started the first session with a full agenda neatly blocked off into timed segments for conversations, activities, and discussions. We introduced the concept of conversations and provided guiding questions. What we found out was that once the small groups got together and were comfortable with each other, they ignored our guidance (a few individuals even resented it) and carried on valuable conversations on their own. In addition, once the conversations had started, they were difficult to stop. Our carefully designed schedule became restrictive and self-defeating.

Cohort II affirmed our notions of the value of conversation as an adult learning strategy. These professionals had been having discussions on all sorts of mundane and necessary operational aspects of their work for so long that having real opportunities to discuss significant moral and ethical issues deeply was, in one associate's words, "stimulating, exciting, and personally and professionally rewarding."

We learned that it was less important to be didactic—to "teach" or give a lecture to drive a point home—than it was to raise a provocative question and allow professional educators to wrestle with it and reflect on their own learnings. We learned what a powerful tool unstructured conversations around a common topic of interest could be. We learned, or perhaps relearned, that adults learn best by sharing their experiences and insights with one another and then reflecting on those experiences and insights. We also learned how valuable an inquiry project can be for opening up questions of professional practice and policy. Engaging in an inquiry project can begin the change process in a school in ways that are nonthreatening and exciting to observe.

Notes

1. The session, held at Breckenridge, Colorado, introduced graduates of the IEI Leadership Program to their new and expanded role as facilitators of their colleagues' learning. Participants worked with the handbook prepared by Wilma F. Smith and Donna Hughes, *Leadership Program Resource Package* (Seattle: Institute for Educational Inquiry, 1995).

2. See Michael Fullan, *Change Forces: Probing the Depths of Educational Reform* (Bristol, Pa.: Falmer Press, 1993), for an extensive discussion

of the educator's role in bringing about change through combining "moral purpose" with "change agentry."

3. The moral dimensions of teaching in a social and political democracy are described in John I. Goodlad, Roger Soder, and Kenneth A. Sirotnik (eds.) *The Moral Dimensions of Teaching* (San Francisco: Jossey-Bass, 1990).

4. Smith and Hughes, *Leadership Program Resource Package*.

5. See John I. Goodlad, *Educational Renewal: Better Teachers, Better Schools* (San Francisco: Jossey-Bass, 1994), and John I. Goodlad, *In Praise of Education* (New York: Teachers College Press, 1997).

9

The Metropolitan St. Louis Consortium for Educational Renewal

Katharine D. Rasch

Picture twenty adults, each involved in education for a very long time, sitting around a circle listening to preservice teacher education students—a rather unlikely event. Then imagine that one of the young women in this group declares that she has come to understand her community through a series of experiences. She also indicates that a lesson that she had been taught throughout her life—not to trust white people—is simply wrong. In a few moments, the support for this new professional is pouring out of every person in the room. Within this picture are education professionals from seven different parts of the St. Louis educational community. They have committed to a year of work, study, and conversation, not knowing each other when they first began. What commitments brought these educators to work together? How are they stronger in collaboration than any might be individually in his or her own workplace? And why are teacher education students involved? The answers to these questions begin to explain the Metropolitan St. Louis Consortium for Educational Renewal's Leadership Program.

The St. Louis Setting

In a setting where rather atypical partners had come together to make application to the National Network for Educational Renewal (NNER), it is, in fact, the Leadership Program that has moved the vision of our work from that of a few participants at each institution to the broader community. What began as a commitment on the part of the Leadership Associates from Cohort III of the Institute for Educational Inquiry's (IEI) Leadership Program as they returned to St. Louis in August 1995 has become a powerful community-building and professional development vehicle for participants from all parts of the setting. We have extended an intense conversation to dozens of school stakeholders: parents, teachers, central office administrators, and college and university faculty. The inclusion of our advisory council in the November session enabled yet another forty to fifty people to begin to understand the depth and the complexity of the work of simultaneous renewal, as well as the urgency of this work in our community.

The partnership began as a rather awkward alliance. In 1994, Harris-Stowe State College (a historically black institution with roots in training elementary teachers for the St. Louis Public Schools) and Maryville University (a comprehensive, private, suburban university), along with partner schools in the St. Louis Public School District and the suburban St. Louis Parkway School District, decided to submit a joint application to the NNER. Although the partners had worked with each other on projects and experiences in St. Louis, the level of collaboration that would be required for this work was new for all. Preliminary exploration by all partners resulted in commitment to four of John Goodlad's postulates—numbers Ten, Eleven, Thirteen, and Sixteen (see Appendix A)—as initial points for discussion and collaborative work. The application was endorsed by a small group of faculty, and, with its acceptance into the NNER, the Metropolitan St. Louis Consortium for Educational Renewal began a journey that had no charts, no road maps, and no precise sense of the direction in which the work might proceed.

Creation of the Leadership Program

A newly formed board of directors met to plan a course of action and determined that the participating institutions would develop two intensely collaborative activities. These were to be significant endeavors, different from any of the work that the partners were already doing in their own institutions. Further, the activities would not only have to help more people understand the intellectual underpinnings of their work but would also have to create a critical mass of people who could move forward together and individually. The two activities endorsed by the board were a collaborative set of year-long experiences for preservice teachers from the two institutions and—the subject of this chapter—a local leadership program.

The four IEI Associates from the St. Louis setting had already launched a small, pilot leadership program for a local professional development school collaborative. This experience helped to build the Associates' confidence and strengthen their commitment to developing a local replication of the IEI program. Because of their experiences with the national and the pilot programs, the Associates ensured that the design for the larger local program called for the inclusion of all partners and a year-long schedule for the work together.

The call for nominations for the first cohort of twenty in the new leadership program went out in January 1996. Board members from Maryville and Harris-Stowe and their respective partner schools were designated to coordinate the circulation of invitations to participate and to collect the nominations to the cohort. The grounds for selection would be determined by each of the partners, and selection would not be competitive. In some places it was easy to recruit potential members of the first cohort; in others it took a great deal of time and encouragement.

Program Purposes

The purposes of the Metropolitan St. Louis Consortium for Educational Renewal's Leadership Program, described in the call for nominations, are consistent with those outlined in the Leadership Program Resource Package that the IEI Leadership Program's Cohort III Associates received in September 1995 during a training program in Colorado.[1] Local leadership associates would

- Develop a deeper understanding of the moral dimensions of teaching in a democracy

- Collaborate with P–12 educators, education professors, and arts and sciences professors toward the renewal of schools and the preparation of educators

- Become agents of change in their own institutions

- Conduct inquiry into the nature of simultaneous renewal in the Metropolitan St. Louis Consortium for Educational Renewal

- Contribute to the work of simultaneous renewal in the St. Louis setting

Program Participants

Potential participants were required to commit to completing an intense series of readings, meeting for four sessions throughout the year, and carrying out an inquiry project to look willingly and critically at their own work. It is not clear that the members of either of the first two cohorts had any real sense of the nature of the inquiry project when they made their initial commitments. Administrators at each institution had to agree to the participants' attending all of the program sessions. Potential leadership associates were also advised that their participation would entail an ongoing obligation to provide leadership in the setting: to share what they learned with others in their own institutions and throughout the St. Louis Consortium.

Those designing the program explicitly intended that it would prepare faculty in all parts of the setting to begin to work together toward a common understanding of the nature of simultaneous renewal and its challenges and opportunities in the St. Louis area. This required careful selection of the cohort to make it representative of all elements of the partnership. We ensured that central office personnel as well as teachers and administrators from each partner school were to be included. Both the St. Louis Public School District and the St. Louis Parkway School District continued to look at how the partnership would benefit teachers in the partner schools and those throughout the districts.

In addition to one central office administrator and three to four teachers from each partner school, education and arts and sciences faculty from both Maryville and Harris-Stowe were selected to participate in Cohort 1. That pattern continued into Cohort 2, which also included two parents of pupils in the partner schools. This diverse composition ensured that cohort members had support at their home institutions and that they would interact with at least sixteen people with whom they had had little or no interaction before the experience. Differences in cohort members' occupational settings has been one aspect of diversity; another is the racial composition of each cohort. We have struggled more with achieving diversity by gender: there have been more women in the program than men. Participation by arts and sciences faculty has been more difficult to secure than that by other groups. The second cohort was easier to recruit: members of the first cohort helped to spread the word about the experience, and direct invitations proved effective.

Program Sessions

The program required a significant and sustained time commitment on the part of the participants. Each participant pledged to devote four full days in August, two in November, one in May, and another two the following August. The November session included a Saturday. During the year, it was a challenge for the administrators to attend every session because they were called away often. Sessions were held at a conference site in August and alternated between school and college or university sites for the other meetings.

The tone of these sessions followed from the unlikely mix of partners. The St. Louis setting had committed not only to the simultaneous renewal of schools and the preparation of teachers, but to doing so with a shared set of experiences that would bring together the teacher education students of both institutions into a collaborative program designed by Harris-Stowe and Maryville faculty and teachers from the schools. Those who planned the leadership program recognized that it would be crucial to the development of trust and a sense of community for future work.

Throughout each session, there was constant interplay between the issues that we would explore in common and the ways in which the readings and understanding reached would affect each participant in his or her own institution. Sessions were planned so that they would focus not only on the readings about simultaneous renewal and the Agenda for Education in a Democracy, but also sharply on the St. Louis setting.

We began with an environmental scan of the area provided by a leading local political scientist. Issues that required leadership within our own community were highlighted and discussed. For example, the community has been painfully divided by racial polarization in housing and in the schools. A voluntary interdistrict desegregation plan buses many students from the St. Louis Public Schools to schools in the surrounding county. Teacher preparation programs at Harris-Stowe and Maryville prepare teachers for both urban and suburban districts. During that first session, we also boarded a bus together to travel throughout the metropolitan area. For many participants, several of the areas that we visited were unfamiliar—or even a bit unnerving. Exploring the entire region, including the areas around each of the schools, gave the group a common frame of reference and a powerful springboard for dialogue about the tough issues facing this metropolitan area.

Conversation

The program developed leaders through much conversation; experiences were structured to ensure both substantive dialogue and opportunities to interact with each other. Session 1, which lasted four days, began with a conversation based on issues in the metropolitan area. Before the community trip, many questions were raised about what would be seen and what it all meant; a debriefing afterward brought participants closer together in their understanding of common problems and issues. On day 3 of session 1, the leadership of group discussions shifted away from facilitators of the program to cohort members themselves. Readings for the initial session, particularly Deborah Tannen's *You Just Don't Understand* and Dorothy Allison's *Bastard Out of Carolina,* provided opportunities for riveting discussions about the critically difficult issues facing many of the children we teach. (All of the readings are listed later in Exhibit 9.1 of this chapter.) Finally, the first session shifted to teacher education. "Unpacking postulates"—examining the postulates carefully to discern their meanings and implications—became the vehicle through which to discuss each participant's role in teacher education. The first session concluded with associates from the same institution formulating personal and site-specific goals for the year.

In the November session, leadership associates, who were now familiar partners, reassembled for a two-day session focusing on enculturation into a social and political democracy and access to knowledge. The leadership cohort was joined on the first day by preservice teacher education students from Harris-Stowe and Maryville who were meeting for their year of common experience. One of the most powerful examples of the St. Louis Consortium's work came through these preservice students who reflected on their experiences by examining the question: "What does it mean to be a morally responsible teacher in a diverse and democratic society?" They talked resolutely about their insights into the teacher's moral responsibility to ensure equal access to a good education for all students. They spoke of the need for the teacher to relate her or his pedagogy in nurturing ways to the individual needs of the students. They talked passionately about the importance of the school's enculturating young people into the democratic society in which they live. The energy and synergy they communicated about their experiences together sharpened our awareness of changes in teacher education. The rest of the day focused on how those students were learning about their roles in the public schools.

The second morning of the November session combined a conference for the broader community with the work of the leadership cohort. (This activity has not been successful for the leadership group and is being rethought for future cohorts.) Finally, conversations led by participants about access to knowledge returned attention to the specifics of the St. Louis setting. An inquiry project update reminded participants of the focus needed for the rest of the year.

In May 1997, the cohort began to reflect a sense of longevity about the work. Using Michael Fullan's principles of change,[2] the group discussed change as it relates to our setting specifically and to the events of the year. There was individual and collective commitment to change, although many institutional tensions surrounded that change. Greater understanding of the work of simultaneous renewal was producing arduous and painstaking changes in direction within each of the institutions and subunits of those institutions that were represented in the cohort. Every participant continued to grapple with the question of how to make substantive changes happen in our consortium.

Cohorts 1 and 2 came together for joint meetings in August 1997. The second cohort had the opportunity to benefit from the work of the first. Shared conversation about Jonathan Kozol's *Amazing Grace* set the stage for ongoing work regarding access to knowledge within our consortium. And members of Cohort 1 presented their inquiry projects to this combined audience, prompting the participants in the second cohort to begin to examine potential topics for their own inquiry. The program was structured so that each participant chose a project of interest from topics addressed in the four sessions. The variety within the sessions provided many opportunities for choice and for all to share the work of colleagues. There was high interest in the presentations of those faculty from the arts and sciences and a deeper appreciation of their changing perspectives on the consortium's work.

Readings

The program coordinators chose a combination of texts used by the IEI and some that were more locally focused (see Exhibit 9.1). They intend to vary at least some of the readings each year to infuse new publications and different conversations into each institution within the consortium. Modifications to the second year's reading list reflected new resources available and suggestions from the group.

Inquiry Projects

The most difficult part of the leadership program for members of the first cohort was completing the inquiry projects. Only two or three members had had experience with action research, and it took quite a while for the group to formulate areas of inquiry. The program required that the projects be focused on some aspect of simultaneous renewal and the work of the Metropolitan St. Louis Consortium, but the connection could be quite loose. We were more directive with the second cohort regarding this connection and, of course, the second cohort benefited from seeing and hearing the projects of Cohort 1.

Lessons Learned

Participants evaluated every session before they left. These evaluations allowed program facilitators to gauge with a good degree of accuracy the success of specific sessions and readings. All participants reported that the cross-site conversations and the time shared among participants had been extremely valuable. In some cases, participants reported that they had taken on work at home that directly related to the Agenda. In other cases, there was seemingly no change in practice or new linkages to the Agenda. Communication

Exhibit 9.1. Readings for the St. Louis Consortium Leadership Program

Allison, Dorothy. *Bastard Out of Carolina*. New York: Penguin, 1992. Cohort 1.

Auspitz, Josiah Lee. "Michael Oakeshott: 1901–1990." *American Scholar* 60 (Summer 1991): 351–370.

Berliner, David C., and Bruce J. Biddle. *The Manufactured Crisis: Myths, Fraud, and the Attack on America's Public Schools*. Reading, Mass.: Addison-Wesley, 1995.

Clark, Richard W., Donna M. Hughes, and Representatives from the National Network for Educational Renewal. "Partner Schools: Definitions and Expectations." Seattle: Center for Educational Renewal, University of Washington, 1995 (orig. 1993).

Focus St. Louis. *Currents*. A publication about the Metropolitan St. Louis area.

Fullan, Michael. *Change Forces: Probing the Depths of Educational Reform*. Bristol, Pa.: Falmer Press, 1993.

Goodlad, John I. *Teachers for Our Nation's Schools*. San Francisco: Jossey-Bass, 1990.

Goodlad, John I. "Beyond Half an Education." *Education Week*, February 19, 1992, pp. 34, 44.

Goodlad, John I. *Educational Renewal: Better Teachers, Better Schools*. San Francisco: Jossey-Bass, 1994.

Goodlad, John I., and Pamela Keating (eds.). *Access to Knowledge: The Continuing Agenda for Our Nation's Schools*. Rev. ed. New York: College Entrance Examination Board, 1994 (orig. 1990).

Kozol, Jonathan. *Amazing Grace: The Lives of Children and the Conscience of a Nation*. New York: Crown, 1995. Read and discussed jointly by both cohorts.

Osguthorpe, Russell T., R. Carl Harris, Melanie Fox Harris, and Sharon Black (eds.). *Partner Schools: Centers for Educational Renewal*. San Francisco: Jossey-Bass, 1995. Cohort 1.

Tannen, Deborah. *You Just Don't Understand: Women and Men in Conversation*. New York: Ballantine, 1991. Cohort 1.

Wasley, Patricia. *Stirring the Chalkdust*. New York: Teachers College Press, 1994.

Wasley, Patricia, Robert Hampel, and Richard W. Clark. *Kids and School Reform*. San Francisco: Jossey-Bass, 1997. Cohort 2.

patterns among the institutions in the consortium have not changed drastically, except for students in the preservice cohort.

We have learned a number of important lessons through creating and implementing the leadership program in the St. Louis Consortium. We have reconfigured and modified the program, for example, to include cohorts from each institution who will focus on a specific aspect of the work. The most notable lessons that we learned seem to fall into five main categories. To be successful, a local leadership program such as ours must provide participants time to reflect on practice, foster collaboration and connections, help participants to change perceptions and build new understandings, select and mentor participants carefully, and have a dedicated group of facilitators to lead the leaders.

Time to Reflect on Practice

Time for thought produces marvelous results. As has been documented in many other teacher development processes, having sustained time to reflect, discuss, and focus on practice permits fuller consideration of difficult dilemmas and produces better results. The shared conversation also creates a common focus, vocabulary, and commitment to the work of simultaneous renewal. Participants made reading and study a top priority, and each person took seriously the obligation to come to sessions ready to discuss the assigned readings. Interestingly, some people questioned whether this diverse group would commit to extensive reading. Dog-eared pages and highlighted passages were evidence that this fear was unfounded. And evaluations indicated that some participants were frustrated that there was not more time scheduled to discuss the readings.

Getting released time for teachers after the program ends is difficult. We had built in resources for cross-site visits during the program, but it remains difficult to free teachers (and, for that matter, many of the college faculty) from day-to-day responsibilities to make those visits. The reconfiguration of time and scheduling continues to be a vexing problem in our partnerships.

Collaboration and Connections

Genuine renewal of schools and teacher education programs begins to occur when all three groups of participants are together. Teacher education is the responsibility of arts and sciences faculty and school personnel, as well as education faculty. Although it took some careful cultivation to recruit arts and sciences participants, their contributions were valued by all, and they came to recognize much more clearly the role that they play in teacher education. We were fortunate to have arts and sciences participants who came with open minds and were willing to listen as well as contribute.

Linkages between the leadership program and the preservice cohort were important. The teacher education part of simultaneous renewal became a much bigger part of the conversation after the preservice students came to the leadership meeting and reported on the work that they had done together. As each preservice cohort becomes a student teaching cohort, we expect that group to engage in more conversation with teachers in the partner schools about the knowledge and skills they have gained through their joint experiences in the preservice cohort.

Changing Perceptions and Building New Understandings

Certain concepts of simultaneous renewal seem difficult to achieve in the light of prior experiences. For example, not everyone embraced the idea of a partner school's emphasizing the professional development of practicing teachers. Some participants did not see the role of the partner school as anything more than a host site for student teachers. Comprehensive school improvement plans varied in the ways that linkages were made with the university and the teacher education program. Linkages between arts and sciences faculty and the schools were easier to conceptualize at the secondary level than at the elementary level.

Inquiry project results have been mixed. We aspire to have inquiry sustained in the program but are not aware that any participant has continued the inquiry after the program ended. One of our partner schools has developed an excellent model for teachers and student teachers to conduct action research jointly, and perhaps that model will be embraced throughout the setting. Changing the way a setting does its work takes time, but we hope that sustained inquiry into simultaneous renewal will gradually become a part of the culture of our setting.

Participants

The selection and mentoring of participants requires careful attention. An invitation to participate was not sufficient. It took conversations, careful persuasion, and deliberate cultivation to ensure that individuals would consider participating in the leadership program. Institutions that were further along in their own understanding and commitment to the consortium had an easier time lining up participants, especially the first year. The second year was easier in some cases, because satisfied participants from the first cohort helped to sell the program to their colleagues. Even after the publication of session dates and a signed letter of commitment, attendance was a problem for some participants, particularly those with administrative responsibilities. When meetings were held on-site, participants from that site tended to get pulled away on other business. The initial sessions also had to be carefully planned around summer school, leaving little time for those participants to take vacations. We had to coordinate four academic calendars, all with different schedules. One spring session had to be rescheduled, and attendance at that session dropped.

Many do not see themselves as leaders when they come into the program. We have not yet systematically studied what the nature of each participant's leadership is perceived to be as he or she leaves the program. As they enter, however, although many associates express an interest in learning and a willingness to consider their own roles or classrooms, they often confess that they do not consider themselves to be leaders in their home institutions. We are not clear about the extent to which the program helps them to redefine their own roles, responsibilities, and commitments related to simultaneous renewal. The most dramatic change has been for those who coordinate and implement the joint preservice teacher cohort. Those faculty have used readings, replicated leadership program experiences, and created a unique program with significant outreach into the St. Louis community. Other participants have returned to their own work sites and contributed to discussions differently, but only a few have been directly involved in initiating new structures or conversations. We need to determine how to get more sustained engagement and initiative from those who graduate from our leadership program.

Leaders of Leaders

Sustaining a leadership program takes tremendous commitment and leadership. During the first year, two colleagues helped our two IEI Associates with planning and facilitating the sessions. After the first year, we also had a coordinator to help with communication and logistics. However, the time and energy required to sustain the program were significant, especially since the leadership of the program was taken on in addition to regularly assigned teaching and administrative responsibilities. The consortium is now seeking local leadership participants who will assume responsibility for sustaining the program. This next iteration of the program will require long-term cultivation and support. The Associates' training in the IEI Leadership Program provided a strong model and continued support for our local program's successes. Not only were we able to import some readings and ideas into our own program, but the Leadership Program Resource Package,[3] put together by Wilma Smith and Donna Hughes, guided us and helped focus the group's time and energies. The visit to our site by both of these senior associates also brought national visibility and credibility to what our leadership program was trying to accomplish.

Hard work has produced some positive, affirming results for our set-ting. This has been perhaps our most gratifying lesson learned—but also our most challenging. Knowledge of the Agenda for Education in a Democracy has reached many more people in each partner insti-tution and has created a group committed to it. But much hard work remains. Together we continue to focus on figuring out how to get that work done. Our commitment to children will allow no less.

Notes

1. Wilma F. Smith and Donna Hughes, *Leadership Program Resource Package* (Seattle: Institute for Educational Inquiry, 1995).

2. Michael Fullan, *Change Forces: Probing the Depths of Educational Reform* (Bristol, Pa.: Falmer Press, 1993).

3. Smith and Hughes, *Leadership Program Resource Package*.

10

The Nebraska Network for Educational Renewal

Marilyn B. Hadley, Jeanne Surface

The Nebraska Network for Educational Renewal (NeNER) consists of nine institutions of higher education together with their sixteen partner school districts and twenty-one partner schools, as well as the Nebraska Department of Education (NDE). In January 1996, the NeNER became the sixteenth setting to be accepted into the National Network for Educational Renewal (NNER).

The NeNER is the result of a long tradition of collaboration among schools and institutions of higher education in the state. The Nebraska Council on Teacher Education, formed in 1947, is one example of such collaborative relationships. It brings together equal numbers of teacher education leaders, teachers, administrators, and school board representatives to make recommendations about teacher education programs and certification through the NDE to the state board of education.

The Nebraska Consortium for the Improvement of Teacher Education through Research, another example of statewide collaboration, included in its membership all of the teacher education institutions in Nebraska. Formed in 1981 by Robert Egbert, then dean of Teachers College at the University of Nebraska at Lincoln, the Nebraska Consortium sponsored an annual conference to promote the sharing of research and practice among state teacher educators for sixteen years until 1997, when the NeNER assumed this responsibility.

This tradition of collaboration, combined with strong support for schools and teacher education, has resulted in a high degree of what James S. Coleman refers to as "social capital."[1] Local control of decisions by school boards is very important to Nebraskans, and consolidation of school districts has happened only slowly in the state. Recent tax reform, however, has resulted in increased con-solidation and a decline in the number of school districts—from 905 in 1996 to 890 in 1997—and the trend is expected to continue. Nebraska is one of only three states that has not developed cur-riculum standards; however, the state board of education has re-cently endorsed voluntary standards in selected areas.

The nine NeNER institutions of higher education vary in size, mission, and partnership arrangements. The smallest site prepares approximately 14 new teachers a year and has one partner school, and the largest site prepares 442 teachers a year and has five part-ner schools plus numerous other collaborative school arrangements. The NeNER institutions represent all categories in the Carnegie Foundation for the Advancement of Teaching's classification sys-tem.[2] Partner schools and school districts are found in both rural and urban communities ranging in population from 1,000 to more than 350,000. Five institutions of higher education have formal relationships with one or more school districts, three have rela-tionships with one or more partner schools, and one has formal re-lationships with a school district and selected partner schools within that district. Within the NDE, personnel from three divisions are working together as partners on issues connected to the simultane-ous renewal of schools and the education of educators.

The 1997 NeNER Leadership Institute

The NeNER began its first Leadership Institute in April 1997. The institute's purpose was to create a critical mass of informed and com-mitted leaders from teacher education, the arts and sciences, and the P–12 schools to guide the simultaneous renewal of schooling and the education of educators at each site and for the Nebraska Network as a consortium. A DeWitt Wallace–Reader's Digest Fund Incentive Award in Teacher Education was used to employ two senior associates of the Institute for Educational Inquiry (IEI) as facilitators and to pay the expenses of forty-one participants. Because the NeNER had only recently joined the National Network for Educational Renewal, we wanted to launch two cohorts of about twenty associates simultaneously to build quickly the critical mass mentioned in the institute's purpose. Fortunately, both the executive director of the NeNER and a principal of a K–12 partner school were then completing their year-long experience as members of Cohort V of the IEI's Leadership Program conducted in Seattle. They were able to assist with the design, organization, and facilitation of the NeNER Institute.

Participants

Selection of the participants was made at the site level, based on the individual's past participation in renewal efforts or potential leadership capacity, or both. The number of associates who could be selected varied with the size of the site: the smallest sites were allocated three participants, and the largest was allocated nine. Because some of the smaller sites did not identify three participants, the actual representation varied from one to ten. Table 10.1 lists the numbers of participants in each institutional role.

Table 10.1. NeNER Institute Participants by Role

	Teacher Education	Arts and Sciences	P–12 Schools	Nebraska Department of Education
Faculty	16	7	6	0
Administrators	5	0	5	2
Total	21	7	11	2

The forty-one NeNER leadership associates met in two cohorts for eight days spread across three separate sessions from April to September 1997. The two cohorts met at the same location during the same time, which afforded the associates opportunities to work in cross-cohort small groups as well as in one large group.

The associates varied as to their knowledge about the Agenda for Education in a Democracy, their participation in the NeNER, and their involvement in site renewal efforts. Five associates served on the NeNER board of directors, and nine were actively involved in partner school efforts. A number of the associates, however, had had very little involvement with NeNER activities and came with a limited understanding of the Agenda.

Program

One goal of the NeNER Institute was to develop leaders at each site who would come to understand more deeply the mission of simultaneously renewing schools and the education of educators. This goal was addressed through a focus on the moral dimensions of the four-part mission of teacher education in a democracy: (1) enculturating students into a social and political democracy, (2) providing all students access to knowledge, (3) connecting with students through a nurturing pedagogy, and (4) serving as stewards of schools. A second goal of the institute was to strengthen the school-university partnerships that the NeNER sites had focused on building during the previous two years. The four parts of the morally grounded mission of teacher education and the development of partner schools thus became the five themes of the program of the NeNER Institute.

Enculturating Students into a Social and Political Democracy

As a prelude to discussing the meaning of this theme, participants read and discussed the article "Dialogical Pedagogy in Teacher Education: Toward an Education for Democracy" by Juan-Miguel Fernández-Balboa and James P. Marshall.[3] This essay advocates using dialogue and conversation in the classroom not only for pedagogical purposes but also to advance civil discourse and democratic society. As they explored this concept, associates became acquainted with each other through conversations in which they built their ideas on others' thoughts and thereby extended the thinking of everyone.

Moving further into the theme of enculturating the young into a democracy, associates asked themselves and each other such questions as: What moral dimensions are basic to teaching in a democratic society? What decisions have you made about classroom practices or leadership that have presented moral dilemmas for you? Why did these situations make you feel uncomfortable? How did you resolve them? Wrestling with these questions prompted associates to contemplate teachers' moral responsibility for enculturating their students into our social and political democracy. They grappled with the meaning of the word *moral* and pursued the implications for teachers' relationships with students. Readings from *The Moral Dimensions of Teaching* served as stimuli for deep reflection and intense conversation.[4]

Access to Knowledge for All Students

How do we as educators ensure that all students have equal opportunities to learn, regardless of gender, learning style, race, or socioeconomic status? Lively discussions resulted from the associates' reading of John Goodlad and Pamela Keating's edited work, *Access to Knowledge*,[5] and the associates returned to their sites determined to examine their own practices to ensure that their students did indeed have equal access to a sound education.

Nurturing Pedagogy

How do educators connect with students in a way that supports the individual learner and creates high expectations for all? Vivian Paley's *White Teacher*,[6] the account of one teacher's journey to understanding of how to work with children from different ethnic backgrounds, provoked stimulating and soul-searching discussions. Participants explored the value of recognizing and honoring differences rather than trying to ignore them. They also related the messages of Paley's work to the themes of access to knowledge and enculturating students into a democracy, taking the perspectives of a P–12 teacher and a teacher educator. How do we ensure that our students in teacher education programs can demonstrate such a nurturing pedagogy and that they can work with their colleagues to help schools provide access to knowledge equitably for all students? they asked. Pushing these themes and questions even further, the participants spent a morning discussing, categorizing, and synthesizing six of John Goodlad's postulates that relate specifically to a nurturing pedagogy: numbers Five, Six, Nine, Ten, Twelve, and Thirteen (see Appendix A).

Stewardship of Schools

Paul Theobald, author of *Teaching the Commons,* spoke to the cohorts about what it means to be a steward of the school, and he expanded the implications of stewardship for our work of simultaneous renewal.[7] Following a discussion of Theobald's ideas, small groups developed scenarios to illustrate what it means to serve as a steward of the school. These scenarios were entitled "A day in the life of a teacher (or administrator or teacher educator . . .) who is a steward of the school."

Partner Schools

Since very few of the ten NeNER sites had well-established partner (or professional development) schools, we used videotapes of several partner schools from across the country at different grade levels and different stages of development. We showed the videotapes to all of the participants and followed with a discussion in which we asked them to contrast and compare what they saw in the videotaped partner schools with the four purposes of NNER partners' schools: to educate children and youths, prepare educators, provide professional development, and conduct inquiry (see Appendix B). Following this activity, the site teams prepared descriptions of theoretical partner schools at three stages of maturity: beginning, developing, and exemplary. Each team shared information about the creation and current status of partner schools at its site. These activities helped participants gain a broader understanding of the possibilities of strengthening both school renewal and teacher education in the partner school setting through collaboration of the partner school faculty, education faculty, and arts and sciences faculty.

Advancing the Agenda for Education in a Democracy

Each leadership associate is expected to take on the role of change agent at his or her site to help advance the work of simultaneous renewal in Nebraska. Three specific activities in the IEI Leadership Program focused attention on this role: a persuasion speech, an action plan to develop and strengthen partner schools, and a site team inquiry project. The persuasion activity was designed to help participants sharpen their skills in engaging their colleagues back home in the work of simultaneous renewal. Each associate selected an issue related to this Agenda and prepared a speech intended either to secure his or her colleagues' participation in renewal efforts or to build understanding and support from a supervisor or official. We organized the associates in cross-cohort groups of three or four members so that they could role-play the speech, with the other members giving them critical (and friendly) feedback to help them improve, strengthen, or extend their persuasive arguments. The assignment for the persuasive speech was given to the associates at the second session so they could prepare for giving it during the third session. The IEI Associates demonstrated such a speech and asked the combined cohort group to critique it. During the feedback session, one of the NeNER associates, a professor of speech, greatly contributed to the value of the activity by suggesting a format for giving helpful feedback to the speaker. During this second session, many associates began to take on leadership roles within their cohorts and to make the simultaneous renewal work their own.

At the conclusion of the third institute session, site teams were asked to develop specific action plans to extend their work with partner schools during the coming academic year. The teams became very specific with these plans, describing purposes, missions, or visions for their partner schools; designing organizational charts or time-task-responsibility charts; and making plans to involve others in the work. A few examples of the tasks that were outlined illustrate the site teams' commitment to the work as well as the individual nature of each of the sites with regard to its partner schools: establishing a steering committee for the school-university partnership; submitting grant proposals to secure funding for renewal efforts; meeting for conversations about renewal; creating web sites and on-line discussions; providing professional development workshops for P–12 teachers, arts and sciences faculty members, and teacher educators; modeling the democratic arts of listening, deliberating, compromising, arguing, and persuading (that is, civil discourse); presenting ideas at school and department meetings; conducting campuswide discussions of *White Teacher*; establishing study groups; holding book talks; and conducting a miniconference.

The third activity intended to build each leadership associate's capacity to serve as a change agent was the completion of an inquiry project to be conducted individually or as a team. We provided structured time and guidance during each session for the site teams to work together in identifying and developing inquiry topics, and by the end of the third session the participants had settled on an array of projects to be carried out over the next academic year. Associates at eight sites chose to assess the development of four new college- or university-school partnerships and the strengthening of five existing partnerships. Five projects were related to teacher education programs, ranging from reviews of the literature about partnerships or a specific curriculum area, to the development of a new course, to assessing faculty and student attitudes about their moral responsibilities as teachers. Two inquiry projects focused on factors affecting change in schools: one collected feedback from all first-year teachers in the state, and the other investigated implications of Nebraska's state educational policies for the NeNER. The results of these inquiry projects were reported at the spring 1998 institute and disseminated to all NeNER sites.

The 1997 associates volunteered to assist in identifying participants for the 1998 institute and to provide an orientation for those who were nominated by their respective sites. A number of them also offered to assist with planning upcoming institutes, and some volunteered to facilitate portions of the sessions.

As a result of the Leadership Institute, members of two cohorts of associates from eleven geographically separate sites now know one another, share a common language about the Agenda for Education in a Democracy, and have a common, vested interest in the renewal of schools and the preparation of educators.

Several steps are being taken to provide ongoing support for leadership associates who have completed the program. For example, a Level II Leadership Institute was added to provide opportunities for discussions of one or more publications, as well as interaction with a resource person from the NNER. A computer listserv has been established to facilitate the sharing of ideas and continuing conversations among the associates until a NeNER web site can be created. To facilitate communication among associates and leaders at each site, the executive director sent a report about the institute to the NeNER board members. In addition, the executive director will make at least one visit to each site during the year following the institute, at which time she will meet with associates and site leaders to discuss progress with and challenges to their work. The NeNER state office is assembling a lending library of print and nonprint materials that can be loaned to associates to support their work in partnerships, on inquiry projects, and with recruiting participants for future institutes. Finally, a manual for conducting a Leadership Institute and a videotape of NNER settings will be sent to each site team.

What Did We Learn?

One of the major lessons we learned was how difficult it is to select dates for the institute that fit the schedules of P–12 school people, arts and sciences faculty, and teacher educators. We had an especially difficult time during the June session because it was scheduled at the end of the year for several school districts. As a result, attendance was not regular for some of the participants, and their colleagues felt the impact of their absence. To alleviate this problem for future cohorts, session dates will be announced to the associates earlier, and facilitators will try to avoid scheduling sessions at times that make it difficult for some members to attend.

We learned as well that not all associates had had enough time to read the materials, in some cases because insufficient time was allowed between the sessions, in others because books or articles were not sent out early enough. As a result, future Leadership Institutes will allow at least three months between sessions to provide adequate time for reading the assigned literature, and materials will be made available earlier. Associates will also be reminded that the discussions will focus specifically on the reading material; this advance notice should be an incentive to read all of the assignments on time.

Having two senior associates from the IEI lead the first NeNER Institute was an excellent decision; their guidance provided a model for NeNER leaders to build on in the future. Nebraska graduates of the IEI Leadership Program, together with several NeNER leadership associates, will facilitate future sessions with assistance from NNER resource persons on specific topics.

In order to provide a residential experience for everyone and encourage social interaction outside the structured schedule, upcoming institutes will be held in cities where no partner school or NeNER college or university is located. The institute will be shortened from eight days to six days, but the same themes will be addressed by including evening meetings.

During the first session of the 1997 institute, the associates were excited about the opportunity for intellectual challenges, frustrated that there never seemed to be enough time for conversations, and determined to get closure on issues and questions raised. By the end of the second session, associates saw more connections among the agenda topics and developed a sense of ownership of both the institute and the Agenda for Education in a Democracy. For example, after viewing Part I of a videotape entitled *The Public Purpose of Education and Schooling*, several associates asked to see Part II.[8] They watched it on their own time and returned the next day recommending that Part II be added to the Leadership Institute's agenda—which was done. By the third session, true cooperation and collaboration permeated the program, and distinctions among P–12, arts and sciences, and education faculty were not apparent. At the conclusion of the final session, associates demonstrated their understanding of simultaneous renewal through discussions about the moral dimensions of teaching and through developing specific action plans to advance the simultaneous renewal work at their own sites.

Impact of the Leadership Institute on NeNER Sites

Three months after the conclusion of the Leadership Institute, facilitators conducted telephone interviews with heads of teacher education at NeNER sites. Several patterns appeared in their observations about how the leadership associates had strengthened and helped the local sites.

First, members of site teams initiated new relationships or strengthened existing relationships with colleagues at other institutions, in other disciplines, or in other professional positions. This was particularly true of relationships between teacher educators and P–12 school educators and between teacher educators and arts and sciences educators. For teams that chose to conduct a collaborative inquiry project, such relationships were particularly strengthened.

Second, the inquiry projects themselves benefited the sites. The projects provided focus for site teams and for individuals who were making needed changes at the local level. Developing a product through applied research energized not only the associates but also others at the sites.

Third, almost all site representatives indicated that associates had gained a better understanding of the Agenda for Education in a Democracy and had reached out to their colleagues in discussing aspects of that Agenda. Such sharing of knowledge typically occurs within the associates' workplaces, so that P–12 associates usually share their knowledge with other educators at their schools, while teacher educators generally share with other teacher educators. One Nebraska Department of Education associate is conveying knowledge of the Agenda to members of the state board of education, as well as to the leaders of the NDE.

Finally, many associates have increased their teacher education and school renewal efforts at their sites. Associates from the arts and sciences have become involved in such formal ways as advising and serving on teacher education committees. Teacher educators have begun program renewal efforts at three sites, with these efforts ranging from reconsidering field experiences to planning a review of the entire teacher preparation program. A school associate has asked for and received approval to participate in a professional development opportunity that allows teachers at her school to pursue graduate study at a reduced tuition rate. Another school associate is using a grant to investigate links between multiple intelligences and the four moral dimensions of the four-part teaching mission.

Conclusion

The NeNER Leadership Institute was a powerful experience that generated excitement among participants and a greater understanding of the Agenda for Education in a Democracy, which the associates carried back to their sites. The institute provided an opportunity for intellectual conversations often not possible during the regular work schedule. Because they met for at least two days at a time, associates were able to wrestle with several issues in some depth. A network of educators from different levels of schooling has been founded that should help strengthen cooperation among sites and create a unified leadership across the NeNER. Some higher education associates indicated that they felt closer to Leadership Institute colleagues from other institutions than to many in their own departments.

We believe that we achieved our major purpose: to create a critical mass of informed and committed leaders from teacher education, the arts and sciences, and the P–12 schools to guide the simultaneous renewal of schooling and the education of educators at each site and for the Nebraska Network as a consortium. Further, we met (and sometimes exceeded) our two goals: to develop leaders at each site who would come to understand more fully the mission of "simultaneous renewal of schools and the education of educators" and to develop and strengthen the school-university partnerships initiated during the two years prior to the creation of the Leadership Institute.

Notes

1. See, for example, James S. Coleman, *Foundations of Social Theory* (Cambridge, Mass.: Belknap Press of Harvard University Press, 1990), p. 304.

2. Carnegie Foundation for the Advancement of Teaching, *A Classification of Institutions of Higher Education* (Princeton, N.J.: Carnegie Foundation for the Advancement of Teaching, 1987).

3. Juan-Miguel Fernández-Balboa and James P. Marshall, "Dialogical Pedagogy in Teacher Education: Toward an Education for Democracy," *Journal of Teacher Education* 45 (May–June 1994): 172–182.

4. John I. Goodlad, Roger Soder, and Kenneth A. Sirotnik (eds.), *The Moral Dimensions of Teaching* (San Francisco: Jossey-Bass, 1990).

5. John I. Goodlad and Pamela Keating (eds.), *Access to Knowledge: The Continuing Agenda for Our Nation's Schools*, rev. ed. (New York: College Entrance Examination Board, 1994).

6. Vivian Gussin Paley, *White Teacher* (Cambridge, Mass.: Harvard University Press, 1989).

7. Paul Theobald, *Teaching the Commons: Place, Pride, and the Renewal of Community* (Boulder, Colo.: Westview Press, 1997).

8. *The Public Purpose of Education and Schooling: A Symposium*, Seattle: Institute for Educational Inquiry, 1996, videotape. The videotape features a panel discussion from a November 1995 conference of representatives and friends of the NNER. John Goodlad served as the moderator; the other panelists were Benjamin R. Barber, Linda Darling-Hammond, Gary D Fenstermacher, Donna H. Kerr, Theodore R. Sizer, and Roger Soder. Part I of the videotape features the panelists' conversation, and Part II highlights panel members' responses to an array of questions from the audience on the public purpose of education and schooling.

11

Montclair State University and the New Jersey Network for Educational Renewal

Tina Jacobowitz, Nicholas M. Michelli

A shared vision is not an idea. It is not even an important idea such as freedom. It is rather a force in people's hearts, a force of impressive power. It might be inspired by an idea, but once it goes further—if it is compelling enough to acquire the support of more than one person—then it is no longer an abstraction. People begin to see it as if it exists. Few, if any, forces in human affairs are as powerful as a shared vision.[1]

Peter Senge

The Leadership Associates Program at Montclair State University (MSU) is more than a professional development program. It is a carefully designed strategy to promote the development of a shared vision of America's schools and the education of educators. Our shared vision, which focuses on the primary purpose of public schools, is consonant with Dewey's notion of democracy and democratic education. More than a form of government, democracy was to Dewey a way of building up the common good and the community. Seeing the school as a "little community," he wrote, "When the school introduces and trains each child of society into membership within such a little community, saturating him with the spirit of service, and providing him with the instruments of effective self-direction, we shall have the deepest and best guarantee of a larger society which is worthy, lovely, and harmonious."[2]

We agree also with James W. Fraser's view that schools must prepare citizens for a democratic society and that meaningful school reform must begin with a commitment to building an American democracy in which the contribution of all citizens is developed and valued; where racism, sexism, and other forms of divisiveness are challenged and ultimately eliminated; where the society is structured for the benefit of all citizens and not a small elite.[3]

This shared vision has been evolving over many years, beginning with our focus on critical thinking and continuing through our involvement in the National Network for Educational Renewal (NNER). It is reflected in our "Portrait of a Teacher"—a set of ideals developed by faculty and administrators from the university and public schools as well as MSU graduate and undergraduate students (see Exhibit 11.1). Our shared vision is also reflected in the purpose and goals established for our Leadership Associates Program (see Exhibit 11.2).

A shared vision such as ours cannot be given by one individual to another, or by a group of individuals to another group, any more than a teacher can "give" knowledge to a student. There is no doubt that a shared vision can be extremely powerful when it evolves through a reflective process that involves the critical players.

Senge's assertion that a shared vision becomes a reality when it is held by more than one person is an overstatement. We know that for change to happen, many individuals in many settings must share the vision. The task of developing a critical mass of individuals who share the vision was therefore the major goal of our Leadership Associates Program.

Beginning in 1992, the Institute for Educational Inquiry (IEI) invited the NNER settings to nominate school, college, and university faculty to serve as Leadership Associates. These individuals spent four weeks over the course of the year studying in Seattle with

Exhibit 11.1. Montclair State University Portrait of a Teacher

The Montclair State University community is committed to the continuing development of teachers who exemplify the character, dispositions, and habits of mind reflected in this portrait. They

- Continue to inquire into the nature of teaching and learning and reflect upon their own learning and professional practice.

- Believe in the educability of all children and seek to ensure equal learning opportunities for every student.

- Possess the literacy, critical thinking, and technology abilities associated with the concept of an educated person and are committed to lifelong learning. They speak and write English fluently and communicate clearly.

- Have content knowledge which includes a strong sense of the concepts, purposes, and intellectual processes associated with the discipline they will teach.

- Understand the effects of human development on the learning of children, adolescents, and adults and are committed to providing a nurturing and caring environment for all students.

- Possess the skills and dispositions necessary to establish a classroom environment that stimulates critical thinking and inquiry.

- Understand principles of democracy and plan instruction to promote critical reflection on the ideals, values, and practices of democratic citizenship.

- Understand and are committed to the moral, ethical, and enculturating responsibilities of those who work in the school.

- Model respect for individual differences and an appreciation of the basic worth of each individual. They plan instruction and assessment with sensitivity to issues of class, gender, race, ethnicity, sexual orientation, and special needs, and work to foster an appreciation of diversity among students and co-workers.

- Are committed to their role as stewards of renewal and best practice in the schools, and they possess the interpersonal skills and dispositions to work cooperatively and collaboratively with colleagues.

- Are willing to explore a career in a variety of settings—urban, suburban, and rural.

Exhibit 11.2. Montclair State University/New Jersey Network for Educational Renewal 1997 Leadership Associates Program

Purpose: To create a cohort of leaders who will move us into the next level of our efforts toward the simultaneous renewal of the schools and the preparation of educators

Goals: During the course of the year, Leadership Associates are expected to

- Develop a deeper understanding of the moral dimensions of teaching in a democracy
- Collaborate with K–12, education and arts/science faculty and administrators toward the renewal of schools and the preparation of educators
- Become agents of change in their institutions
- Conduct inquiry into the nature of simultaneous renewal in the MSU Teacher Education Program and/or the New Jersey Network for Educational Renewal
- Contribute to the agenda of simultaneous renewal by serving as presenters, advisors, facilitators, and friendly critics to the New Jersey Network for Educational Renewal and the MSU Teacher Education Program

John Goodlad and his associates. Together, they engaged in reading and discussing texts and issues relevant to the Agenda for Education in a Democracy. From the inception of the Institute's Leadership Program, our setting has had at least one participant each year from either education, the arts and sciences, or the schools.

This core of leaders has developed a local Leadership Associates Program at Montclair State, using personal experience as well as the *Resource Package* provided by the IEI as guides.[4] Through this program, twenty faculty members each year, balanced between the schools and the university and between education and arts and sciences, complete a two-week program of reading, discussion, and study. The session takes place in the summer, with attendance at all meetings a requirement. The cohort then meets several times during the year and reconvenes each summer to discuss progress toward simultaneous renewal and to delve further into the Agenda. Each associate is required to undertake an inquiry project designed to advance the work of renewing the schools and the education of educators. The focus of the program is on refining, clarifying, and implementing the shared vision.

To date, fifty-nine participants have completed the program and constitute the leadership core. Our goal is to develop a group of committed faculty who understand and share our vision and are willing to act on it. These individuals, many of them recruited because they are opinion leaders in their own areas, have a responsibility to involve others they work with in the renewal efforts.

Setting

Montclair State University, with a student body of sixty-five hundred full-time undergraduates, thirty-five hundred part-time undergraduates, and some thirty-five hundred graduate students, is located fifteen miles west of Manhattan in northern New Jersey. It is part of the state college/university system. Its Center of Pedagogy opened in November 1995 after four years of planning. In the rationale and description published at MSU, the center is defined as "a place where the education of educators is conceptualized, planned for and carried out. Its members include all those committed to, and whose participation is necessary for, that endeavor. Its goal is the facilitation of the ongoing simultaneous renewal of the education of educators, the educational program of the University, and the educational program of the schools in the interest of student learning."[5]

The center includes members from education, the arts and sciences, and the schools, which we refer to as the "tripartite." Physically, the center is housed in the education building, but conceptually, it is an umbrella-like structure that goes beyond the university, embracing the tripartite. Associates automatically become members of the center when they complete the summer program.

The New Jersey Network for Educational Renewal (NJNER) promotes the simultaneous renewal of schools and the education of educators through a collaboration between the university and member school districts as equal partners. To date, eighteen urban and sub-urban districts are members of the NJNER, and four hundred public school educators serve as clinical faculty. The Montclair Leadership Associates Program is one element of an extensive array of profes-sional development opportunities for clinical faculty offered by the NJNER.

The Leadership Associates Program

Issues in the Recruitment and Selection of Associates

Criteria for selection of associates, like those of the IEI's Leadership Program, focus on stewardship and relate directly to the program's overriding purpose and specific goals (see Exhibit 11.2). In late fall, information about the program, including the selection criteria, is sent to all faculty in education and to faculty in the arts and sci-ences who have been involved in teacher education in some capac-ity. ("Faculty" applies to teachers and administrators at both the university and school levels.) In addition, deans of all colleges are asked to recommend faculty to participate in the program, and beginning in year 2, associates from previous cohorts have been asked to assist in recruitment. (This tack has been very successful with arts and sciences faculty: two arts and sciences faculty from Cohort 1 were responsible for recruiting five other arts and sciences faculty into Cohorts 2 and 3.) Application information is also sent to district coordinators, as well as superintendents of NJNER dis-tricts. In this way, the information is disseminated in an efficient and cost-effective manner to all who may be interested. Individu-als planning to apply are asked to call for the application; in this way, we are able to keep track of who has requested applications.

To ensure equality in the application process, both university and school faculty are asked to provide the same information. First, applicants are asked to provide a one- to two-page statement that shows how they meet the selection criteria outlined in the application information. In addition, we ask applicants to give the names of two individuals who will serve as references. Applicants also sign a statement verifying their commitment to attend all eight days of the summer session and to make every effort to attend other meetings during the year. Finally, they agree to conduct inquiry into the nature of simultaneous renewal.

The selection committee consists of the NJNER's IEI Leadership Associates and representatives of the tripartite selected from former cohorts. The directors of the Center of Pedagogy and the NJNER also participate in the selection process.

Our goal is to have twenty participants each year—ten from the schools and ten from the university, with half from education and half from the arts and sciences. Every effort is made to achieve a balance among the tripartite as well as to diversify the group. The committee reserves the right to invite additional applications if a balance cannot be achieved with the original group of applicants. The numbers in Table 11.1 show that these goals of diversity and balance were achieved to some extent in the first three years of the program.

Because we feel that we increase the potential for change in a school when administrators and teachers work together, preference is given to administrator and teacher teams. In the first three cohorts, eight of the public school participants were district- and school-level administrators. Similarly, two of the university associates were department chairs whose faculty also participated.

Table 11.1. Collective Demographics of the First Three Cohorts

	White		African American		Latino		Asian	
	Male	Female	Male	Female	Male	Female	Male	Female
Education	3	7	0	2	1	0	0	0
Arts and Sciences	5	2	2	2	1	1	1	1
Public School	12	16	1	2	0	0	0	0

Organizational and Administrative Issues

Because the Montclair State University/New Jersey Network for Educational Renewal program was adapted from the national Leadership Program conducted by the Institute for Educational Inquiry in Seattle, its purposes (see Exhibit 11.2), as well as some of the readings and activities, are similar to those of the national program. The New Jersey program, however, is held for only eight days in July and therefore cannot cover each of the dimensions in as much depth as we would like. Meetings are scheduled during the academic year to continue the discussions on topics relevant to the moral dimensions of teaching, to share progress on inquiry projects, and to maintain contact. One example of such a meeting was a day-long visit to the Harold Wilson Professional Development School in Newark. Associates had an opportunity to visit classrooms and share their reasons for entering the teaching profession with the students. At another meeting, we invited a guest speaker, Jean Anyon of Rutgers University, to discuss her work with teachers in Newark, a partner district, and provide a historical perspective of the city. A third meeting was devoted to a presentation by one of the associates related to his research on the Holocaust.

The Agenda

During the eight days in the summer, participants are introduced to the Agenda for Education in a Democracy. The program focuses on the four-part mission of teaching described by John Goodlad (access to knowledge, enculturation of the young into a social and political democracy, nurturing pedagogy, and stewardship of schools) and the moral dimensions of each.[6] Each of the four themes is studied through readings and discussions. (See Exhibits 11.3 and 11.4.)

Almost every session begins with a discussion of a reading relevant to the topic of the day. On most days, these are small-group discussions led by one of the participants. Prior to the two-week

Exhibit 11.3. Summer Leadership Associates Program

Agenda: Week 1

Monday	**Purposes and Goals**
Morning topics:	Welcome and introductions
	Criteria for a good conversation
	Fernández-Balboa and Marshall article discussion
	Agenda and goals for the Associates Program
	The four themes of teaching
Afternoon topics:	Purposes of education and schooling
	Relating the themes to our own work

Tuesday	**The Moral Dimensions of Teaching**
Morning topics:	DeLorenzo article discussion
	The moral dimensions of teaching
Afternoon topic:	Inquiry projects: Presentations by Cohort 2

Wednesday	**Access to Knowledge**
Morning topics:	Kotlowitz book discussion
	Access to knowledge
Afternoon topic:	Trip to Newark Museum (luncheon and educational tour)

Thursday	**Nurturing Pedagogy**
Morning topics:	hooks book discussion (whole group)
	Pedagogical nurturing
Afternoon topics:	Unpacking the postulates
	Action plans

Agenda: Week 2

Monday	**Enculturation into a Political and Social Democracy**
Morning topics:	Villegas article discussion
	"Culturally Responsive Teaching"
	Guest speaker, Ana Maria Villegas, Department of Curriculum and Teaching, MSU
	Preparation for open space
Afternoon topics:	Open space
	Work on action plans

Exhibit 11.3. Summer Leadership Associates Program, cont'd

Tuesday	Expanding the Concept of Teacher Education
Morning topics:	Apple book discussion
	What is a democracy?
Afternoon topics:	Democracy discussion continues
	The role of arts and sciences faculty at the university and in the schools in simultaneous renewal (Soder article discussion)
Wednesday	**Stewardship of Best Practice**
Morning topics:	Fullan book discussion
	Stewardship and effecting change
Afternoon topic:	The Change Game
Thursday	**Effecting Change**
Morning topics:	What is a center of pedagogy?
	Looking ahead, staying together, planning for the future
	Reflections on the past two weeks
Afternoon topic:	Lunch and farewell ceremony

seminar, every participant is randomly assigned to facilitate discussion of a specific reading, and each decides how to conduct this half-hour conversation. This strategy provides every associate with a leadership role. The discussions give the group an opportunity to develop a mind-set for the day's work, as well as a chance to share thoughts about the reading. Participants are asked to keep a journal of their reactions to help them recall what they read for these discussions.

We begin the eight days with a discussion of "Dialogical Pedagogy in Teacher Education: Toward an Education for Democracy," by Juan-Miguel Fernández-Balboa and James P. Marshall.[7] This article presents some provocative ideas about discussion as well as criteria for "good" dialogue. According to Fernández-Balboa and Marshall, good dialogue is, among other things, a free act, social,

Exhibit 11.4. Reading List for the Leadership Associates Program, Summer 1997

Books

Apple, Michael W., and James A. Beane (eds.). *Democratic Schools*. Alexandria, Va.: Association for Supervision and Curriculum Development, 1995.

Fullan, Michael. *Change Forces: Probing the Depths of Educational Reform*. Bristol, Pa.: Falmer Press, 1993.

Goodlad, John I. *Educational Renewal: Better Teachers, Better Schools*. San Francisco: Jossey-Bass, 1994 (Chapters 1, 2, 3, 8).

hooks, bell. *Teaching to Transgress*. New York: Routledge, 1994.

Kotlowitz, Alex. *There Are No Children Here: The Story of Two Boys Growing Up in the Other America*. New York: Barnes & Noble Press, 1991.

Articles

Cochran-Smith, Marilyn. "Uncertain Allies: Understanding the Boundaries of Race and Teaching." *Harvard Educational Review* 65 (August 1995): 541–550.

Cole, Susan A. "Open Discourse in Our Society Appears to Be in Jeopardy." *Chronicle of Higher Education*, March 17, 1995, p. B5.

DeLorenzo, Lisa. "Teaching as Moral Stewardship: A Guide for Teacher Preparation." Inquiry Project Report. Seattle: Institute for Educational Inquiry, 1994.

Delpit, Lisa D. "The Silenced Dialogue: Power and Pedagogy in Educating Other People's Children." *Harvard Educational Review* 58 (August 1988): 280–293.

Fenstermacher, Gary D. "What's Missing from Education Reform?" *Education Digest* (November 1994): 4–7.

Fernández-Balboa, Juan-Miguel, and James P. Marshall. "Dialogical Pedagogy in Teacher Education: Toward an Education for Democracy." *Journal of Teacher Education* 45 (May–June 1994): 172–182.

Giroux, Henry A. "Teacher Education and Democratic Schooling." In *Schooling and the Struggle for Public Life: Critical Pedagogy in the Modern Age*, pp. 173–202. Minneapolis: University of Minnesota Press, 1988.

Goodlad, John I. "Reasonable Expectations." In *Teachers for Our Nation's Schools*, pp. 46–53. San Francisco: Jossey-Bass, 1990.

Michelli, Nicholas, Tina Jacobowitz, and Robert Pines. "Renewing Teacher Education Through Critical Thinking." *Record in Educational Leadership* 14 (Spring–Summer 1994): 45–48.

Oakes, Jeannie, and Martin Lipton. "Tracking and Ability Grouping: A Structural Barrier to Access and Achievement." In John I. Goodlad and Pamela Keating (eds.), *Access to Knowledge: The Continuing Agenda for Our Nation's Schools*, pp. 46–53. Rev. ed. New York: College Entrance Examination Board, 1994.

Exhibit 11.4. Reading List for the Leadership Associates Program, Summer 1997, cont'd

Quan, K. Y. "The Girl Who Wouldn't Sing." In Gloria Anzaldua (ed.). *Making Face, Making Soul/Haciendo Caras*. San Francisco: Aunt Lute Books, 1990.

Soder, Roger. "Teaching in a Democracy: The Role of the Arts and Sciences in the Preparation of Teachers." Occasional Paper no. 19. Seattle: Center for Educational Renewal, University of Washington, 1994.

Villegas, Ana Maria. "Culturally Responsive Pedagogy for the 1990s and Beyond." Trends and Issues Paper no. 6. Washington, D.C.: ERIC Clearinghouse on Teacher Education, 1991.

---

inclusive, and transformative.[8] Our hope is that as a result of this interaction, the group will establish its own criteria for "good" discussion that we can refer to during the two weeks. Some lively arguments have arisen during these sessions related to the right to remain silent, men's domination of the discussions, and whether there is a need for hand raising. This initial discussion about discussion starts the group's bonding process in a positive way.

During the next seven days, issues around the purposes of education and schooling are addressed using the framework of the moral dimensions and the four curricular themes. In the first three years of the program, we incorporated a variety of activities in addition to readings to make the themes come alive. For example, on the third day of each session, we have delved into access to knowledge in the morning, and then in the afternoon have taken the cohorts to the Newark Museum for lunch and an educational tour. Our goals have been threefold: to provide a bonding activity, to introduce the group to a valuable educational resource near the university, and to take the associates to an urban environment similar to the one they have read about in *There Are No Children Here*.[9] During the debriefing on the next day, we discuss museums and access to knowledge, as well as the poverty that exists so close to our university that precludes children from gaining access to knowledge. We show videos and invite guest speakers to help us

further our understanding of nurturing pedagogy and enculturation. We use "open space," an unfilled block of time during which
people can lead or participate in conversations on topics of their
choice—for example, how university faculty are rewarded for their
work in P–12 schools. We discuss stewardship and then play The
Change Game,[10] an exciting team game that reinforces many of the
important concepts presented by Michael Fullan in his book
Change Forces.[11] Both the game and the book show the importance
of involving all key players in the change process, rather than just
relying on those in top positions, and of being flexible and open to
change.

Readings

The readings are selected with the following criteria in mind.

- They relate to the four themes and their moral
  dimensions.

- They achieve an appropriate balance between theory
  and practice.

- They offer diversity of authors in regard to race and
  gender.

- They are not only provocative but even emotionally
  upsetting, because we feel that strong emotions may
  inspire people to action.

Participants receive the books in early May, which gives them
adequate time to complete the readings. So as not to overwhelm
the groups, we have not required a complete reading of all of the
books. We have also prioritized them so that some are required for
discussions and others are merely recommended for background
information.

Inquiry Projects

Over the first three years of the MSU/NJNER Leadership Program, inquiry projects fell into several broad categories: "Advancing the Agenda," "Improving Communication at and Among Our Sites," "Teaching to Diversity," "Retention of Underrepresented Groups in Teacher Education," "Nurturing Pedagogy," and "Access to Knowledge." All inquiry projects must relate to the Agenda for Education in a Democracy. Several faculty conducted study groups within their departments related to the Agenda. Others focused on ways of using technology in education. One university arts and sciences faculty member developed a service-learning course in anthropology and is now serving on the university service-learning committee. Of course, many other inquiry projects have been carried out or are currently under way at the university and in the schools.

Cost

The Leadership Associates Program was originally funded through external grants, including a DeWitt Wallace–Reader's Digest Fund Incentive Award, but the costs of any future cohorts will come from ongoing university funding for our efforts toward increasing our cadre of leaders. We will also use this funding to continue holding meetings during the year to maintain contact and to assess and ensure progress of the Associates Program.

The approximate budget for each two-week program is $40,000. Table 11.2 shows a breakdown of the costs.

Additional costs were incurred in the second and third years, when we brought members of Cohorts 1 and 2 back for one or two days in the summer. We also held three meetings over the course of each year, and there were costs for food and materials.

Troublesome Issues

At times during the two-week sessions, troublesome issues have arisen, and decisions have had to be made about how to deal with them. Three examples stand out as indicative of the kinds of prob-

Table 11.2. Costs of the Leadership Associates Program

Description	Cost
Coordinator	$ 4,000
Facilitators (4 @ $2,000)	8,000
Consultants	600
Participant stipends (20 @ $1,000)	20,000
Books and materials	4,000
Postage and mailings	250
Food and beverages	3,000
Total	$39,850

lems that may occur in such an intensive setting where emotional and provocative issues are being discussed. In one cohort, a female participant became distraught when she was not called on after patiently raising her hand and waiting. Other associates, primarily males, were jumping in, interrupting, and basically dominating the discussion. No rules for discussion had been established at that point, and the topic was the Fernández-Balboa and Marshall article on discussion. Her distress became apparent when she shouted out, "Look, either we raise our hands or we don't! It can't go both ways. The way it's happening now, only men are getting to speak." This outburst upset many of the participants, but we forged ahead and used it as a springboard for discussing rules for discussion.

In another situation, the group had just watched an extremely provocative video that showed graphic examples of abusive behavior toward women. During a break, the female graduate assistant who was participating came to one of the leaders and reported that two of the associates (both male faculty) had made some extremely sexist comments to her, and it was her belief that the film had provoked their comments. The group of leaders discussed the incident and decided to bring the issue to the whole group, without mentioning names, in the context of building group respect. This tack backfired; several people in the group became paranoid, feeling that they had said something inappropriate. After clarifying what was said, most calmed down. Although the offenders did not apologize publicly, they did apologize privately to the graduate assistant.

A third problem arose when two Asian participants said that they felt excluded because none of the readings came from an Asian perspective. To remedy this, we included a relevant short story by a Chinese woman in the readings for a follow-up session for that cohort, as well as in the readings for the next cohort.

All three incidents served to bond the group. We learned from situations such as these that conflict can have value and can result in growth of understanding as well as group cohesiveness. It was important to address these conflicts directly (perhaps more directly than we did in the second instance) and use them as vehicles for exploring the Agenda. These three examples relate directly to en-culturation, and participants were able to make these connections in later discussions.

Evaluation and Results

At the end of each summer session, participants are asked to provide feedback on the program. In addition, members of Cohorts 1 and 2 were given a questionnaire related to the impact of the program on them over time. This questionnaire was developed so that we could have feedback to help us improve the program in regard to curriculum, readings, activities, and recruitment of future associates.

Comments pertaining to the meaningfulness of the program indicated that participants were pleased with almost every aspect. They cited several elements as particularly meaningful: the free exchange of ideas, philosophical discussions, the readings and the opportunities to exchange ideas about them, and interaction with and collaboration among colleagues. When asked to jot down their favorite readings, participants named several texts. Michael Fullan's *Change Forces* led the list. Other favored readings were *There Are No Children Here*, by Alex Kotlowitz; *Teaching to Transgress*, by bell hooks; "Dialogical Pedagogy in Teacher Education," by Fernández-Balboa and Marshall; and "Teacher Education and Democratic Schooling," by Henry Giroux.

The most frequent suggestion for strengthening the program was that the program be longer, with more discussion of readings. Some participants felt that the scope of the program should be smaller and that we should incorporate more application of the ideas discussed. Several requested that we continue to bring the group together to discuss progress on inquiry projects and continue the discourse on topics relevant to the Agenda. To augment dissemination of information and communication, some associates suggested that we create a web site and a newsletter.

A variety of reasons were offered for why individuals joined the program, including professional development and self-renewal, networking, gaining a better understanding of democracy, and getting more involved in our work with the NJNER. Associates reported that the program was different from other work they had done with colleagues in that it allowed for more intimacy, fostered interaction with people who believe in democratic practice, was more focused on a specific agenda, and provided more interchange with educators at different levels of schooling. Respondents unanimously said that they would recommend the program to colleagues. Several even commented on the good food. Overall, the feedback from the questionnaires was highly positive and quite useful for improving future programs.

Participants have found the Leadership Program extremely rewarding. This does not mean that we can rest on our laurels and maintain the status quo. We must continually revise the program curriculum to maintain currency and meet the needs of each group. Obviously, we cannot implement all of the suggestions participants made, but we hope to accommodate as many as possible as long as they support the goals of the program. One important lesson is to give high consideration to creature comforts when planning the program. Good food, comfortable seating, frequent breaks, and time for socialization all serve to maintain energy and motivation to learn. In addition, it would be ideal if we could conduct the program off campus, to preclude university faculty from going to their offices during breaks, which can result in loss of focus.

Unfortunately, the costs for this are prohibitive, given our current budget.

Conclusion

We are very encouraged by our progress to date. The fifty-nine participants who have completed the program have created a strong base of leadership for our ongoing work; they continue to gather for meetings and work together on inquiry projects. Their influence goes beyond the scope of our program as they take what they have learned back to their schools and university departments. We hope that there will be continued interest in the program as past participants communicate their positive experiences to their colleagues. Indeed, we have begun preparation for our fourth Leadership Associates Program (pending additional funding). Our shared vision is being shared by more and more people, and this can only benefit future generations of students and educators.

Notes

1. Peter Senge, *The Fifth Discipline* (New York: Doubleday, 1993), p. 206.

2. John Dewey, *The School and Society* (Chicago: University of Chicago Press, 1899, 2nd ed., 1915), p. 29.

3. James W. Fraser, *Reading, Writing, and Justice: School Reform as if Democracy Matters* (New York: State University of New York Press, 1997), p. 54.

4. Wilma F. Smith and Donna Hughes, *Leadership Program Resource Package* (Seattle: Institute for Educational Inquiry, 1995).

5. Nicholas M. Michelli, "The Center of Pedagogy" (Upper Montclair, N.J.: Montclair State University, 1997), p. 2.

6. See John I. Goodlad, *Educational Renewal: Better Teachers, Better Schools* (San Francisco: Jossey-Bass, 1994), pp. 4–5.

7. Juan-Miguel Fernández-Balboa and James P. Marshall, "Dialogical Pedagogy in Teacher Education: Toward an Education for

Democracy," *Journal of Teacher Education* 45 (May–June 1994): 172–182.

8. Fernández-Balboa and Marshall, "Dialogical Pedagogy in Teacher Education," p. 174.

9. Alex Kotlowitz, *There Are No Children Here: The Story of Two Boys Growing Up in the Other America* (New York: Anchor Books, Doubleday, 1991).

10. Susan E. Mundry and Leslie F. Hergert (eds.), *Making Change for School Improvement* (Andover, Mass.: NETWORK, 1988).

11. Michael Fullan, *Change Forces: Probing the Depths of Educational Reform* (Bristol, Pa.: Falmer Press, 1993).

12

The South Carolina
Summer Institute of Leaders

Barbara L. Gottesman

I s it possible to provide a leadership program on a large scale for a very diverse group to meet the purposes of statewide as well as institution-specific goals? A resounding yes would have startled many educators when we began our collaborative efforts in 1990 as a setting in the National Network for Educational Renewal (NNER). We agreed to implement the Agenda for Education in a Democracy when we were in the confederacy state, a loose organization of like-minded institutions with a common purpose but little idea of how to achieve it. Our partners represented a cross-section of the state's population and colleges. Benedict College is a historically black institution; Columbia College is an independent women's college; Furman University is a Baptist-related, private liberal arts institution; the University of South Carolina (USC) is the state's largest research land-grant institution; and Winthrop University is a regional university that was formerly a teacher training institution. The coordinating agency, the South Carolina Center for the Advancement of Teaching and School Leadership (SCCATSL), was a statewide, legislatively funded restructuring center.

These institutions had several commonalities that made them think that they could implement the Agenda for Education in a Democracy. First, all five expressed the desire to improve on the conditions that were so vividly depicted in the five-year study of the education of educators.[1] Second, whereas these five institutions represented the range of teacher preparation programs and types of students in the state, they recognized that no one college could renew its teacher education programs alone. The five institutions believed Benjamin Franklin's axiom, "We all must hang together or surely we will hang separately" and John Goodlad's comment, "If they can do it in South Carolina, they can do it anywhere." The point of Goodlad's recommendations in *Teachers for Our Nation's Schools* was that renewing teacher preparation in one college was not enough; renewal had to spread to other partnerships and eventually influence state policy. In South Carolina, models had been funded and successfully implemented in individual colleges, but no model had been successfully transferred. If our five diverse institutions and their partner schools could renew teacher preparation, we could build a case for other partnerships in the state to renew also.

Our task was more complicated than the task of other single institutional initiatives. We had to raise our own level of involvement from simple awareness to effective application and increase our sparse cadre of leaders and believers to a critical mass in each college and throughout the statewide collaborative. The initial work of the SCCATSL had focused on creating awareness; eight regional dialogues were held on college campuses around the state, with all surrounding school districts invited to become part of the renewal effort. By holding the dialogues on the college premises, with educational reformers addressing key issues,[2] we sought to build a common understanding. Half of each meeting was a genuine conversation. The large audience was broken up into groups of five or seven to answer the two questions: "What can colleges do to assist in life-long staff development for teachers?" and "What can schools do to assist in preparing more effective teachers?" This was ground that few had dared to tread before; typically the mission and goals of each separate institution—the P–12 school and the teacher preparation program—were kept quite separate. The audiences of P–12 schoolteachers, education faculty, and administrators were surprised to be equal partners in dialogue, but even more surprising were the forty to fifty pages of recommendations that each ultimately developed for the others' programs. Given the experience of the eight statewide dialogues during the first year, the South Carolina Collaborative to Renew Teacher Education (formerly the SCCATSL) had a small but powerful base from which to begin.

At its first meeting, the collaborative's leadership group consisted of the five education deans or chairs and the center director. Among the six, four would soon leave their leadership positions. Clearly the work of the center in restructuring had to inform the direction of the initiative in the state. Many skeptical, politically minded educators estimated that the center's state funding would have only a three-year lifeline; many gave it less, and none gave it more. The uncertain luxury of state money to make changes in schools and in teacher preparation was recognized as a window that most likely would not open again. The six leaders spent the first meeting staking out their territorial imperatives, but at the same time they recognized the pressing need to collaborate in a once-in-a-lifetime opportunity.

Collaboration

The key element obvious to the six leaders was the need to educate a sufficient number of people at the five sites so that membership in the NNER would not waste away into a bandwagon effort. The most difficult part was to pool the resources, human and otherwise, to the mutual benefit of the collaborative, when each of the partners had been ingrained in the tradition of jealously guarding its successful strategies and carefully hiding its failures. Although the University of South Carolina had been involved with the Holmes Group—the organization of education deans seeking to improve teacher education—and had some definitions for professional development schools, all of the institutions started at operational ground zero. The collaborative went ahead with keynote-type conferences on partner schools (held at Furman), cultural diversity (held at

USC), and school-college partnerships (held at Winthrop). The center's work with restructuring schools improved the design of future meetings and seminars by asking participants to contemplate a major concept (presented by a keynote speaker or keynote book) and then engage in dialogue about the concept's implications for their renewal work in South Carolina. This technique created a valuable synergy: with many people participating in finding solutions to problems, the result was a whole greater than the sum of its parts.

Structure

The collaborative decided that the establishment of working professional development schools (PDSs) would provide a vehicle for change. Three different methods for establishing these partnerships emerged: one college held a series of informative meetings and welcomed school proposals as a culminating activity, another conducted year-long focus groups with schools on the four-part mission of teaching in a democracy, and one invited a state panel to do site visits and judge PDS applicants. None of these methods, however, produced the desired cooperation for moving toward effective PDSs. Finally, true collaboration took place as the fourth partner invited a state panel composed of teachers as well as administrators to select among PDS applicants.

The physical reality of having professional development schools (also called partner schools) stimulated a working relationship that repeated the first stage of what we came to know as the collaborative process: What can we do together to renew our schools and teacher education simultaneously? Through trial and error and the "hang together" philosophy, the South Carolina Collaborative had compelled its members to pool their resources, at least on the surface. Creating and cultivating partnerships with public schools was an extension of hanging together—but as five separate sites. Both the college of education professors and the public school personnel, who had often been graduate students of those professors, viewed these initial contacts as professor-student relationships. Building the trust that would sustain us over the long haul for the mutual benefit of schools and teacher preparation programs took almost three years of working hard together, of admitting ignorance, and of wanting to learn.

Naturally, we encountered false starts and dead ends. For example, one lengthy argument with a scholarly professor who wanted to conduct a year-long study of PDS literature and present a research paper to "his" PDS resulted in the scholarly paper, blank looks from "his" school, and a new effort that began with a round table, identical chairs for professors and teachers, and a blank agenda. Focus groups composed of equal partners were created to discuss the meanings of the words *professional, development,* and *school*. We began to see that the school was the site where teachers, teacher candidates, and college teachers could learn together and develop as professionals.

One example illustrates the success of the process after three years. At one school, a college professor taught a graduate course in conceptual science to teacher leaders. The professor then observed as each teacher implemented the concepts in her or his classroom with a student teacher and with the P–12 students. The graduate course participants then gathered to critique the work and go on with their studies. The professor spent about half of her time in the PDS and was welcomed as a colleague and as a part of the school. Another college added the feature of having the college professor substitute for each P–12 teacher as he or she peer-coached another teacher who was either implementing the concepts or teaching student teachers in the on-site seminars.

Having developed a physical structure for working as partners in the PDSs, the five colleges began holding twice-yearly sharing conferences among all the partners to learn the successes to replicate and the failures to avoid.

The Summer Institute of Leaders

The structure for success was now evident to all of us: a firm knowledge and skills base, collaborative efforts, and a physical space from which to work. Early in 1994, it became evident to the six leaders of the South Carolina Collaborative that all our efforts were not enough to sustain and increase the critical mass working on simultaneous renewal. True, we were forging some working partnerships in PDSs, and the center's restructuring work was providing training in participatory decision making, managing change, team building, action research, and learning styles. But we knew that we needed to take a giant leap forward and engage in an intensive effort to involve our partner schools, our education faculties, and our arts and sciences colleagues in teacher preparation.

The Institute for Educational Inquiry (IEI) announced the availability of DeWitt Wallace–Reader's Digest Fund (DWRDF) Incentive Awards just as the South Carolina Collaborative had decided on a strategy for the giant leap forward: intensive training and interaction to develop leaders to carry on simultaneous renewal. The collaborative received one of the first awards, but it was difficult for five sites to reach consensus on committing the sum to one venture for the mutual benefit of all. Nevertheless, the outline for the Summer Institute of Leaders soon appeared: an entire week would be set aside for teams from each partnership site representing education, arts and sciences, and PDSs.

A knowledge base was crucial for the new and diverse groups. Who was to present it, and in what form? Skills needed to be developed: how and by whom? The desired final product was evident: action plans for each of the five partnerships to create what John Goodlad calls "centers of pedagogy."[3]

Planning: Leading the Leaders

Once we determined that the institute would take place during the third week in July of the next year at Furman University, we had fifteen months to plan the institute and bring it into being. At that time, our setting had six graduates of the IEI's Leadership Program. Despite the knowledge and training each had gained from four weeks in Seattle interacting with leaders in the field of simultaneous renewal, the South Carolina Leadership Associates had been underused as leaders in their own setting. They were to be the second generation of leaders, but they had no significant experience with collaboration. Nor was it clear, then, that friction would develop between the first generation of leaders and the second generation.

Tensions arose partly because the six first-generation leaders, who had worked together for four years, turned over the planning for the Summer Institute to the six Leadership Associates without guidance or interaction. The South Carolina Leadership Institute would include those who were already active in partnership work or those who wanted to become active. The IEI Program included long reading lists, four weeks of sessions in Seattle, and intensive work with leaders who had years of experience and a sound knowledge base. The Leadership Associates who were creating the Summer Institute hoped to replicate their IEI experience for a group of fifty in a quarter of the time with few, if any, national experts. The six first-generation leaders thought that replication of the IEI Leadership Program would not satisfy the collaborative's need to achieve the goals of forging teams and producing action plans. We needed more interaction among sites and more skill building. We needed genuine collaborative learning if the collaborative were to survive in a state notorious for each going his own way.

Just as the Russian psychologist Lev Vygotsky uses the term "zone of proximal development" to refer to the understanding that lies just beyond our current knowledge and ability or what we can learn alone,[4] we can move on to what we are capable of learning next with help. At that time, we needed to have our collective knowledge base intensified and spread in a way that would allow us to learn from each other by constructing our own meaning. We realized that it was the right time to forge five teams at five sites that could take us a giant step forward toward developing real tripartite partnerships in centers of pedagogy. No one could tell us how to do it: we would have to forge our own teams.

Our "chief worriers" from the IEI came to our assistance just as the two generations of leaders had ceased communicating with each other four months before the Summer Institute was scheduled to take place. After a consensus-building day with the two worriers from Seattle, the planning group moved ahead, now composed of some first-generation leaders, some Leadership Associates, and some worker bees, such as assistant deans and team leaders.

Orientation, Final Preparations, and Pre-Institute Readings

The time and place for the institute were important considerations. To accommodate conflicting schedules from three separate educational communities, we chose a week in the summer. And to make the DWRDF Incentive Award go further, we arranged housing in the Furman dormitories. We insisted that each college's team be composed of equal numbers of representatives from education, professional development schools, and the arts and sciences. We had learned from the IEI Leadership Program that advance reading was important for meaningful conversations. We added our own criterion: each of the participants was required to attend a half-day orientation to the Agenda as advance preparation for the intensive July institute week.

The success of the April orientation day was due largely to the presentation of the keynote speaker, a senior associate with the IEI. She enlightened all participants about the original five-year Study of the Education of Educators and the founding of the NNER. The day also provided an opportunity to distribute copies of the following five books to each participant in the Summer Institute of Leaders:

John I. Goodlad, *A Place Called School* (New York: McGraw-Hill, 1984)

John I. Goodlad, *Teachers for Our Nation's Schools* (San Francisco: Jossey-Bass, 1990)

Holmes Group, *Tomorrow's Teachers* (East Lansing, Mich.: Holmes Group, 1986)

Holmes Group, *Tomorrow's Schools* (East Lansing, Mich.: Holmes Group, 1990)

Holmes Group, *Tomorrow's Schools of Education* (East Lansing, Mich.: Holmes Group, 1995)

In addition to the five books, each participant was given a notebook with a number of articles related to the Study of the Education of Educators and an article written by Paul Dixon and Richard Ishler on professional development schools.[5] Each participant was required to read the five books and the articles before the July session. The five partnerships organized focus groups for the discussion of these required readings, delving into the background of the Study of the Education of Educators that resulted in *Teachers for Our Nation's Schools* and examining implications from the three books by the Holmes Group.

The orientation stimulated so much interest that four of the colleges wanted to bring more than their ten allocated participants. The list of participants grew to seventy-two.

When participants arrived on the first day of the institute in July, they received an additional set of books:

Michael Fullan, *Change Forces: Probing the Depths of Educational Reform* (Bristol, Pa.: Falmer Press, 1993)

John I. Goodlad and Pamela Keating (eds.), *Access to Knowledge: The Continuing Agenda for Our Nation's Schools*, rev. ed. (New York: College Entrance Examination Board, 1994)

Shirley M. Hord, William L. Rutherford, Leslie Huling-Austin, and Gene E. Hall, *Taking Charge of Change* (Alexandria, Va.: Association for Supervision and Curriculum Development, 1987)

Russell T. Osguthorpe, R. Carl Harris, Melanie Fox Harris, and Sharon Black (eds.), *Partner Schools: Centers for Educational Renewal* (San Francisco: Jossey-Bass, 1995)

These books, together with the five already distributed in April, formed the basis for all of the conversations and activities.

The Evolving Institute Agenda

Before the Summer Institute of Leaders began, its agenda was changed several times to use more appropriate pedagogy and to reflect new circumstances. In the original agenda for the institute, it was plain that we had learned very little from the literature on managing change or from the center's experience in holding seminars on managing change. The six days were planned along traditional lines, including dinner and a keynote speaker for the opening. Each of the next five days centered on a keynote speaker or workshop leader, who would provide what we thought was an extension of the knowledge base. We allowed some time for the five teams from each site to meet and discuss, but had no real action plan for their products and no way to hold them accountable.

We needed skills in team building to forge education faculty, arts and sciences faculty, and public school faculty into one center of pedagogy responsible for reconstituting the operations and governance of teacher preparation. The second version of the agenda moved away from the traditional keynote speakers and workshop leaders to give us time to teach and learn skills essential for developing teams to reach consensus on one-year and five-year action plans. We eliminated from the schedule several keynote speakers on managing change and consensus building and instead decided to use our local talent to teach each skill, lead a practice exercise, and identify a part of the intended action plan on which to use the skill. For example, we would teach a skill like participatory decision making, give each team a practice problem to work with, and then give them the task of using participatory decision making for working out the governance of their center of pedagogy action plan.

The third rendering of the institute agenda (see Exhibit 12.1) removed all but two of the keynote speakers, one for a welcome at Sunday dinner and one to set the agenda on Monday morning. We included a variety of exercises on participatory decision making,

Exhibit 12.1. Summer Institute of Leaders Agenda, Version 3

Sunday	Monday	Tuesday	Wednesday	Thursday	Friday
	"Moral Dimensions"	*Change Forces*	Exercise: Participatory Decision Making	Donna's Delphi: The Moral Question as Part of the Action Plan	Formal Presentations of Five Action Plans for Centers of Pedagogy
	Teams: Local Beliefs	Exercises: Circle Teamwork and Strength Deployment Inventory	Team Practice	Teams: Short-Range Goals	
"The Background of the NNER"	"The Social and Political Dimensions"	Job-Alike Site Teams	Leadership and the Wizard of Oz	Team Building with Little White Boxes	Challenge for Next Year
Team Focus Groups: "Access to Knowledge"	Teams: Tripartite Relationships		Teams: Action Planning II	Teams: Long-Range Goals	Formal Debriefing
	Teams: Action Planning I	Teams: Needed Changes	Teams: Action Planning III	Picnic: Plans for COP	

strength deployment, team building, and goal setting. Each morning session and each afternoon session began with a skill- or team-
building exercise. The bulk of each session was devoted to teams'
practicing the skill or incorporating it into their action plans.

Version 4 of the agenda only slightly modified version 3 and
evolved during the last week of June, when it became apparent that
the state legislature would end funding for the South Carolina Center for the Advancement of Teaching and School Leadership.
SCCATSL had been the coordinating agency, the training center,
and the source of grants and funding that would cease abruptly on
June 30. The Summer Institute of Leaders was scheduled for the
third week in July. The first-generation leaders began meeting daily
instead of weekly or monthly to revise the institute plan in the face
of what seemed to be ultimate disaster. Each vowed to lead his or
her institution ahead, to continue to implement the Agenda for
Education in a Democracy, and to plan for centers of pedagogy, even
without the center's money and leadership. It required a certain
amount of courage, foresight, and commitment to take this leap of
faith in the midst of upheaval and change.

The fifth version of the agenda was developed on the Thursday
before the Sunday on which the Leadership Institute was to begin.
We learned then that our Monday keynote speaker was unable to
come to South Carolina. Roger Soder, codirector of the Center for
Educational Renewal, agreed to replace her. In his erudite manner,
he persuaded the arts and sciences faculty on each team that the
Agenda for Education in a Democracy was an initiative worthy of
their commitment. Soder's afternoon discussions with the teams
took place at the same time that the institute agenda was being
revised once more to permit teams to spend more time together
practicing their newly learned skills, bonding, and forging their
action plans.

It may sound as if our planning were haphazard, but such was
not the case. As we learned more from each other and remembered
the success of our efforts to manage change, we incorporated feed-

back from previous conferences and the developing group dynamics we were observing. We were astute enough to have two Leadership Associates recording and documenting each morning and afternoon session. They also collected brief written evaluations twice a day during the institute. These instant feedback forms helped the institute leaders revise and plan the modification of activities to meet the emerging needs of the group.

Union

As the institute days moved swiftly along, it became evident that the whole was indeed becoming more than the sum of its parts. The dormitory housing that had originally brought cries of outrage from full professors resulted in communal bonding and late-night planning and discussion that none had ever found time to indulge in at work. Groups from the same colleges who carefully sat together during opening sessions and lunches during the first days blended together with other participants by Friday. Benedict administrator, Corley Elementary principal, University of South Carolina music professor, high school history teacher, fourth-grade teacher—it was difficult to see separate institutional or role groups by Friday.

Two brief vignettes give some flavor of the institute. As institute leader, I was exhausted by Wednesday afternoon after, among other things, facilitating the exercise in participatory decision making. I decided that the seventy-two individuals could do without my guidance for a few hours if I really believed in the team process. So I dropped into a nap that stretched into six hours. When I awoke and returned to the common room after dinner, I saw the twenty-two-member USC team so intensely involved in the process of participatory decision making that I could scarcely believe it. They, as well as the other groups, worked on the process until about eleven o'clock that night.

The second vignette started Thursday at dinner when an Airport High School biology teacher related her experience at the University of Georgia in the late 1980s. She had been ready to drop out of teacher education when she was invited to discuss the ills of teacher preparation with a visiting researcher, John Goodlad. On Friday morning, as the USC team presented its five-year action plan for its center of pedagogy, she related her earlier contribution to the identification of the problem. She was proud to be part of the team that now was working on the solution.

Team Presentations: Action Plans

On Thursday, each of the five teams spent every spare minute reaching consensus on the various aspects of their action plans: the structure of the center of pedagogy, the governance and membership of each center, strategies for creating a critical mass on each campus, strategies for administrative support, the one-year action plan, the five-year action plan, and the plans for collaborating with the other four partnerships in South Carolina. We invited local college administrators and local school district administrators to participate when the partnership teams presented their action plans on Friday morning.

Each of the five teams had completed plans for its center of pedagogy and had reached agreement on the critical elements of the design, including even naming its center. Each naming involved long, philosophical discussions of issues peculiar to the institution, but each center of pedagogy adhered to the principles John Goodlad set forth in *Educational Renewal*. Benedict chose the name "Center of Pedagogy"; Winthrop, "Center for Pedagogy"; USC, the "Academy for Educational Renewal"; Columbia, the "Alliance of Educators"; Furman, the "Forum for Educational Inquiry."

The dormitory housing, the late-night planning, and the team bonding that had taken place was evident in each team's presentation of its action plan for a center of pedagogy. Benedict presented its plan in the form of a court trial of the moral imperative. Columbia chose to illustrate the tripartite nature of the center with equal parts for each partner group. Winthrop presented its plan with mime and song, waving little American flags to illustrate the moral and political imperative for preparing teachers for America's democracy. USC's three partners illustrated their equality in governance with a choral response from all parts of the room. And Furman's partnership banded together in a group sing. The fun and creativity did not overshadow the hard work that had gone into five days of intensive collaboration or the concrete plans for establishing centers of pedagogy. Each participant was firmly convinced that he or she was responsible to help change the traditional preparation of teachers into a tripartite endeavor better suited to preparing teachers for America's democracy.

Evaluations

A mathematics professor from USC commented that he had learned new ways to teach his students, what to expect from the public schools in which his children were enrolled, and about his own responsibility for preparing teachers. An African American fourth-grade teacher from a school serving a low-socioeconomic neighborhood was surprised that she was listened to and treated as an equal by a participating college vice president and one of her former professors. An education dean who had joined the activities late was enculturated into the new team processes and began functioning as a team member rather than an administrator accustomed to leading by fiat. A full professor of music at the research university commented that this had been the most significant week in education in the state and that he was glad to have been a part of it.

We were all glad to have been a part of it, but the next five years would also be crucial. Could we establish centers of pedagogy? Could we maintain the equality of professional development schools, arts and sciences faculty, and education faculty as partners in the preparation of teachers for an American democracy? Could we demonstrate that educating teachers in this new way provides better teachers and, consequently, increased learning for P–12 students? Could we enlighten the new generation of leaders and worker bees as the old deans retire and leaders move to new positions outside the South Carolina Collaborative?

Participants left from the mountaintop of a great experience as a united group and with a determination to change the future. The center staff left with the same exhilaration to disband the now-unfunded center but to continue its collaborative restructuring work in other settings in other roles.

During the two years after the South Carolina 1995 Summer Institute of Leaders, two significant events occurred: the 1996 Summer Renewal Institute was held, and the South Carolina Collaborative leaders decided on a strategy for using a second DWRDF Incentive Award. For two days in June 1996, the participants in the Summer Institute of Leaders reconvened with about thirty new participants. No team-building exercises were needed: it was old-home week for all participants, new and old. Most of the time was spent on intensive team planning for the centers of pedagogy and sharing each partnership's progress. We listened carefully to our guest from the Connecticut partnership, a high school principal who welcomed 100 to 150 University of Connecticut students into her school each year to improve P–12 learning, student teaching, and college teaching. For the first time, superintendents participated in our gathering. It was gratifying to see PDS teachers and principals among the most outspoken members of the group.

The second Incentive Award was split among the five partnerships to further the work of their own centers of pedagogy. This was perhaps an error because again it seemed to indicate that we had learned little about collaboration. The award did support the establishment of each center of pedagogy, but it also shifted concentration from the strength of the collaborative: collaboration.

Coming Down from the Mountain

Was the Summer Institute of Leaders worth the time and effort in a climate of disaster with the withdrawal of state funding? Not one participant would say nay. The lack of state funds, the dissipation of the collaborative effort during two years, and the errors made in the name of territoriality—coupled with turnover among faculty of education, in the professional development schools, and in the arts and sciences—has not diminished the efforts of the worker bees. An agenda for the new way of preparing teachers for an American democracy has been institutionalized. Five-year action plans? No, we are engaged in a lifetime of work. This is the way we do things now.

Notes

1. The findings, conclusions, and recommendations of the Study of the Education of Educators were published in John I. Goodlad, *Teachers for Our Nation's Schools* (San Francisco: Jossey-Bass, 1990).

2. The educational leaders who addressed key issues at colleges around the state were John Goodlad, Phil Schlechty, Dean Corrigan, Phyllis Edmundson, Michael Cohen, Terry Peterson, Ted Sizer, and Art Wise.

3. John I. Goodlad, *Educational Renewal: Better Teachers, Better Schools* (San Francisco: Jossey-Bass, 1994).

4. Lev S. Vygotsky, *Mind in Society: The Development of Higher Psychological Processes*, ed. Michael Cole, Vera John-Steiner, Sylvia Scribner, and Ellen Souberman (Cambridge, Mass.: Harvard University Press, 1978).

5. Paul N. Dixon and Richard E. Ishler, "Professional Development Schools: Stages in Collaboration," *Journal of Teacher Education* 43 (January–February 1992): 28–34.

13

The Utah Associates Program for Leaders

Robert S. Patterson, Kathleen H. Hughes

Throughout the history of the Brigham Young University–Public School Partnership (BYU-PSP), there has been a close correspondence between ideas originating in the Center for Educational Renewal (CER) and the Institute for Educational Inquiry (IEI) and practices ensuing in our Utah-based setting of the National Network for Educational Renewal (NNER). This alignment certainly was apparent in the decision our partnership made in 1995 to launch an associates program, one intended to follow closely the model established and operating under the auspices of the IEI.

The reasons for commencing an associates program were simple. Primary was the need to expand the number of well-informed, committed supporters who would be both able and inclined to assist in advancing the agenda of renewal that our partnership had pursued since its inception in 1983. Although we had been functioning for over a decade, relatively few people within our partnership could articulate the central ideas and purposes undergirding our activities. Questions that arose among faculty and administrators of the university and its partner school districts—questions such as "Why do we pay so much attention to John Goodlad's ideas?" or "What are the moral dimensions of teaching?"—vividly revealed that we lacked a foundation of common understanding essential to our purpose.

Further, too many colleagues in the schools and across the university thought that the partnership was nothing more than the interest or preoccupation of a few senior administrators. It meant even less to the majority of university and partnership district personnel. Our vision was not shared extensively enough to sustain the creative capacity of those who make the difference with the students. Using a metaphor from the history of our semiarid land, we perceived that the life-giving water, that is, the vision of the partnership, was not flowing through our irrigation channels to the parched plants at the ends of the rows.

The experiences of the three people from the BYU-PSP who had participated in the IEI's Leadership Program in Seattle by 1995 showed the difference in attitude and behavior that could result from the exploration of ideas central to our mission. The richness of their contribution in applying the fundamental philosophy that the NNER sites shared caused us to seek to increase the number of people who could make similar contributions. We knew that the only way to build such a group was to establish our own local leadership associates program. The three participants from the first two IEI Leadership Program cohorts would serve as a nucleus of experienced, knowledgeable leaders to provide direction for our own associates group.

With the need for more people to appreciate the basic ideas of our partnership and with a model for a partial solution in the IEI's Leadership Program, we launched our own initiative. The idea was presented to the governing board of the BYU-PSP at its January 1995 meeting. The proposal contained two programs, each designed for a different audience, but each targeting the need to increase the number of people in the organization who understood the key ideas of the partnership and could add to the generative leadership capacity of our NNER setting. The first program called for a leadership retreat to be held twice annually for the purposes of building a shared education base and encouraging a more proactive leadership stance that would develop strategies and related projects for improving teacher education and schooling. The leadership group, primarily centered on the membership of the governing board of the

BYU-PSP, was to consist of approximately twenty people, including superintendents, assistant superintendents, directors of curriculum, deans, associate deans, department chairs, and vice presidents. The second proposed program was to create an associates cohort of eighteen to twenty people chosen from the faculty and administration of the five school districts and the university. The governing board endorsed the launching of the two programs. However, more than policy approval was required to make things happen.

A fortuitous confluence of four factors made the successful launching of the associates program possible. First, a positive model existed in the IEI's Leadership Program. We benefited greatly from having had people participate in the successful operation of a leadership training program conducted by a group of colleagues on the staff of the IEI. These same colleagues, sensing the possible interest of a number of NNER settings in conducting their own leadership groups, provided the second factor that was timely in launching the BYU-PSP Associates Program. Wilma Smith, who led the IEI Leadership Program, and her colleague, Donna Hughes, assembled a curriculum *Resource Package* that was made available to interested NNER settings.[1] In addition, a training meeting was convened in May 1995 at the University of Texas at El Paso (UTEP). Our team of facilitators participated and gained further ideas about conducting and operating an associates program. With only the UTEP and BYU partnerships involved in these meetings, local leadership program facilitators had ample opportunity for questions and discussion. The third factor that helped bring the associates program into being was the decision of Kathy Hughes, one of our participants in the IEI's Cohort I, to take a sabbatical leave from the Provo School District. In part, her sabbatical was arranged for the purpose of allowing her to serve as the leader and key facilitator of the BYU-PSP Leadership Program's first cohort. The essential fourth element needed to launch the initiative, financial support for both the program and the leadership retreats, came through the decision of the dean of the BYU McKay School of Education to provide $15,000 to the partnership for this purpose.

Planning for Cohort I

Having received a mandate to organize and conduct an associates program for the BYU-PSP, the planning team began making preliminary decisions. The six-person planning team consisted of the four people who had participated in the UTEP training sessions with the IEI personnel, the governing board chair, and the site director of the partnership. The school year for most teachers and schools in the five districts was only two weeks from its finish when the planning team began deliberating. There was no time to announce the program and to solicit applications, so a list of potential participants was prepared, in consultation with school and university leaders, and those on the list were invited to participate. Each district nominated three members, two were included from the state Department of Education, and the remaining members were selected from the School of Education and from the various colleges and departments of the university. Twenty-six people committed to join this initial venture.

Little publicity accompanied the launching of the associates program. Many of the participants had limited understanding of the experience, and several participated only because their deans or superintendents had encouraged them to do so. Although identification and enlistment of the associates were inadequate because of the late start, and facilitators did not have the opportunity to weigh the attitudes and interests of the cohort members, a good cross-section of partnership participants was assembled. The group of twenty-six was divided evenly between the sexes and included a mix of classroom teachers, school principals, professors from the School of Education, and representatives from departments of the arts and sciences. Of the school personnel, seven were from elementary schools and ten from secondary schools. The inclusion of two leaders from the state Department of Education—the state curriculum director and the assistant director of evaluation—added a rich perspective to the conversation; these individuals became strong supporters of both the BYU-PSP and its associates program. Their positive reaction to the experience helped open the door to special funding support from the state superintendent of education for a major expansion of the program two years later.

The planning team gave consideration to logistics, venue, and curriculum for the program. Early on we recognized that it was unrealistic to expect twenty days for the meetings, the time allotted for the IEI's Leadership Program. The superintendents were reluctant to have teachers and principals absent from their schools for so many days. Instead, fifteen days were designated and spread over the year. We designed a schedule that started with three days in September and then alternated two-day sessions off campus with single days spent visiting partner schools or meeting on the BYU campus. As the retreat location we chose Park City, a mountain resort roughly an hour's drive for most participants. Beautiful and accessible year-round, steeped in the interesting history of mining in early Utah, and enriched by a vital art community and delightful restaurants, it proved a good main setting for our meetings.

The readings, discussion topics, and methods of exploration provided challenges in our planning, especially for the group's leader and facilitator, who was responsible for choosing which ideas from the Agenda for Education in a Democracy would be emphasized. She relied heavily on her own experience in the IEI Leadership Program in Seattle and the *Resource Package* provided by the IEI leaders. A consultant who had been hired to help the partnership build a culture of inquiry assisted in the conduct of the cohort meetings, adding a strong inquiry component to the curriculum.

Four multiple-day sessions in Park City highlighted the moral dimensions of the four-part mission of teaching. Session 1 included an introduction to the overriding theme, emphasizing the enculturation of the young to the principles of a social and political democracy. Inquiry was an important consideration in this beginning session and in the following multiday sessions, which examined topics of access to knowledge, nurturing pedagogy, and stewardship of schools in educative communities. Interspersed between these sessions in Park City, which occurred in September, November, January, and March, were single-day meetings comprising visits to partner primary, middle, and high schools. The final single-day session in April and a two-day meeting in May dealt with the establishment of a center of pedagogy and a culminating activity based on the simulation game Making Change for School Improvement.[2]

The Program in Action

As we convened the first meetings and began to see the camaraderie and cohesiveness of the group grow, the value and power of the associates program became increasingly apparent. Frustrations involved with establishing appropriate room temperatures or keeping batteries and tapes changed in the tape recorders used to record group conversations became less bothersome; eventually, over the course of the year, these minor grievances became sources of amusement and banter. Even the consistently late arrival of one of the cohort members became a source of in-group humor. For discussions and interactions, we divided the cohort into small groups gathered around circular tables. The groups commenced the two-day sessions together at breakfast and shared midmorning and midafternoon breaks as well as lunch and dinner. Both of the two days ended at approximately 3:30 P.M., with the groups completing reflections and entering comments on exit cards. On the first day of each of the two-day meetings, a group activity and dinner away from the hotel were provided. Most cohort members chose to participate in these activities, and this contributed to coalescing and bonding the group quickly. By year's end they had become close as colleagues and friends.

Session 1

The first session of Cohort I began with a message of introduction and welcome from the superintendent of schools for the Alpine School District. Although speaking in his role as chair of the partnership governing board, he drew heavily from his own experience as a member of the IEI's Cohort II. He encouraged the group to listen a lot, "learn much, think much, and forget about 'down the road' and enjoy this great experience as we pursue this agenda of simultaneous renewal."[3] The partnership site director and dean of the School of Education then described the partnership and its characteristics, along with the uniqueness of this associates group. The presence of the governing board chair as well as the dean of the School of Education to greet and talk with the new cohort members helped validate the program and encourage participation in it.

Each participant was given a journal for taking notes, recording ideas from conversations, and writing personal reflections on the readings. Time was allotted each morning and afternoon for participants to write in their journals as they reflected on their group experience and individual conversations. Sometimes the group members were asked to share their journal thoughts with the larger group or with a table partner, but most often the journal represented the private musings and thoughts of the individual on the chosen agenda topic.

The first discussions of the moral dimensions of teaching centered on the article, "Dialogical Pedagogy in Teacher Education: Toward an Education for Democracy."[4] This piece was suggested by the Montclair State University group, after they had used it in their first leadership program held earlier in the summer. Permission to copy and distribute the article was purchased for a small fee.

From the outset, we planned for sessions to engage the learners in exploring the topics. We were committed to the goal of creating active learners. Except for occasional formal instruction, multiple methods of presenting and expanding information were used to build meaning from interaction among group members: role playing, small-group activities, panels, picture making, chart work, and open space, to name a few. Desiring to create a strong feeling of esprit de corps within the group as soon as possible, we used small-group discussions early and often, usually for each session and with differing configurations of members. Such strategies seemed to work. Exit card comments, which we used to improve and refine the experience, often noted that participants were pleased with the opportunity to interact with so many other people.

Our efforts at capturing discussions by audio recordings were not entirely successful. The technology was bothersome to the groups, and the frustrations we experienced in trying to make the recording process comfortable led us to abandon the recordings by the end of the first session. We recognized the importance of having a record of our conversations and are still seeking adequate means for accomplishing this.

Session 2

The second main session of our program centered on the topic of access to knowledge. We assigned various individuals chapters from John Goodlad and Pamela Keating's edited book, *Access to Knowledge*, and had each person read Alex Kotlowitz's *There Are No Children Here*.[5] In addition, several chapters from *The Moral Dimensions of Teaching* were assigned.[6] The chapters from *Access to Knowledge* generated some energetic and even heated conversation. One person, a university professor, was adamant in advocating the importance of addressing gender issues. Participants insisted that conversations around the chapters from *Access to Knowledge* be extended into the afternoon. *The Moral Dimensions of Teaching* gave a broader perspective to issues we were discussing. Reading *There Are No Children Here* captured the participants' hearts and enlarged their understandings in ways that no pedagogical text could do. In evaluations at the end of the year, this book, along with *The Moral Dimensions of Teaching*, was most often mentioned as a "must-read" text.

In this session the cohort members used the assigned readings to inform their conversations much more than they had in their first meeting. The discussions were greatly enriched by the referencing of study materials. Interest in the topics was high.

During this session the group responded well to the role play about Zenith Middle School, drawn from the resource package provided by IEI staff. Teachers at Zenith sought to extend their popular humanities program for gifted students to all entering seventh graders by providing educational enrichment activities and special instructional units of study. Parents of students labeled as "gifted" wanted the program to be limited to a select number of seventh graders. Participants in the role play took the positions of teachers, parents, administrators, and students. As they enjoyed this creative experience, this group of professional educators became wholeheartedly engaged in serious deliberations about ideas and issues central to their roles in the schools and the university. One individual who had been a school administrator said: "Part of the value of our spending time learning to critique and question things is that often—as teachers and administrators who have come up through the system—it has not been appropriate to do these things. We have never learned to do things constructively. It is so good to have a forum like this to question and critique."[7]

With each new high point reached in a session, we were curious to see whether such a level could be sustained or exceeded in future meetings. And we found that with each meeting the members of the group were more eager and willing to engage in well-informed, stimulating exchanges of ideas on the various moral dimensions of teaching.

Session 3

The third major session focused on the moral imperative to provide a nurturing pedagogy for students in P–12 schools as well as in colleges and universities. Readings were assigned from *The Moral Dimensions of Teaching*, along with Donna Kerr's fine essay, *Beyond Education: In Search of Nurture.*[8] At this point in our year together, a few associates still lacked understanding of the Agenda for Education in a Democracy and were reticent in their acceptance of it.

But this session captured these individuals. One of the men said, "Isn't this, after all, what school is about? Caring for and nurturing children and each other?"⁹ Although he may have been stating the obvious, it was nevertheless true that the readings and conversations that preceded his comment were a necessary prerequisite to his voicing the observation. The more the group members connected their own experiences to the moral dimensions, the closer together the members grew. The effect was powerful.

One of the associates who was well trained and experienced in action research focused on the difference between what she called "little r" and "big R" research. "Little r," she explained, referred to inquiry-based, experiential, or observational action research; "big R," by contrast, was more theoretical, more regimented, and more typical of the university setting. She created excitement among the group, particularly those in the school sites for whom "little r" research seemed a kind of inquiry that they could do in their own schools and readily use in their teaching. How acceptable and useful this type of research would be for those at the university who are seeking tenure or promotion is a question that was raised, but not satisfactorily answered, in ensuing conversations.

Session 4

The fourth two-day retreat raised the topic of stewardship of the schools in educative communities. Readings for this session included Michael Fullan's *Change Forces*, Robert Putnam's *Making Democracy Work*, and several chapters from John Goodlad's *Educational Renewal*.¹⁰ All participants enjoyed *Change Forces*, but several questioned why *Making Democracy Work* was selected for inclusion in the readings. But after our conversation about social capital, reciprocity, building civic community, and "lessons learned," many expressed appreciation for the book and its ideas.

Group activities and dinners were included as part of the scheduled events on the first evening of the two-day sessions. These experiences added to program costs, but were an expense worth incurring.

The cohort members got to know Park City as an interesting community, and these events also helped associates to develop valuable relationships that spanned district and university boundaries.

Prior to the final meeting, the cohort met in April at Brigham Young University and heard the dean of the School of Education present a vision of the Center of Pedagogy, which was by then becoming a centerpiece of conversation among partnership members. The final two-day session in May built on the discussion that had taken place at the April meeting. The associates were asked to synthesize the knowledge and understandings gained through the previous months and to propose agendas for change in their own settings. To facilitate this thinking, the group played the game Making Change for School Improvement. Some were frustrated with this experience, yet the insights they gained assisted them in thinking about how difficult renewal is to initiate and to maintain. Many came to a fuller understanding of the political nature of the change process through this experience.

During a formal evaluation session at this meeting, participants shared their feelings about their experience in the program and turned in completed evaluation forms, which had been sent to them earlier. If the associates program had offered only pleasant associations and stimulating conversation, it would have fallen considerably short of the intended goal. The experience was intended to stir people to think and act differently, to shape their professional conduct after the program ended. To discern whether these goals had been achieved, participants were asked in the evaluation, "What is the single most important thing you have done in your own setting since the first session as a result of participating in this program?" The answers were exciting and rewarding. We learned that Cohort I associates were thinking and acting differently. Not only were they committed to the central agenda of the program, but they were also determined to make a difference in their own professional settings.

Several school-based individuals indicated that they had taken ideas back to faculty colleagues or that they were creating similar time opportunities for conversation with their peers. Participants from district offices were restructuring training for principals and assistants to examine elements of the Agenda for Education in a Democracy covered in the associates program. One participant mentioned that she and her colleagues were planning to approach their superintendent about beginning their own district-level associates program. Faculty members of the College of Education and university arts and sciences departments reported discovering new ways to work with students and seeing the importance of the Agenda for their colleges. Those from the state Office of Education indicated an interest in having their colleagues continue participating in future programs. They also resolved to see that the readings, especially those focusing on enculturation of the young, were used in working with the state curriculum specialists. All agreed that they wanted networking and involvement with each other at future "reunion" meetings.[11] Such commitment to the Agenda and to each other was significant and provided a sound basis for continuing the associates program into succeeding years.

The final activity was a celebration. Each person completing the program was given a plaque etched with the partnership logo, his or her name, "Associates Program, Cohort I," and the year. Each was honored individually with a formal presentation of the plaque and with comments about his or her contribution to the success of the group.

Spreading the Water

In 1996–1997, the academic year following the first associates program, the BYU-PSP expanded its initiative and held two associates groups: one cohort served the total partnership, and another was directed by and for the Alpine School District. The decision to create the district-based cohort resulted from the work of a committed superintendent and three Cohort I associates who were determined to explore the feasibility and desirability of conducting an associates group in their school district. The results of the two associates programs in year 2 of the initiative confirmed the excellent results of the first cohort of associates.

In 1997–1998, faced with the challenge of preparing a large number of teachers and university personnel to participate in a major redesign of BYU's secondary teacher education program, we decided that an effective strategy would be to expand the number of associates cohorts. Thus, in the third year of operation, six cohorts were created: four were district directed, another drew participants from the schools involved in the Arthur Vining Davis Foundations' Secondary Partner School Project started in 1996–1997, and the sixth group was modeled on the previous two cohorts that had been supported through the partnership. One district declined to sponsor its own cohort, not because personnel were uninterested, but because the superintendent was relatively new to both the job and his association with the BYU-PSP, and he wanted to become better grounded in the Agenda and the nature of the postulates before incorporating an associates program into his overall plans for the district.

All of the experiences with the various associates programs have been outstanding. Leaders in the BYU-PSP are committed to continuing their efforts to support associates programs within the partnership. To use the irrigation analogy, they are committed to keeping the water in the rows.

What We Have Learned and Are Learning

Our experiences during the first three years of the associates programs were significant for the BYU-PSP. We learned a great deal concerning the value of such programs in building a foundation for collaborative renewal of schooling and teacher education; we also learned many strategies for the effective operation or conduct of such a program. Prominent among these insights are several observations.

First, professional development experiences, especially those that offer educators time to read, write, and think with each other, are of great value in promoting personal growth and willingness to change. Given time, support, and information, educators can change both their philosophy and their practice. Those who have engaged in this form of learning in an associates cohort sense a responsibility to share the ideas they have examined and to engage in activities that are designed to help others—students or colleagues—benefit from these ideas.

Second, the content of an associates program is a critical element in the success of the undertaking. As cohorts coalesce, they gain power, and they may attempt to take over decisions concerning what they study and how they study it. The curriculum for the program, as developed and refined by the IEI, has great value. The experience of the leaders and facilitators of the BYU-PSP associates groups underscores the importance of adhering closely to the established topics and readings recommended in the IEI Leadership Program. Often cohort members want to use the forum of an associates program as an arena for discussion of topics that they personally consider important. Persistence in pursuing the established curriculum will lead eventually to agreement among cohort members as to the power and consequence of the moral dimensions of teaching that John Goodlad and colleagues have articulated.

A third variable vital to the success of an associates program is the skills and commitment of the facilitators or leaders who guide the learning experience. The leaders must be well grounded in the central themes of the program and the content of the related readings. They must also be adept at helping groups explore ideas and bond in their relationships in order for the purposes of the program to be met. As the BYU-PSP program expanded in three years from one to six groups, competent group leadership was a prominent concern. The facilitators and leaders met regularly throughout each year to discuss effective functioning of their cohorts and to share accounts of successful experiences.

The variables of released time, content, and leadership are critical considerations, but the details of practical operation are important as well. The organization and conduct of the program influence the attitudes and behavior of the participants and thus deserve attention. It is extremely important, for example, that potential participants be identified early, well in advance of the time when the first session will begin. When fifteen days are to be committed over a year-long period, advance notice of at least six months is not too much. For university professors who may be assigned a teaching load half a year ahead, this advance notice is especially important. Also, the identification of participants requires careful consideration. Over our first three years of operation, all participants in the nine cohorts were nominated by leaders. Using the nominations of superintendents and deans helped to ensure the support of the leaders and the selection of participants who were in strategic positions in schools and the university. However, there is also great value in inviting individuals who seek out the program and choose to participate. Whatever selection process is used, written information on the purpose and nature of the program must be provided. An oral invitation to participate is generally unsatisfactory in providing answers to the invariable question, "Just what is the associates program?"

Capable, positive leadership; a proven curriculum; a secure, adequate budget; and sufficient time in a pleasant setting all contribute to an experience that will be highly rewarding. It meant a great deal to cohort members, especially school-based colleagues, to be well treated. One associate commented, "We've never been treated so well as educators. You made us feel that we were professionals." The attractive setting, the coverage of all expenses, the provision of many books for their professional libraries, and the encouragement by their leaders to participate made them feel valued and important as partnership members.

The Future

Although it is relatively easy to be confident about the value of the professional development for school and university personnel in an extended associates program, such assurance should not convey a message that the ultimate has been achieved. A number of critically important issues remain if the investment of time and money is to be justified by the benefits of the program. It is important that the value of the program be conveyed so that a greater number of discipline specialists from the arts and sciences departments of the university will participate, recognizing that this activity is an important aspect of their role. Persistence, persuasion, and patience are vital in conveying this positive perception.

Helping participants in associates programs experience inquiry as a significant dimension of their learning and professional growth is another major concern. Our efforts in this area have not been as successful as we desire. We are uncertain whether to incorporate more aspects of inquiry into the themes of the four main sessions of the program. Is a project assignment an effective way to try to build a new attitude? If so, are more days required? Should annual reunion sessions emphasize ongoing inquiry?

It is obvious that the associates program does not end when the last session of the fifteen-day experience concludes. Through sharing this experience, participants have formed personal connections that will continue to enrich their personal and professional lives. In addition, participants periodically need to reconnect and recommit to the Agenda for Education in a Democracy and to share ideas and experiences relating to their own pursuit of the Agenda. Because it is relatively easy for the isolation of separate workplaces to cause a weakening of interest and a dissipation of energy and commitment, we continue to search for ways to extend the impact of the associates program through a variety of activities, including at least one meeting annually. The challenge of sharing experiences and ideas with future and past associates groups, both within the

BYU-PSP and possibly across other NNER settings, is an important consideration for the future. We need further discussions and exchanges to enable us to learn more from one another.

The greatest challenge for the future can be related again to the irrigation image. By providing a reasonably effective associates program at the level of an NNER setting, we have effectively channeled the water into the rows. What remains to be seen is whether it will continue to surge onward, providing vital nutrients and moisture to the plants all along the rows—that is, to the students in teacher education and in public schools. Sustained investigation is needed to determine how to overcome obstacles that may impede the flow and how to enrich the stream through our associates program to help ensure the desired growth.

Notes

1. Wilma F. Smith and Donna Hughes, *Leadership Program Resource Package* (Seattle: Institute for Educational Inquiry, 1995).

2. Susan E. Mundry and Leslie F. Hergert (eds.), *Making Change for School Improvement* (Andover, Mass.: NETWORK, 1988).

3. Proceedings of September 1995 Associates session. Tape recording held in Center for the Improvement of Teacher Education and Schooling (CITES) Office, Brigham Young University, Provo, Utah.

4. Juan-Miguel Fernández-Balboa and James P. Marshall, "Dialogical Pedagogy in Teacher Education: Toward an Education for Democracy," *Journal of Teacher Education* 45 (May–June 1994): 172–182.

5. John I. Goodlad and Pamela Keating (eds.), *Access to Knowledge: The Continuing Agenda for Our Nation's Schools*, rev. ed. (New York: College Entrance Examination Board, 1994); Alex Kotlowitz, *There Are No Children Here: The Story of Two Boys Growing Up in the Other America* (New York: Doubleday, 1991).

6. John I. Goodlad, Roger Soder, and Kenneth A. Sirotnik (eds.), *The Moral Dimensions of Teaching* (San Francisco: Jossey-Bass, 1990).

7. Proceedings of November 1995 Associates session. Tape recording held in CITES Office, Brigham Young University, Provo, Utah.

8. Donna H. Kerr, *Beyond Education: In Search of Nurture*, Work in Progress Series no. 2 (Seattle: Institute for Educational Inquiry, 1993).

9. Proceedings of January 1996 Associates session. Tape recording held in CITES Office, Brigham Young University, Provo, Utah.

10. Michael Fullan, *Change Forces: Probing the Depths of Educational Reform* (Bristol, Pa.: Falmer Press, 1993); Robert D. Putnam, *Making Democracy Work: Civic Traditions in Modern Italy* (Princeton, N.J.: Princeton University Press, 1993); and John I. Goodlad, *Educational Renewal: Better Teachers, Better Schools* (San Francisco: Jossey-Bass, 1994).

11. End-of-program evaluations, May 1996.

Part IV

Lessons in Leadership Development

14

What Changed over Time and Why

Wilma F. Smith

E arly in the design phase of the Institute for Educational Inquiry's (IEI) Leadership Program, we knew that changes would occur as we learned from the Associates, found new readings that added value to our conversations, or discovered participants' interests and needs. However, none of us imagined the extent to which the program would actually change or the degree to which the Leadership Associates would cause the program leaders (senior associates of the Institute) to change.

This chapter is dedicated to those who take on the challenges of organizing and conducting their own leadership programs. By highlighting some of the changes we made in the Leadership Program and sharing the lessons we learned, local facilitators of such programs will almost certainly gain useful insights. They will sense, in particular, the importance of routinely gathering feedback and evaluative data from the participants. By acting on this information, facilitators can make desired adjustments to their programs. The changes we made in the IEI Leadership Program pertained to its content, its pedagogy, its emphasis on connections between theory and practice, and our ongoing communication with the Associates. But before we take a closer look at the changes in the program and in ourselves, I would like to emphasize the unique challenges that present themselves to those who choose to organize local leadership programs for their colleagues.

Some Challenges of Teaching and Learning with Colleagues

Anyone who has worked with colleagues to construct professional development experiences can relate to the difficulty of structuring those experiences in such a way that everyone is learning together. This is not the familiar teacher-student relationship of the school or university, nor is it the university professor advising the doctoral candidate or the principal supervising the teacher. The relationship is not quite like the staff developer planning workshops for P–12 educators, nor is it like a teaching team, joint presentation, or grant-writing task force. The relationship of participants and facilitators in a local leadership program features colleagues from different educational cultures immersing themselves in a common core of readings, engaging in ongoing conversations, and contributing to one another's learning about the moral dimensions of teaching in a social and political democracy. It is an increasingly nurturing and supportive relationship among equal partners who are creating new structures, new ways of collaborating, and a new emphasis on the public purpose of education.

Planning a viable leadership program for colleagues is a challenging opportunity. If the program is to succeed, facilitators must seek ongoing feedback from participants in order to shape the program to their learning styles and needs. For the IEI program we adopted Kenneth Sirotnik's framework for critical inquiry for school renewal as our guide for gathering frequent, targeted input from the Associates.[1] We analyzed that information, decided where program adjustments could be made, and carried out the necessary revisions in the program.

Some aspects of our Leadership Program were nonnegotiable: the curriculum and its organizing elements, presenters and speakers, organization and facilitation of the program, cost-sharing elements of the program, and the overall schedule for the sessions. For example, the curriculum, focusing on the mission for teaching in a democracy, assumed that the participants were committed to the moral dimensions of teaching as well as to the nineteen postulates. The themes of the sessions, explained in Chapter Two, were based on the four-part mission of teaching in a democracy: enculturating the young in a democracy, ensuring equal access to knowledge for all students, engaging in a nurturing pedagogy, and serving as stewards of the schools. These curricular organizing elements did not change over the course of the program. To carry out the themes of the curriculum, we brought in presenters and speakers who could offer unique perspectives and experiences. Senior fellows were scheduled to share their work at specified sessions during the year. The facilitators planned and conducted the sessions and took responsibility for arranging all of the logistics. Expenses of the Leadership Program were partially offset by grants, with the remainder covered by the participants' settings. Dates for the four sessions were advertised at the same time the nominations were sought for the program, and the Associates were expected to make a commitment to attend all of the sessions.

Given these nonnegotiables, however, we were prepared to be quite flexible in adjusting other parts of the program to the participants' needs. During each cohort's first session, we asked for participant feedback several times every day and at the conclusion of the session. At the close of each day, we debriefed the activities, asking such questions as, "What did you learn or reaffirm during this day?" "What activities or teaching strategies were helpful to your learning?" "What did not go well?" "What changes would you like to see in tomorrow's schedule?"

We asked them to reflect, write, and discuss their reactions to the program. We also reflected, responded, and listened to their ideas and shared our own impressions of how things were going. At the end of the fifth day of each session, we asked participants to complete a written evaluation, compiled and summarized their comments, and then made changes in the next session, wherever possible and desirable, to accommodate suggestions that were made by the Associates.

The first cohort had much to say to us about their experiences. For example, from the beginning of the nominating process, we had called the participants "fellows." Our thought was that this designation would carry prestige and recognition, as do fellowship programs in academe and learned societies. However, on the second day of the first session, the members of Cohort I protested this designation. Several women stated that they simply did not feel comfortable with the label because it had too many negative connotations for them. Dictionary definitions did not enlighten us as we listened to the participants' points of view, and so we devoted a special problem-solving session to the topic. During a healthy debate, most of the participants spoke on the issue. At the conclusion of that session, the "fellows" had negotiated a new title. They would henceforth be called "Leadership Associates."

We also heard clearly that we had tried to cover too much ground in too little time. (This complaint was similar to Theodore Sizer's conclusion following his analysis of the high school curriculum in *Horace's School* that "less is more" when referring to content coverage.)[2] Not only did we cram too much content into the days, but the schedule was also too intense. Breaks were short and days were long. The intensity of the conversations and complexity of the issues seemed to demand more time for thoughtful reflection and informal conversations. People needed time to process what they had encountered in order to make sense of it and relate it to their own lives. We assigned too many readings to discuss adequately, the participants told us. They wanted to deal with fewer texts in more depth.

Cohort I Associates told us that we kept them in the larger group too often and for too long at a time. They wanted more small-group arrangements, which seemed to encourage a much higher level of participation and to engage quieter people in the conversations.

We continued with these frequent debriefing and formative evaluations throughout the six cohorts of the Leadership Program. We grew better at asking questions and responding to the answers, even when those answers were contrary to what we had wanted to hear. We adapted, flexed, adjusted, and improved the program for each session and for each cohort. Sometimes we agonized over the feedback when we felt that the Associates had missed the point. Sometimes the readings did not accomplish our hoped-for purposes. We had to admit to ourselves that our presentations and explanations were not always as scintillating or clear as we thought they were. We all learned.

Changes in the Leadership Program

The Leadership Program evolved, developed, and embraced new perspectives and strategies for learning. As the Associates changed and enlarged their understanding of the daunting tasks of simultaneous renewal, the program changed to meet them where they stood. Major changes in content, pedagogy, connections between theory and practice, and communication reflected the lessons we learned together as organizers, presenters, and participants.

Changes in Content

Although the curricular themes remained constant throughout the program, we found it to be important to continually scrutinize the readings that formed the basis for many of our conversations about simultaneous renewal. In Chapter Two, I highlighted some of these changes, and in Chapter Three, Roger Soder discussed changes in the readings on the theme of enculturating the young into a democratic society. New books were published that advanced our thinking. For example, Neil Postman's 1995 book, *The End of Education*, together with Roger Soder's 1996 edited volume, *Democracy, Education, and the Schools*, spoke directly to the theme of enculturating the young into a democracy.[3] Jonathan Kozol's *Amazing Grace*, published in

1995, gave a current emphasis to the challenges of providing equal access to education for children of the ghetto.[4] In 1997, *Kids and School Reform*, featuring high school students' perspectives of school renewal efforts, added new dimensions to our readings.[5] Recent publications by John Goodlad and his associates—*In Praise of Education* and *The Public Purpose of Education and Schooling*—synthesized many elements of simultaneous renewal in today's democracy.[6] Russell Osguthorpe and his colleagues from the Brigham Young University–Public School Partnership of the NNER published a timely book about partner schools, giving examples from NNER settings.[7]

At times we found it necessary to insert new content or readings when members of a cohort indicated a need or a high level of interest. For example, the diverse experiences and learning styles of the Associates sometimes resulted in conversations that were monopolized by some voices. We read and discussed texts such as Deborah Tannen's *You Just Don't Understand: Women and Men in Conversation* and Thomas Kochman's *Black and White Styles in Conflict*, after which we analyzed our own communication patterns in cohort conversations to strengthen and improve the ways we chose to talk with and listen to one another.[8]

Another need that we recognized during the first cohort was for information and conversations on the topic of school and organizational change. We brought in presenters from the organizational development field and asked Institute senior associates to develop special sessions on the topic of change in educational systems. Associates read *The Good Society* by Robert Bellah and colleagues, *The Empowered Manager* by Peter Block, and *Images of Organizations* by Gareth Morgan.[9] John Goodlad focused special attention on linear versus ecological change models,[10] and Kenneth Sirotnik spoke about the school as the center of change.[11] Roger Soder developed a presentation and activity on the art and science of persuasion, which gave Associates an opportunity to construct rational arguments to persuade others in their settings to join them in renewal efforts.[12] From the initiation of this persuasion activity with Cohort 1, we kept revising it for each succeeding cohort to make it less a contrived speech to some unknown audience and more an authentic rehearsal for engaging colleagues back home in some aspect of the renewal work. We also created role plays, simulations, and full scenarios in which the Associates had to take on roles of change agents.

Changes in Pedagogy

The four of us who met regularly with the Associates worked constantly to strengthen the art and the science of our teaching. We were striving to model the conditions of Postulate Ten: "Programs for the education of educators must be characterized in all respects by the conditions for learning that future teachers are to establish in their own schools and classrooms."[13] We asked ourselves questions like the ones John Goodlad posed in his chapter, "Unpacking the Postulates," in *Educational Renewal*.[14] For example, were we demonstrating excellence in teaching through the examples we brought to the conversation? Was the content of our presentations relevant to the lives of the Associates and their current work in the settings? Did we truly engage them in conversation with us and with one another? Were we managing the physical environment in such a way that it enhanced their work in small and large groups? Did we know if the Associates were connecting the themes of the curriculum with their work in their settings? Were we willing to retrace our steps when things did not go as well as they should have? Were we willing to bend and change in order to accommodate the varied learning styles and experiences of the Associates?

We critiqued each other's presentations and activities and sought to strengthen our own presentations. Our directions for activities and simulations became more targeted and explicit, and we remembered to pause for feedback to see how well the participants understood them. We stopped to monitor the Associates' perceptions and understandings and to clarify meaning. We became better at stopping the conversation for a quick evaluation of how well we were following the norms set forth in the beginning of the program.

When we failed to follow through on these pedagogical matters, the energy lagged, the conversations became one-sided, or the cohort took off on its own tangents. As it is with any other group of learners, it is all too easy to get the conversation off track. Someone must be responsible for bringing it back to the topic at hand. With a group of one's colleagues, this is much more difficult to do than it is with a classroom of students or an inservice workshop for teachers. We assumed the role of gatekeepers of conversations to keep them focused on the topic and balanced in participation. We encouraged the cohorts to take on responsibility for monitoring their own group processes through the use of a process observer who shared information with the group at the end of the designated time segment.

People who are normally active and on their feet much of the day find that long stretches of sitting and conversing are tiring, sometimes exhausting. We learned to manage the schedule more effectively, allowing for thirty-minute breaks and lunch hours of ninety minutes, during which Associates enjoyed informal conversation or exercise. We placed the intense content in the morning and engaged in more active learning events in the afternoon. We noticed that on the third day of each session, the energy level of the cohort dwindled, so we began scheduling visits to schools and simulations on that day. After Cohort II, we left more evenings open as well.

Discussion groupings became more flexible. We moved from the large group of eighteen to dyads, trios, and quartets. We structured small groups so that every Associate had the opportunity to work with every other one. Sometimes we grouped arts and sciences, college of education, or school people together. Most times we sought to diversify each small group to benefit from the expertise and experiences of the Associates. Associates' feedback affirmed the value of using variable sizes in groupings: more voices were heard, conversations were better, and participants developed respect and understanding for one another.

Responsibility for leadership, facilitation, presentation, and debriefing was spread more widely across the members of the cohort.

From the second session of their program onward, the Associates accepted increasing responsibility for the conversations and activities. The program culminated in presentations of and conversations on their inquiry projects during the NNER annual meeting in August.

We changed the fourth session too, bringing together all of the graduates of the Leadership Program and the deans and directors of the NNER settings for an annual meeting. This three-day event took place in the middle of the last session for the outgoing cohort. We began this arrangement with the fourth session of Cohort III and have continued to modify the schedule since then to benefit from the energy, enthusiasm, and growing expertise of the large cadre of graduate Leadership Associates. Of course, we have asked for evaluative feedback from the annual meeting participants so that we can continue to modify this event. The deans, setting directors, and guests participate in the issues conversations, book discussions, and inquiry project reports, all modeled on the ongoing Leadership Program. This annual event has provided a rare opportunity for Associates from all of the cohorts to interact with one another and with other people from the sixteen NNER settings. It has also provided time for the senior associates of the Center for Educational Renewal (CER) and IEI to meet with a cross-section of representatives from the settings to discuss how they are advancing the work of simultaneous renewal.

Changes in Emphases

Informal feedback and summative evaluations from the Leadership Associates emphasized the need to connect the theory driving the Agenda for Education in a Democracy to their everyday practice. "What does this presentation on the human conversation have to do with my middle school students and our three student teachers back home?" "Do you believe that tracking students is immoral?" "How can we move ahead to develop more partner schools?" "How do others get the arts and sciences faculty involved in teacher education?" These and a host of other questions kept our feet firmly on the ground. The meshing of university and school district cultures continues to present rich and challenging problems to solve together. Connecting research with practice continues to be a perplexing conundrum. And connecting our mission with the necessary conditions for implementation demands thoughtful action.[15] We gave increasing attention to these linkages between theory and practice as time went on.

One way we sought to emphasize the linkages was to take the Associates out to visit partner schools, after which they shared their observations and connected them to the theme of the session. We tried harder to nudge the Associates' inquiry projects toward the implementation of the Agenda. We reconfigured the daily schedules so that a presentation or conversation would be followed by discussions about applications to the world of school-university partnerships. We developed and used videotapes, engaged in role plays and simulations, and asked Associates to share examples from their NNER settings. We tried to make sure that all assignments connected to the implementation efforts. We discussed, over and over again, the Agenda for Education in a Democracy: its four-part mission and its necessary conditions. We are still seeking ways in which this twenty-day experience can become vitally connected to the lives of the teachers, principals, superintendents, deans, professors, and students in the thirty-three higher education institutions, more than one hundred school districts, and roughly five hundred partner schools of the NNER.

Changes in Our Communication

Since the inception of the Leadership Program in 1992, we have increased the frequency of our communications with the Associates before their first session and between sessions. Feedback from many participants indicated that they would appreciate some guiding questions to help focus their reading of the texts. In addition, it became obvious to us that the purposes behind our choices of readings or certain activities were not always clear to the Associates. Midway through the year with Cohort II, we began sending detailed notes along with the schedule for the upcoming session. We shared our intent for the conversation or activity and highlighted responsibilities that the individual Associates would take on: leadership of a book discussion, facilitation of a conversation, or helping to debrief the day, to name a few. We suggested some questions about each of the readings, and asked the Associates to prepare for selected activities. When the topic for the next session included the renewal of programs to prepare elementary teachers, for example, we asked the Associates to come prepared to discuss their partnership's elementary education program. When they were given assigned roles in a scenario, we suggested that they meet with someone who holds that role and discuss the scenario from that person's perspective. Finally, we summarized, published, and mailed the evaluations of each session to the Associates so they could see how their colleagues assessed their experiences as well as how we had adjusted the next schedule to accommodate major concerns or to incorporate good suggestions.

During the session itself, we took time to construct meaning together. For example, we discussed the elements of a healthy conversation in the context of our program and then debriefed different conversations in the light of how well we followed those elements. We clarified terminology and demystified acronyms, recognizing that school-based educators did not always relate to NCATE, AACTE, SCDE; nor did professors from the disciplines always know what was meant by IEP, SBM, ESD, or NASSP.[16] We became more confident about helping the group address conflicts as they arose, respecting differences of opinion but always seeking out common ground.

How the Associates Changed the Leaders

Embedded in the context of the changes made in the Leadership Program are a host of clues to indicate that we were changing our behaviors and attitudes at the same time we were making modifications to the program itself. Asking for evaluations and feedback implies that one is willing to scrutinize one's own performance. Four of us have reflected on how the Associates came to change our views of our roles as leaders, facilitators, presenters, advocates, and colleagues. The most notable changes affected the way we came to understand the Associates as adult professional learners, the importance of beginnings and endings to the program, the fear of conflict and independent inquiry, and the complexity of the mission of teaching in a democracy.

Associates as Adult Professional Learners

Adult professional learners bring their own experiences, learning styles, and commitment to the program. They need the opportunity to explore and reflect on the ideas of simultaneous renewal, to construct their own meaning, and to think through the applications to their lives. We learned, and relearned, that we cannot expect people to sit and absorb ideas; they must play with them, talk about them, try them out in scenarios and case studies, challenge them, unpack them, and reassemble them. This processing takes time—more than we are able to allocate. We learned how difficult it is to lead worthwhile and deeply focused conversations that are satisfying to almost every Associate. We also felt frustrated at times that the "reporting out" from small groups left much to be desired; little interaction and questioning occurred among the presenters and the audience. We are still working on methods to capitalize on the quality of conversation in small groups when sharing thoughts with the larger group.

We changed the way we viewed the materials and concepts we were presenting. For example, one of us remarked: "The Associates had a significant impact on the conceptions of knowledge that I brought to my work on this concept. It was their resistance, in that first cohort, that helped me to see how canonical (Western, Enlightenment) my thinking had been up to that time. It was not that they simply changed the form of my presentation, but that they had a major impact on the substance of the material presented."[17]

These kinds of changes came about because we, as program leaders, recognized and valued the knowledge and expertise that the Associates brought to the table. They caused us to examine our own thinking, read more, and reconsider concepts that we thought had been settled in our minds.

We changed our thinking, too, about the need for structuring discussions of books and other texts. Associates differed markedly in their desire for structure or open-endedness in such discussions. Many Associates in one cohort requested questions to guide the discussions, but others rejected such structure as inhibiting. We have yet to find the best balance to meet the differing needs of individuals. For example, during the second session of Cohort VI, several Associates remarked that they wished we had discussed specific texts in greater depth; they felt we had glossed over the material. But others were delighted with the treatment of the readings, stating that they were motivated to probe more deeply into several of the texts on their own. One of the senior associates expressed this thought: "In the end, people are going to make of a text what they will, despite my intervention or because of my intervention, or some combination of what I'm saying and doing and what they're about, before, during, and after the session."

Perhaps our greatest insight about adult professional learners is that they will always be interesting, full of surprises, and challenging. We must be ever alert in observing the Associates' reactions and be ready to modify the activities.

Beginnings and Endings

We learned and reaffirmed the importance of the first welcome, the first conversation, the first session. In the words of one of our senior associates:

> The tone that is set during the first response to the first Associate's question will govern the remainder of the session unless there is significant intervention. It is clear

that the group is cautious at first, and equally clear that by the end of the morning session most members feel that they will be treated with respect and consideration. They know, too, something of the level of discourse that will be encouraged—thoughtful discourse and the distinctions between opinions and authorized opinion—and they know that they will be expected to participate.

First, and most important, is the matter of ethos. Our respect and concern for [the Associates] as individuals and as a group stem from the center of our character, our ethos. Claims of respect and consideration ring hollow when there is no core.

Second is the matter of process. Since my initial participation in the program, I have watched opening sessions of many groups. Every one has started with, "Let's go around the table and introduce ourselves," in one form or another. I've come to realize the limitations of this approach. (However, there may be cultural contexts in which the "go around the table" approach is precisely the right thing to do.) Even with that caveat, and assuming my own culture, the Oakeshott conversation [described in detail in Chapter Three] makes greater and greater sense to me as a way of encouraging people to talk, a way of quietly showing expectations and strategies.

Endings are important, too. Closure of each day, of each session, looks back at what has been said and done with a critical and appreciative view and then looks ahead at the session to come and the work to be done to continue the connections between our times together and the work at home. Endings should celebrate the worth of the participants and the dedicated work of renewal in which they are engaged. Endings should leave everyone anxious to apply what they have learned and to look ahead to the next time they meet. We have changed in the depth of appreciation that we hold for strong beginnings and endings to the sessions of the program.

Fear of Conflict and Independent Inquiry

During one of the sessions with Cohort II, two senior associates got into an argument, the kind of perfectly normal argument that respected colleagues engage in from time to time. Some Associates seemed quite upset. Others seemed to be embarrassed by unseemly behavior. Still others backed away, looking at nothing, the way people do in a group when they want to carry out an elaborate pretense that nothing has happened. We have continued to notice this reticence among Associates to engage in disagreements with one another or with senior associates. As one of our program leaders put it,

> I had expected that the desire to avoid conflict would decrease as the cohort members got to know each other and trust each other. My own observations, to my surprise, suggest that conflict avoidance behavior actually increases over the four sessions. Perhaps they argue in private with each other, but they don't as a group. Perhaps people get into comfortable roles. Perhaps group members feel that their group is starting to click as a group and they don't want to stop good group work. Or perhaps I am seeing groupthink and tyranny of the majority. What I'm seeing in the group is a microcosm of a democratic civil society—a society that claims to hear diverse points of view but in fact reinforces conformity. We don't really have useful ways to play off each other in efforts to come to more creative solutions. We don't do very well in dealing with the oddballs, the weird, the outré, the wacky, the outrageous, the truly excellent.

We have not solved this problem and have learned that we must continue to work on it. In a democracy, civil discourse is, after all, the stuff of which society is made.

Along with the fear of conflict, we noted that many Associates seemed to fear the inquiry process or to have little idea how to go

about pursuing sustained, independent inquiry. One senior associate said,

> At the same time I recognize that most of the members
> of the cohort are people with terminal degrees, I continue
> to be fascinated by the fear that some of them have about
> independent inquiry and the lack of a sense of how to
> proceed. I am surprised at the continuing difficulty I have
> in getting them to interact in constructive ways with
> other NNER settings to develop their inquiry projects.
> This frustrates me and makes me wonder [whether] lack
> of confidence or interest or understanding (or maybe just
> time) creates this condition.

We have learned that we need to emphasize more strongly the
value of the inquiry projects—the value not only to the Associates
themselves but also to their sites, their settings, and the NNER. We
have made several different attempts to clarify the project itself and
make opportunities for Associates to help one another in defining
inquiry topics, conducting research, communicating across settings,
and planning for the presentations of their projects. We are still
learning about ways to make the Associates' inquiry projects more
satisfying and worthwhile to them and to the other NNER settings.

Complexity of the Mission

The work of simultaneous renewal can be complex and even daunting. Concerning the four-part mission of teaching, the two components that seem to be the least well understood are "engaging in a
nurturing pedagogy" and "serving as stewards of the schools." One
of the senior associates mused: "Perhaps we still have widely different notions about what school stewardship is. The idea of nurturance still dominates the importance of becoming able to master a
number of different pedagogical techniques, and the number of people who are really convinced that all children can learn meaning-

ful things continues to be limited. This is not to say that the themes
are wrong—just that we are still seeking ways of gaining deep and
common understanding of them."

Relationships, Relationships, Relationships

During a conversation with Cohort IV, James Comer, director of the
School Development Program and professor of psychiatry at the
Yale Child Study Center, spoke about the critical importance of
human connections to nurture the development of children. In a
twelve-year cooperative journey toward school improvement, the
interrelationships among children, parents, teachers, and the Yale
multidisciplinary team proved to be all important in bringing the
home and school together. "In the real estate business," Comer
pointed out, "success is tied to location, location, location. In the
work of school improvement, success is tied to relationships, relationships, relationships."[18]

In John Goodlad's Study of Schooling, reported in A Place Called
School, the levels of satisfaction expressed by those connected with a
school were indicative of the quality of the relationships between
the students and the teachers.[19] We have sought, throughout the life
of the Leadership Program, to develop high-quality relationships that
treasure each Associate and value the critically important work that
he or she is doing to renew schooling and teacher education. Over
the life of the program, these relationships continue to deepen and
expand. The changes we see in the relationships of the Associates
with one another and with us are, we believe, a strong indication
that the Leadership Program has moved all of us forward in our
understanding of and appreciation for the daunting work of simultaneous renewal.

In Chapter Two, I related what our thinking had been when we
designed the Institute for Educational Inquiry's Leadership Program:
"We believed that constructing a program for leaders of simultaneous renewal efforts should extend our own learning as well as the

learning of participants. Further, we wanted this program to make a significant difference in the hearts and lives of the participants from the settings. We did not want the experience to be just one more conference, seminar, inservice session, or faculty-development event."

Given the feedback from the Associates from six cohorts, it would seem that we have achieved the goals of extending our own learning as well as making a difference in the hearts and lives of the Associates. Chapter Fifteen presents an evaluation of the Leadership Program from the perspectives of the Associates and NNER setting directors who supported their participation and acknowledged their leadership roles in the partnership.

Notes

1. Kenneth A. Sirotnik, "Evaluation in the Ecology of Schooling: The Process of School Renewal," in John I. Goodlad (ed.), *The Ecology of School Renewal: Eighty-sixth Yearbook of the National Society for the Study of Education*, part I (Chicago: National Society for the Study of Education, 1987), pp. 41–42. Critical inquiry is described as a dialectic around sets of questions such as: "What goes on in the name of X? How did it come to be that way? Whose interests are (and are not) being served by the way things are? What information and knowledge do we have—or need to get—that bear upon the issues? Is this the way we want it? What are we going to *do* about all this?"

2. Theodore R. Sizer, *Horace's School: Redesigning the American High School* (Boston: Houghton Mifflin, 1992). See the nine common principles of the Coalition of Essential Schools, pp. 207–209.

3. Neil Postman, *The End of Education: Redefining the Value of School* (New York: Random House, 1995); Roger Soder (ed.), *Democracy, Education, and the Schools* (San Francisco: Jossey-Bass, 1996).

4. Jonathan Kozol, *Amazing Grace: The Lives of Children and the Conscience of a Nation* (New York: Crown, 1995).

5. Patricia A. Wasley, Robert L. Hampel, and Richard W. Clark, *Kids and School Reform* (San Francisco: Jossey-Bass, 1997).

6. John I. Goodlad, *In Praise of Education* (New York: Teachers College Press, 1997); and John I. Goodlad and Timothy J. McMannon (eds.), *The Public Purpose of Education and Schooling* (San Francisco: Jossey-Bass, 1997).

7. Russell T. Osguthorpe, R. Carl Harris, Melanie Fox Harris, and Sharon Black (eds.), *Partner Schools: Centers for Educational Renewal* (San Francisco: Jossey-Bass, 1995).

8. Deborah Tannen, *You Just Don't Understand: Women and Men in Conversation* (New York: Ballantine Books, 1990); and Thomas Kochman, *Black and White Styles in Conflict* (Chicago: University of Chicago Press, 1981).

9. Robert N. Bellah, Richard Madsen, William M. Sullivan, Ann Swidler, and Steven M. Tipton, *The Good Society* (New York: Random House, 1991); Peter Block, *The Empowered Manager: Positive Political Skills at Work* (San Francisco: Jossey-Bass, 1987); and Gareth Morgan, *Images of Organizations* (Thousand Oaks, Calif.: Sage, 1986).

10. For a review of these models see Goodlad, *In Praise of Education*, pp. 103–107.

11. Associates read and discussed Kenneth A. Sirotnik's, "The School as the Center of Change," in Thomas J. Sergiovanni and John H. Moore (eds.), *Schooling for Tomorrow: Directing Reforms to Issues That Count* (Boston: Allyn & Bacon, 1989), pp. 89–113.

12. Soder brought in a veritable mountain of books to illustrate different types of persuasion and asked the Associates to read two articles: George Orwell, "Politics and the English Language," in Sonia Orwell and Ian Angus (eds.), *The Collected Essays, Journalism and Letters of George Orwell*, vol. 4: *In Front of Your Nose, 1945–1950* (New York: Harcourt, Brace & World, 1968), pp. 127–140; and James Boyd White, "Constituting a Culture of Argument," in *When Words Lose Their Meaning* (Chicago: University of Chicago Press, 1984), pp. 231–240.

13. John I. Goodlad, *Educational Renewal: Better Teachers, Better Schools* (San Francisco: Jossey-Bass, 1994), pp. 84–85.

14. Goodlad, *Educational Renewal*, pp. 67–95.

15. Michael Fullan identifies the critical importance of linking moral purpose with change agentry in *Change Forces: Probing the Depths of Educational Reform* (Bristol, Pa.: Falmer Press, 1993). See especially pp. 8–18.

16. NCATE: National Council for Accreditation of Teacher Education; AACTE: American Association of Colleges for Teacher Education; SCDE: school, college, or department of education; IEP: Individual Education Program; SBM: Site-Based Management; ESD: Educational Service District; NASSP: National Association of Secondary School Principals.

17. Staff comments have been excerpted from an e-mail conversation on the topic of "How the Leadership Program Changed Us," October 1997.

18. James P. Comer is a senior fellow of the Institute for Educational Inquiry. He made these remarks during a presentation to the Leadership Associates in Cohort IV, March 24, 1996, in Seattle, Washington. A videotape of this presentation, *School Power: A Conversation with James Comer*, is available through the Institute for Educational Inquiry.

19. See the chapter entitled "The Same But Different," in John I. Goodlad, *A Place Called School: Prospects for the Future* (New York: McGraw-Hill, 1984), pp. 246–270.

15

The Impact of the Leadership Program

Wilma F. Smith

The mission of the Institute for Educational Inquiry's Leadership Program—"to empower a cadre of leaders deeply committed to the Agenda who will work to carry out the vision of renewing simultaneously America's schools and the education of educators" (see Chapter Two)—was to be fulfilled through the accomplishment of five major objectives. Participants would

- Develop a deeper understanding of the moral dimensions of teaching in a democracy

- Collaborate with P–12 educators, education professors, and arts and sciences professors toward the simultaneous renewal of schools and the education of educators

- Become effective agents of change in their institutions and settings

- Conduct inquiry into the nature of simultaneous renewal in the National Network for Educational Renewal (NNER)

- Contribute to the work of simultaneous renewal by serving as presenters, advisers, facilitators, and friendly critics to the sixteen settings of the NNER

During the sixth year of the Leadership Program, we set out to assess its effectiveness in fulfilling these five objectives. To do this, we relied on three sets of data: summative evaluations by the Associates themselves at the conclusion of their year in the program, individual interviews with each of the NNER setting directors, and Associates' annual reports of their accomplishments and specific activities to promote simultaneous renewal within their own settings and across the NNER.

Participants will develop a deeper understanding of the moral dimensions of teaching in a democracy.

Most Leadership Associates believed that they had personally fulfilled this objective.[1] One graduate of the program said,

> The Leadership Program has given me a greater vision of what can and should be done in American education, based on the moral dimensions of education. It has also given me a greater sense of how I can contribute to accomplishing that educational mission.

Another Associate put it this way:

> My understanding of the issues and challenges of the Agenda for Education in a Democracy is both broader and deeper than before. The grounding of educational renewal on bedrock, moral elements, and the need to consider ecological dynamics was more an intuitive position twelve months ago than it is now.

The acquisition of a deeper understanding of the moral dimensions of teaching seemed to move many individuals beyond their own disciplines or areas of interest to a much broader appreciation of education writ large. Observed one Associate,

> The Leadership Program has demonstrated through well-chosen readings and discussion that the role of educator

transcends the content (discipline) area. As such, teaching takes on a much higher purpose. My inquiry project on the moral dimensions of teaching, for instance, truly reflects a compelling need on my part to fully understand what it means to be a moral steward in schools. I cannot underscore enough the importance and impact that this idea, along with simultaneous renewal, has had on my teaching and my willingness to serve in a leadership capacity at my institution.

Graduate Associates spoke of their heightened awareness of the moral dimensions of teaching. One Associate remarked,

I am, if possible, more urgent about my work. I am more grounded in knowledge about the moral dimensions and believe wholeheartedly in the possibility of equal access to learning for all children.

Another Associate remarked that prior to the Leadership Program he had not thought very deeply about how education should connect to democracy. Now he is anxious to get others to consider the question "How do we, in a nation dedicated to personal freedoms, instill in our nation's teachers the need to promote important ideas about citizenship?" He knows that the work will not be easy but concludes, "We must engage our colleagues 'back home' in this important conversation."

One Associate said that she previously had focused most of her concern on the moral dimensions of providing access to education for all students. However, since participating in the Leadership Program, she stated,

My knowledge is broader and more integrated, and I have some basic understandings of how and why all of the moral dimensions are essential for teaching in a

democracy. I am not as naive. I realize the importance
and urgency of directly addressing the Agenda at all levels of education.

All sixteen of the NNER setting directors remarked that Associates who are active leaders in their settings embrace and act on a
deep understanding of the moral dimensions of teaching in a
democracy, and the directors provided countless examples that rein-
forced this belief.[2] They talked about ways in which the Associates'
commitment to the moral dimensions has permeated their work in
the school-university partnerships. Some of the directors' comments
highlight their unanimous belief that the Leadership Associates
have become well grounded in the moral dimensions.

It's quite apparent to us that the Associates have studied, learned, understood, and embraced the moral dimensions. The moral dimensions were, in fact, a feature
of the Agenda that really facilitated our partnership's
players to more fully commit to a common agenda.

Moral dimensions of teaching has become a theme in
Associates' work, their own scholarship, their own teaching at higher education or K–12 level—and they keep
reminding us of it (in our own decision making as a
school of education).

An overwhelming majority of the faculty continually
brings the moral dimension theme to faculty discussions.
The mental model of the moral dimensions piece is very
evident in the talk and behavior of our Leadership Associates—our dean, a school principal, and a school district administrator.

Although the Associates themselves may have developed a thorough understanding of the moral dimensions of teaching, it is not

always easy for them to share their thinking with colleagues or to make the topic central to their day-to-day work:

> Associates come back entrenched in the philosophy. They begin immediately to impact the sites. Nurturing, stewardship, and access are well received. Democracy is harder. Some of the people say, "Oh, that is social stud-ies," and it is brushed off. One principal has really tried to change her school and give students a voice. "Teach-ing democracy in a multiage, nongraded environment where teachers have a voice is beyond the realm of understanding of many people," she says.

"Although somewhat subtle," commented another setting direc-tor, "the Associates continually raise matters of the moral dimen-sions in their conversations with others."

Participants will collaborate with P–12 educators, education professors, and arts and sciences professors toward the simultaneous renewal of schools and the education of educators.

When we asked the Leadership Associates to give examples of ways in which they are collaborating to advance the Agenda for Edu-cation in a Democracy, their responses naturally varied with the indi-vidual and the setting. In some NNER settings, strong collaborative efforts have been forged between college of education faculty and school faculty, but it has been more difficult to engage the faculty from the various disciplines in the arts and sciences colleges. Tripar-tite collaboration continues to be a major emphasis across the NNER, however, and some settings are splendid examples, many in working centers of pedagogy. A few quotations from Leadership Associates illustrate how they perceive the collaborative efforts to be developing:

> Our school has a long history of working with our partner college. Most recently, we were served by the Industrial

Technology Department in developing a modular technology lab. This lab is being used by our students but also as a training area for new teachers coming into the field. In the summer, the lab is used by practicing teachers to assist them in making curricular changes.

Collaborative opportunities with our college of education and schools has come through partner school meetings and through participation in a regional institute that follows the IEI Leadership Program agenda. Arts and sciences faculty participate in this institute.

Through our center of pedagogy we have developed integrated units of curriculum with the school of education, the colleges of arts and sciences, and the professional development center.

NNER setting directors reported that the Leadership Program has had a marked effect on the Associates' efforts toward tripartite collaboration (among teacher educators, arts and sciences professors, and school faculty). All of the directors said that the program had helped to build overall capacity for such collaboration—for example:

Candidates for the Leadership Program have been carefully selected, based in part on the institution where he or she works and the position he or she holds in that institution. Thus, collaboration has been integrated so fully into the structure and process of our partnership that it constitutes, in a very real sense, part of the very nature of the partnership.

We have dramatically changed the nature and responsibility of our Teacher Education Council. It now includes some P–12 people, in addition to education and arts and sciences faculty.

However, some directors believed that their Associates returned to the setting without a strong, practical capacity for building tripartite collaboration or that they had not developed the communication skills necessary for collaborative relationships. "Conversation is occurring among our education faculty," noted one setting director, "although we have not cracked the arts and sciences faculty." Other directors made similar comments:

> We have a partnership council that brings people together for decision making. The Associates serve on the partnership council as liaisons or faculty. The Associates have not done much as a group until this year, which is the first time they have met together to discuss what they could do as a group. Before that, they acted quite independently.

> We still lack some participants from the arts and sciences, but beyond that, the group of eight Associates has been helpful since the start of the program. The dean and the partnership director have talked about including arts and sciences faculty in simultaneous renewal; now they must start over.

In summary, the Leadership Program has had mixed success in strengthening tripartite collaboration. Where the setting leadership was already strongly moving toward this goal, the Associates have been able to advance collaborative endeavors. Also, where the setting carefully selected its cadre of Associates to represent all three partners—arts and sciences faculty, education faculty, and school faculty—the efforts to extend collaboration were greatly strengthened.

Participants will become effective agents of change in their institutions and settings.

The Cohort I Associates seemed uncertain about their responsibilities and roles as change agents in their settings. Some of them said that they were not sure why they had been nominated by their setting directors. The experience of the Leadership Program itself was judged to be extremely valuable in fostering the Associates' personal growth and learning and their commitment to the ideas of simultaneous renewal. However, not all Associates were clear about the changes desired at their settings, nor were they certain about what their role was expected to be in that change process. As the second cohort engaged in the program, the Associates appeared to have clearer notions about the expectations for their taking on leadership roles in bringing about change at their settings.

The graduates of each cohort had a marked impact on the selection and orientation of succeeding cohorts. As a critical mass of Associates evolved at the setting, teams began conscientiously working toward the advancement of the Agenda. Also, an increasing number of setting directors realized the potential benefits of selecting Associates who were poised to assist with the major changes that were desired in creating exemplary partner schools and education programs.

During Cohort I's year with us, we began to emphasize the Associates' role as change agents in their settings. However, as we realized the importance of providing not only conceptual bases for change but practical skill development for the Leadership Associates, we scheduled many more opportunities for Cohorts II through VI to translate theory into specific practice.

In the words of the graduate Associates, arranged below from Cohort I to Cohort V, they were indeed increasingly conscious of their growing impact as agents for change in their NNER settings.

I have become an unrelenting yet, I hope, kind voice in advocating the postulates and in pushing for school renewal. There are now some things that I would like to see altered in the College of Education. The state office of education is hearing now about my experience.

As a result of my inquiry, we are going to begin changing the admissions process to make it more reflective of the postulates. I have also been instrumental in involving more clinical adjuncts [cooperative teachers] in the planning of staff development efforts. Through reports I have given, committees I have chaired, and a retreat that I co-coordinated, people at the college and in the schools are more aware of what we are trying to accomplish.

I find myself advocating for the postulates in large and small groups. I find that I truly "own" these. They've become mine. I'm a believer. It's made a distinct change in me, and now I am using my influence to assist others to understand and do something about them. In January, I participated in our own associates program with three of our principals and university people. It was an experience, together with my work with Cohort II, that changed me. Out of it we designated a high school and junior high school as partner schools. We'll move from diluting the resources to focusing them. That's a 180 degree reversal for me, and it has come about because of the Institute experiences.

I worked with others at my setting to continue the transition from a very traditional teacher preparation program to a field-based one. Our setting has made tremendous progress. I would not have been able to participate in these conversations and activities had I not been part of this program.

The nature of my inquiry project drove me to initiate what I feel are beneficial activities relative to the purposes and intent of promoting the Institute's Agenda. We have been able to expose about thirty principals to the purposes and value of developing partner school sites, which has resulted in a firm commitment from ten elementary schools, three middle schools, and four high schools to date.

I have increased my understanding of educational change a great deal! For example, although I always knew relationships were important, this is much clearer to me now. I also have increased my repertoire of ways to build professional relationships. Coming to work closely with deans and arts and sciences faculty in my cohort has given me confidence and greater understanding of the views of the people in these roles. I have also improved my ability to articulate the Agenda and to frame arguments persuasively.

As a superintendent, I am in a position of influence in my district. The Leadership Program has given me knowledge and understanding of the Agenda. I believe in it, and our administrators and board know I am committed to moving it forward. As I meet with people, interact with them, and live my life, I am trying to model that the Agenda is important.

Certainly not every Associate felt that she or he had made a significant impact on changing the school or university programs of the setting. Further, Associates' connections to their settings, like those of deans, provosts, superintendents, and principals, evolve and sometimes end. Some Associates have moved on to other campuses or schools, several of which are not affiliated with the NNER. A few who continue to work at the settings have become distanced from the simultaneous renewal efforts. Table 15.1 depicts the number of Associates who are active or not currently active at their settings.

Table 15.1. Current Status of Leadership Associates

NNER Setting	Number of Associates	Active at Setting	Moved from Setting	Not Active
Brigham Young University–Public School Partnership	7	7	0	0
California Polytechnic State University	7	5	2	0
Colorado Partnership for Educational Renewal	10	8	2	0
Connecticut School–University Partnership	3	3	0	0
Hawaii School University Partnership	10	10	0	0
Miami University	10	9	1	0
Montclair State University/ New Jersey Network for Educational Renewal	7	7	0	0
Nebraska Network for Educational Renewal	5	4	1	0
Metropolitan St. Louis Consortium for Educational Renewal	8	6	0	2
South Carolina Network for Educational Renewal	9	5	1	3
Southern Maine Partnership	4	4	0	0
Texas A&M University	5	2	3	0
University of Texas, El Paso	5	5	0	0
University of Washington	7	4	1	2
Wright State University	5	3	2	0
Wyoming School–University Partnership	8	7	0	1
Non-NNER Settings	3	–	–	–

All sixteen of the NNER setting directors attest to the leadership activity of those Associates who continue with the work of simultaneous renewal. The most frequently mentioned change or renewal activity that affects the entire setting is the establishment of leadership programs designed for tripartite members of the simultaneous renewal effort. To date, nine settings have already conducted at least one leadership program, and three other settings are either planning or beginning their first program. In the words of the setting directors, these local leadership programs are generating cohesiveness and enthusiasm while broadening the scope of involvement of people from the schools, the arts and sciences, and the colleges of education:

> Probably the strongest evidence of the Associates' ability to move the Agenda forward—expanding its sphere of influence as well as its applicability to local needs and issues—is the spawning of the Partnership Associates Program. There are currently six groups of Associates, with each group consisting of twenty members from different organizations. IEI Associates serve as facilitators.

> All Associates work on our replication of the Leadership Program. To date we have three cohorts, for a total of sixty people who have had a similar experience at the local level. All Associates have served on the faculty. Half of the participants have been from the schools, one-fourth from the arts and sciences, and the remaining one-fourth have come from education. They have been very careful in their process to select "opinion leaders" in the setting.

In addition to designing and conducting local leadership programs, Associates are making other significant contributions to advancing the Agenda for Education in a Democracy. Setting directors observe,

We have been creating lots of partnerships here, and I have seen our Associates lead the meetings. They are also prime movers in the development of our secondary program, and they continually raise the issue of moral dimensions in these discussions and planning sessions.

Two Associates serve as codirectors of our center of pedagogy. Our program is a work in progress all of the time. We have undergone numerous significant changes in the past, and we are doing a major review of the program right now in order to fine-tune it.

One Associate is the director of teacher education—so he is involved with many P–12 people. We are developing a preeducation program, and that includes contact with P–12 people. Five of our Associates are meeting to develop a plan for partner schools.

Two NNER setting directors pointed out that although several of their former Leadership Associates have left their settings, others who are not Associates have become active in promoting the work of simultaneous renewal. For example, at one setting the director remarked,

Although our first Leadership Associate has left our setting, she sparked an interest in some faculty who are not Associates. One continues to raise the Agenda in her work with student teachers and now with the faculty at large. There is a ripple effect of the Agenda's being picked up and carried by other non-Associates.

Participants will conduct inquiry into the nature of simultaneous renewal in the NNER.

The Associates generally gave favorable evaluations of the worth of their inquiry projects. They were pleased when their inquiry resulted in desired changes within their settings. "As a result of my inquiry," reported one Associate, "we are going to begin changing the admissions process to make it more reflective of the postulates." Other Associates commented,

> I plan to continue the inquiry on my project topic: a study of exemplary partnership schools that promote simultaneous renewal. The information may be of use to others in the NNER and also will contribute to my dissertation, which is still in a formative stage.

> Because of our work with another national school reform effort, I was able to bring classroom teachers and an arts and sciences professor to inquire about simultaneous renewal in a rural setting. We all gained!

Fourteen of sixteen setting directors responded that their Associates have continued to conduct inquiry into aspects of simultaneous renewal "as a natural aspect of their careers."[3] Some of the stronger responses follow.

> In a very real way, it can be said that our entire partnership is inquiry driven. Using the model developed by the Institute, the local associates meet to discuss selected readings and inquire into the actions and processes of simultaneous renewal at the local level. By carefully and patiently fostering relationships based on trust, the partnership leaders and IEI Associates have engendered cultures of inquiry within schools and school districts. The inquiry projects undertaken by the IEI Associates have been useful in specific areas. For example, one Associate has chosen to conduct inquiry on the manner and extent

to which personnel in his school district (serving about sixty thousand pupils) understand the Agenda. Another example of the culture of inquiry is evident in the Partnership Leaders Retreat, held twice each year for about twenty of the partnership's leaders. During this year, some of the retreat time will be spent discussing the research findings of the Associate mentioned above.

The fifth-year interns in the P–12 schools conduct an inquiry that is based on a need or issue emerging from the public schools. P–12 teachers are coming to campus to do research. Two of them completed dissertations on the moral dimensions. Everyone in our program is involved in inquiry in some way.

We have restructured using the inquiry method. Coordinators shifted to inquiry-based instruction. The faculty has implemented graduate courses using action research related to classes or within schools. Undergraduates are doing inquiry collaboratively. Elementary education has worked with dissemination. A research conference features collaborative inquiry and research with a college professor. In April 1997, a staff development aspect brought total school involvement.

Inquiry is done primarily through the secondary preparation program. Establishment of the teacher inquiry groups at PDSs was initially led by Associates and now has been taken over by school personnel. As an example, one teacher group is conducting inquiry into the question of why there are so few minority students in high school advanced placement classes.

We are getting into quite a bit of assessment work to try to figure out what effects we have had. Individuals in their own scholarship have worked in this area. Others work on a variety of things, including projects, action research, grant writing, assessment of pilot projects, and examination of professional preparation of school leaders. We allocated $4,000 to each partner school to do collaborative action research. We are doing inquiry on how to do collaborative teacher education. We created a series of seminars to develop inquiry-based school leadership, and supported minigrants for inquiry. We are studying outcomes for kids and families as well as outcomes for our students in teacher education.

One director gave a qualified yes response to the question of whether the Associates continued their inquiry as natural elements of their careers, and two stated simply that their settings have not been able to make inquiry part of their organizational or partnership culture:

I do not know the answer to that very well. One Associate did some things, but once back into his job he got very busy. Another Associate's whole research is about teacher leaders.

A lot of people were very bothered by the inquiry expectation. They found it a burden because they couldn't tie it to their daily work. In the second generation leadership program at our setting, we have struggled with it and have changed it from an individual to a group project—but even that has not worked well.

There has been less inquiry than I would like. However, our associates are very busy and in great demand, so they realistically have not had any time to conduct inquiry.

Participants will contribute to the work of simultaneous renewal by serving as presenters, advisers, facilitators, and friendly critics to the sixteen settings of the NNER.

Our fifth objective sought to use the talents of the Leadership Associates across the sixteen NNER settings. After six years of the Leadership Program, this objective has been realized to a much lesser degree than the other four. Certainly a number of Associates have pushed beyond the boundaries of their own settings to present at national conferences, to serve as advisers and critical friends to other settings, and to facilitate conversations about simultaneous renewal. However, the major impact of the Associates' work has been the development of necessary conditions for renewal at their own settings. We must remember that this is, after all, the highest priority for the program.

Each August since 1994 we have surveyed the graduate Associates to ascertain the kinds of outreach activities in which they have been engaged. The results of the 1996 and 1997 surveys indicated that such intersetting activities clustered around several major areas of involvement: publishing articles and books, presenting at national and regional conferences, facilitating conversations at NNER settings, assisting non-NNER sites to form networks or engage in simultaneous renewal, serving on national boards, assisting with NNER setting visits, and serving on NNER task forces and work groups.

The overall impact of the Associates' work is yet to be seen, as many of them are now moving into new leadership positions at their own settings or in others. Their contributions will be substantial with regard to several major NNER initiatives in progress at the time of this writing: the Secondary Partner School Project (featuring tri-partite teams at sixteen high schools), Diversity in Teacher Education (focusing on recruitment and retention of minority teachers), the General Education Work Group (developing a model curriculum for teachers), and the Arts in Teacher Education and Teaching (developing joint partner schools with the Getty Education Institute for the Arts). A Futures Caucus has been meeting to determine the future organization of the NNER; seven of the steering committee members are Associates. Several books are currently being written about the work of the NNER, and nearly twenty Associates are writing their stories. Sixteen Associates are helping to plan major exhibitions of their settings' work at a national conference in 1999 entitled "In Praise of Education."

Overall Impact of the Leadership Program on the NNER Settings

All sixteen of the NNER setting directors affirmed that their partnerships had been well served by sending their Associates to participate in the Leadership Program. Several spoke of the Associates' deeper understanding of the mission of teacher education in a democracy and the broader perspective they now bring to local issues:

> A continuity of vision and purpose has been maintained in spite of personnel changes at all institutions. The Leadership Program provided an opportunity for members of the tripartite organizations to learn about and focus on a common set of understandings and a shared vision or mission for their work together on simultaneous renewal.

> It is the single most important thing that has happened. They have a clear and shared sense of mission and the Agenda. Working with a core of leaders, they have replicated the leadership program at the local level. The support for the IEI Associates and the sixty local associates is the best money I've ever spent!

It has helped in that when we get people together to talk, the Associates have a broader perspective to bring to the table.

They were already leaders, but the program helped them develop deeper understandings, gave a moral grounding, and has strengthened partnership. They want more now than organizational leadership. The program has opened doors. They have developed into strong collaborative leaders. It has been really, really good.

The program increased and deepened our Associates' capacity for leadership. We chose people in positions that would move the program or had the potential means and a firm philosophical grounding. It makes planning easier, and they talk more deeply on issues. They are strengthened as leaders and given confidence as change agents.

The Leadership Program gave them content, a belief system, and contacts to take the initiative. They have had the courage to move beyond NNER and to make it our own setting's agenda. They are getting into partner schools and districts more.

Other directors related examples in which the Associates had experienced self-renewal:

All of our Associates left the program more knowledgeable about education in a democracy and have been advancing the ideas in curriculum development and democracy education.

The Leadership Program gave our Associates a new knowledge base and a renewed way of viewing themselves. One Associate had seen herself as "just a teacher"; she sees herself more now as an equal member of our partnership. Another Associate probably got some interpersonal skills out of it: he tended to be quite dominating, and now he has moderated his approach, helping him to work more collaboratively.

Three of our Associates were not setting leaders before they participated in the Leadership Program. It has helped them tremendously. They have really grown. It has helped them in their inquiry; it has provided direction in offering others readings and then in leading discussions; and the ideas are reflected in their instruction and in working with others.

Two of our Associates in particular have gained knowledge, self-confidence, a belief in the moral dimensions, an increased ability to interact and hold their own with others, and a better understanding of diversity.

The Associates have taken responsibility for leadership on their own, and I keep putting them in meetings where they really have to carry the ball on their own. I am convinced that the Leadership Program has given them tremendous confidence to speak up and be leaders. It's such a coherent, powerful voice that they get people to come along. The content information in the Leadership Program is very important. The Associates become masters of the content. The third important piece is the national connection: to see others do it and then be part of a bigger thing increases one's stature in the eyes of peers and oneself.

Participation in the Leadership Program helped Associates in several NNER settings to revise the total teacher education program or to immerse themselves more fully into the work of partner schools:

> Most clearly, their leadership has been instrumental in the development of our new five-year undergraduate teacher education program. We are having a conference with our partner schools this week (seventy to eighty people), and the Associates are very heavily involved in this.

> The Leadership Program is a good investment in people. It helped them in redesigning the teacher education curriculum. It has generated many in-house conversations. It provided impetus for our university to collaborate with P–12 schools.

> The postulates can be seen in the new teacher education curricula currently being developed. The Agenda serves as a good framework around which we are developing thematic strands for the secondary teacher education program. The Agenda has been embedded in the search and screen process for eight new faculty positions: we are looking for people who are willing to move the Agenda ahead.

> The largest single benefit was that participation in the IEI Leadership Program prompted our associates to develop partnerships not only within the university, but also with P–12 schools.

Advancing the Agenda

The strongest successes of the IEI's Leadership Program related to the Associates' performance on objectives 1 and 3: to develop a deep understanding of the moral dimensions of teaching in a democracy and to become effective change agents in their settings. Evidence from the graduate Associates and their setting directors affirms that significant gains have been made with regard to these two objectives.

Objective 4, to conduct inquiry into the nature of simultaneous renewal in the NNER, received strong positive responses in thirteen of the sixteen settings. Many of these settings have incorporated inquiry into the culture of the partnership, where it has become the basis for renewal efforts. However, in three NNER settings, inquiry is a hit-or-miss activity that is not the top priority at this time. We continue to urge these settings to embrace collaborative inquiry as a prerequisite to initiating changes and stimulating true renewal of the schools and the programs that educate all educators.

Objective 2, to participate in tripartite collaboration, has had a mixed measure of success. The determining factor appears to be the degree to which the setting has moved forward with authentic collaboration and engagement of all three parties to simultaneous renewal: the education faculty, the school faculty, and the arts and sciences faculty. In NNER settings where tripartite relationships have been formalized through centers of pedagogy, the collaboration has become part of the way the partners "take care of their business." We continue to urge the settings to build these critical tripartite relationships, especially with the professors from the disciplines in the colleges of the arts and sciences.

Objective 5, to contribute to the advancement of simultaneous renewal across the NNER settings, is the least fulfilled of the objectives at this writing. However, although the number of Associates who have traveled to other sites is quite small, a growing number of them have been publishing, presenting at conferences, and serving on NNER task forces and work groups. We expect to see an ever-increasing involvement of the Associates in leadership throughout the NNER and the country as the Agenda for Education in a Democracy is advanced.

As we review all of the comments from the graduate Associates of the Leadership Program and their setting directors, we are affirmed in our belief that this program has succeeded in building momentum for advancing the Agenda through simultaneous renewal of schools and teacher education. We look forward to continuing our relationships with the 113 graduates of Cohorts I through VI and to strengthening our collective work together.

The Agenda for Education in a Democracy permeates the lives of hundreds of educational leaders across the country. We strongly believe that this major educational renewal initiative has taken firm root because it has a clear and compelling agenda. This Agenda has two parts: a moral mission and the conditions that are necessary to fulfillment of that mission. As we have repeatedly emphasized throughout this book, the moral dimensions that serve as the grounding or bedrock of that mission are embedded in four themes: enculturating the young in a social and political democracy, ensuring that all students have equal access to knowledge, engaging in a nurturing pedagogy, and serving as stewards of the schools. These themes constitute the curriculum of the IEI's Leadership Program as well as the curricula of those leadership programs being carried out at settings across the Network.

We believe that the IEI's Leadership Program has succeeded as a major change strategy, fulfilling its programmatic mission "to empower a cadre of leaders deeply committed to the Agenda who will work to carry out the vision of renewing simultaneously America's schools and the education of educators." This cadre of educational leaders is growing rapidly at each NNER setting, and the Agenda for Education in a Democracy is now beginning to permeate every program, every school, and every role within the partner institutions of that setting. If the renewal process is to continue to thrive and grow, the Agenda cannot belong solely to the dean or the superintendent or a handful of positional leaders. Truly, the Agenda must drive the intentions and the efforts of all of the responsible academic and clinical faculty members, who "must have a comprehensive understanding of the aims of education and the role of schools in our society and be fully committed to selecting and preparing teachers to assume the full range of educational responsibilities required."[4]

We are well aware that we have only just begun to realize that education and democracy are ecologically intertwined. As John Goodlad states dramatically in his recent work, *In Praise of Education,* "Rising above the narcissism of the egocentric ethic to one that encompasses the common good is a theme that has challenged human civilization throughout its history. Until schools are guided by such an ethic, they will have great difficulty in, at best, getting beyond the provision of a caring custodial habitat to the cultivation of a caring educational pedagogy. Absent this cultivation, not just the American democracy but the global habitat is at risk."[5]

The Agenda for Education in a Democracy has guided the work of the Institute for Educational Inquiry, the Center for Educational Renewal, and the sixteen settings of the National Network for Educational Renewal for fifteen years. This Agenda has withstood the test of time. It remains a strong, compelling force driving the work of an increasing number of educators who have committed themselves to answering the question, "What does it mean to be a morally responsible teacher in a pluralistic social and political democracy?"

Education. Democracy. Simultaneous renewal. Moral mission. Conditions. These ideas now permeate the thoughts and actions of the Leadership Associates and all of their colleagues throughout the National Network for Educational Renewal. The Agenda moves us forward on our journey toward fulfilling the promise of education for ourselves and our posterity.

Notes

1. The quotations are taken from written end-of-year evaluations compiled for Cohorts I through V in, respectively, August 1992, 1993, 1994, 1995, and 1996. At the time of this writing, Cohort VI was halfway through its year-long program.

2. Comments are taken from individual interviews with the NNER setting directors conducted between August 1997 and January 1998 by Donna Hughes, senior associate of the Institute for Educational Inquiry, and Robert Burke, education professor at Ball State University.

3. This expectation comes from Postulate Eleven. See Appendix A.

4. This wording is taken from Postulate Five. See Appendix A.

5. John I. Goodlad, *In Praise of Education* (New York: Teachers College Press, 1997), p. 114.

Appendix A

Nineteen Postulates
for Educational Renewal

Postulate One. Programs for the education of the nation's educators must be viewed by institutions offering them as a major responsibility to society and be adequately supported and promoted and vigorously advanced by the institution's top leadership.

Postulate Two. Programs for the education of educators must enjoy parity with other professional education programs, full legitimacy and institutional commitment, and rewards for faculty geared to the nature of the field.

Postulate Three. Programs for the education of educators must be autonomous and secure in their borders, with clear organizational identity, constancy of budget and personnel, and decision-making authority similar to that enjoyed by the major professional schools.

Postulate Four. There must exist a clearly identifiable group of academic and clinical faculty members for whom teacher education is the top priority; the group must be responsible and accountable for selecting diverse groups of students and monitoring their progress,

---

Source: John I. Goodlad, *Educational Renewal: Better Teachers, Better Schools* (San Francisco: Jossey-Bass, 1994), pp. 72–93.

planning and maintaining the full scope and sequence of the curriculum, continuously evaluating and improving programs, and facilitating the entry of graduates into teaching careers.

Postulate Five. The responsible group of academic and clinical faculty members described above must have a comprehensive understanding of the aims of education and the role of schools in our society and be fully committed to selecting and preparing teachers to assume the full range of educational responsibilities required.

Postulate Six. The responsible group of academic and clinical faculty members must seek out and select for a predetermined number of student places in the program those candidates who reveal an initial commitment to the moral, ethical, and enculturating responsibilities to be assumed, and make clear to them that preparing for these responsibilities is central to this program.

Postulate Seven. Programs for the education of educators, whether elementary or secondary, must carry the responsibility to ensure that all candidates progressing through them possess or acquire the literacy and critical-thinking abilities associated with the concept of an educated person.

Postulate Eight. Programs for the education of educators must provide extensive opportunities for future teachers to move beyond being students of organized knowledge to become teachers who inquire into both knowledge and its teaching.

Postulate Nine. Programs for the education of educators must be characterized by a socialization process through which candidates transcend their self-oriented student preoccupations to become more other-oriented in identifying with a culture of teaching.

Postulate Ten. Programs for the education of educators must be characterized in all respects by the conditions for learning that future teachers are to establish in their own schools and classrooms.

Postulate Eleven. Programs for the education of educators must be conducted in such a way that future teachers inquire into the nature of teaching and schooling and assume that they will do so as a natural aspect of their careers.

Postulate Twelve. Programs for the education of educators must involve future teachers in the issues and dilemmas that emerge out of the never-ending tension between the rights and interests of individual parents and interest groups and the role of schools in transcending parochialism and advancing community in a democratic society.

Postulate Thirteen. Programs for the education of educators must be infused with understanding of and commitment to the moral obligation of teachers to ensure equitable access to and engagement in the best possible K–12 education for *all* children and youths.

Postulate Fourteen. Programs for the education of educators must involve future teachers not only in understanding schools as they are but in alternatives, the assumptions underlying alternatives, and how to effect needed changes in school organization, pupil grouping, curriculum, and more.

Postulate Fifteen. Programs for the education of educators must assure for each candidate the availability of a wide array of laboratory settings for simulation, observation, hands-on experiences, and exemplary schools for internships and residencies; they must admit no more students to their programs than can be assured these quality experiences.

Postulate Sixteen. Programs for the education of educators must engage future teachers in the problems and dilemmas arising out of the inevitable conflicts and incongruities between what is perceived to work in practice and the research and theory supporting other options.

Postulate Seventeen. Programs for the education of educators must establish linkages with graduates for purposes of both evaluating and revising these programs and easing the critical early years of transition into teaching.

Postulate Eighteen. Programs for the education of educators require a regulatory context with respect to licensing, certifying, and accrediting that ensures at all times the presence of the necessary conditions embraced by the seventeen preceding postulates.

Postulate Nineteen. Programs for the education of educators must compete in an arena that rewards efforts to continuously improve on the conditions embedded in all of the postulates and tolerates no shortcuts intended to ensure a supply of teachers.

Appendix B

Partner Schools:
Definitions and Expectations

Partner schools in the National Network for Educational Renewal (NNER) share a commitment to the nineteen postulates John I. Goodlad enumerated in *Teachers for Our Nation's Schools* (1990) and further developed in *Educational Renewal: Better Teachers, Better Schools* (1994). Each of these postulates has a bearing on the way partner schools are created and operated, with the fifteenth postulate speaking most directly to the subject:

> Programs for the education of educators must assure for each candidate the availability of a wide array of laboratory settings for simulation, observation, hands-on experiences, and exemplary schools for internships and residencies; they must admit no more students to their programs than can be assured these quality experiences.

In addition to the nineteen postulates, NNER settings share common values that influence the ways in which they approach

---

Source: This appendix is drawn, with slight modifications, from Richard W. Clark, Donna M. Hughes, and Representatives from the National Network for Educational Renewal, "Partner Schools: Definitions and Expectations" (Seattle: Center for Educational Renewal, University of Washington, 1995 [orig. 1993]).

their overall mission of simultaneous renewal of schools and the education of educators. These shared beliefs include the following:

- Partner schools of the NNER ensure that all learners have equitable access to knowledge.

- Partner schools recognize and honor diversity, commit to multicultural curricula and culturally responsive practice, prepare individuals for active participation in a democratic society, and promote social justice.

- Partner schools contribute to the growth of students as citizens in a democratic society, as contributors to a healthy economy, and as fully human individuals versed in the arts and ideas that help them take advantage of their talents. In short, they are schools prepared to enculturate learners for participation in a democratic society.

- Partner schools enable educators to make educational decisions with students and other stakeholders.

- Partners in partner schools create educative communities that seek to develop a more just and sustainable society.

Whether called professional development schools, centers for teaching and learning, or some other name, NNER partner schools are not an end but a means by which schools and universities seek to accomplish four purposes:

1. Educate children and youths
2. Prepare educators
3. Provide professional development
4. Conduct inquiry

The general expectations follow, arranged in relation to the four major purposes of partner schools. School and university educators from the NNER settings met on four occasions to help develop the following general expectations and associated examples. The term *university-based educators* includes representatives from the departments of arts and sciences involved in preparing teachers as well as those from colleges, schools, and departments of education.

As partner schools in NNER settings develop, they will use these guidelines to help them determine how well they are accomplishing each of the four major purposes, how consistent their work is with the nineteen postulates, and whether their work is truly guided by the set of shared values.

Each NNER setting is unique. Consequently, no two settings are likely to make the same amount of progress. Nevertheless, the settings have agreed that these expectations will assist them in assessing growth. They expect to renegotiate the contents of this document from time to time so that it can serve as a dynamic guide to difficult work.

Purpose One: Educate Children and Youths

Expectations:

- Establish a Learning Community

  Partners communicate in such a way as to create a learning community.

  Example:

  – Parents, community members, educators, and students commit to lifelong learning.

- Seek Equity and Excellence

  Partners seek equity and excellence for all enrolled students and other members of the learning community.

  Examples:

  – Partners ensure that the curriculum and instruction of the partner school help students achieve common, high expectations.

- Partners ensure access to learning by all students.

- Partners work so that differences in student achievement are not associated with factors such as race, gender, or social class.

- Written descriptions of curricula in partner schools reveal high expectations in keeping with local, state, and national standards.

- Classroom observations in partner schools reveal that educators make effective use of a variety of instructional techniques.

- Students develop a variety of learning strategies such as problem framing and questioning in order to construct meaning.

- NNER settings demonstrate progress in implementing alternatives to tracking of students in partner schools.

- Partners use "best practices" to assess student performance.

Purpose Two: Prepare Educators

Expectations:

- Engage in Collaboration

  Educator preparation programs in partner schools are based on continuous collaboration among partners to ensure that the partner school is an integral part of the total preparation program.

  Examples:

  - Partners communicate a common vision of the goals and purposes of the partner school in written and oral communications about the school.

  - Partners deal regularly with essential linkages between what happens at the partner school and the campus-based segments of the education preparation program.

  - NNER settings share meeting minutes to demonstrate growing collaboration concerning partner schools.

  - NNER settings demonstrate through testimony of preservice candidates and school and university faculty that the work in the partner schools is an extension of work that occurs on campus.

- Construct Pedagogy, Curriculum, and Attitudes

  Partner schools help preservice teachers construct the pedagogical skills, curriculum knowledge, and attitudes necessary to educate all learners.

  Examples:

  - Preservice teachers' experiences are based on a shared understanding among school- and university-based educators of current best practices in classroom teaching and learning.

  - Preservice teachers integrate theory and practice as they plan and carry out classroom instruction.

  - Preservice teachers develop the ability to apply the wide variety of instructional techniques and strategies required to help students with differing learning styles and backgrounds.

  - Observations in partner schools reveal that sound learning theories and best practices are integrated into the everyday life of the students.

  - Observations, interviews, and course descriptions reveal that campus-based courses and partner school learning activities for preservice teachers exemplify the conditions of learning that the prospective teachers will be expected to create in their future classrooms.

- Acquire and Exhibit Academic Knowledge

  Partners exhibit knowledge of relevant academic disciplines from the arts and sciences.

  Examples:

  - Preservice teachers in partner schools participate in a general education that enables them to enter into the human conversation.

  - Preservice teachers demonstrate appropriate proficiency in the disciplines they are expected to teach.

  - Preservice teachers have the pedagogical content knowledge needed to link student learning to the key elements of the major disciplines.

– Faculty from arts and sciences and education work with faculty from the schools in continuous renewal of the substance of the curriculum in partner schools.

Purpose Three: Provide Professional Development

Expectations:

- Collaborate and Define Programs Based on Student Needs

  Professional development for educators is collaboratively defined and is based on the diverse needs of students to be served by the educators.

    Examples:

    – Observations of school- and university-based educators who work with partner schools reveal instructional practices consistent with professional development collaboratively derived from analysis of the need of students in the partner school.

    – Professional development builds the capacity of educators to engage in school-centered renewal.

- Establish Linkages

  Professional development links theory, research, and practice.

- Work with Special Needs Students

  Professional development helps professionals work with special needs students.

- Develop Interprofessional Relationships

  Professional development helps educators understand how professionals from various fields can best work together as part of an "educative community."

Purpose Four: Conduct Inquiry

Expectations:

- Engage in Critical Social Inquiry

Partners engage in critical social inquiry concerning school and teacher practices.

Examples:

– Partners collaborate in action research groups using such categories as race, class, gender, and/or ethnicity as frameworks for analysis of school curriculum and instructional practices.

– Partners share examples of critical social inquiry regarding their school and the broader community of which it is a part.

- Engage in Reflective Practice

  Partners engage in reflective practice as a means of generating continuous improvement of education in the partner school.

  Examples:

  – Adults and children in the partner school generate questions about teaching and learning, gather information, develop practices, and assess the consequences of those practices on student learning.

  – Preservice teachers (and others at the setting) reflect on classroom experiences with other preservice teachers and their university- and school-based teachers and mentors.

  – School- and university-based educators use reflective practice in order to grow professionally.

  – The results of such reflection are used to inform school practice and educator preparation.

- Engage in Inquiry as Scholarship

  Partners use the partner school as a setting for scholarly examination of professional practice.

  Examples:

  – Partners conduct inquiry in accordance with norms of scholarly research, including review by and discussion with colleagues.

– Results of scholarly inquiry at the partner school are disseminated through such vehicles as conference presentations, scholarly journals, videotapes, professional development workshops, and infusion into college curricula.

– Representatives from each setting within the NNER publish scholarly examinations of professional practice conducted by school- and university-based educators at partner schools.

Resources

Sufficient resources are vital to the realization of each of the previous four purposes of partner schools.

Expectations:

• Provide Sufficient Resources

Partner schools are supported by sufficient people, time, and money.
Example:

– University and school faculty responsible for conducting teacher preparation programs are allocated sufficient time for planning, conducting, and assessing such programs.

– Sufficient numbers of well-qualified school- and university-based educators enable the partner school to accomplish its responsibilities related to teacher preparation, professional development, inquiry, and the education of P–12 students.

– Necessary and sufficient support is provided for professional development, including time, peer support, and opportunity for reflection.

– Collaborative work engaged in by all partners will be weighted equitably in connection with all personnel decisions, including compensation.

– Sufficient supplies and equipment support the learning of P–12 students and preservice teachers at the partner school.

– Comparisons of partner schools with nonpartner schools at NNER settings reveal that the partner schools have the time, staff, and money required by the multiple purposes they are expected to accomplish.

Index

A

Access to knowledge, 105–127, 241; the Agenda mission goal of, 14–15, 73, 82, 223, 278–279; inequities in, 107–110, 244; the moral imperative of, 105–107, 123; Postulate Thirteen on, 21, 339; putting the ideal into practice, 122–123; removing the barriers to, 116–118, 121; in renewing partner schools, 118–122; school barriers to equal, 110–116. *See also* Knowledge, conceptions of

Accountability: responsibility rather than, xviii; and stewardship, 178; and student performance standards, 115–116

Acronyms, use of, 301, 310n.16

Action plans, leadership program participant future, 200, 226, 266–267

Adler, M. J., 37, 62, 76–77, 81

Adorno, T., 134

Adult learning: with colleagues, 292–295; importance of conversations to, 201; and the Leadership Associates, 302–303

Advanced placement classes, 107–108

African American students, 107–108, 109, 111

Agenda for Education in a Democracy, the, 3–27; advancing, 225–227, 331–334; books on, xiv; conceptual differences about, xxiii–xxvi; core initiative of, 6, 23; epistemic grounds of, 11–12, 82; experiencing, xxi–xxiii, 23–25; exploring the ideas of, xxiii–xxvi, 18–22, 240–245, 300; and the five IEI Leadership Program objectives, 311, 312–328; the four-part mission of, 10–12, 222, 230, 240, 333; genesis of, xiii, xix–xxi; mission overview, 10–18; moral dimensions critical to, 11–12, 279–280, 334; ownership of, 229, 319; postulates overview, 18–22; sharing of, 230; simultaneous renewal basis of, 6–10; the strength and endurance of, 334. *See also* Leadership Program (IEI)

Agendas, educational renewal: about, xix–xxi; importance of commonplaces in, xxii; onion-like quality of, xxii–xxiii

Allison, D., 209, 212

Anderson, R. H., 157

Annenberg Rural Challenge, School at the Center Project of the, 167

Annual meetings, NNER: The Conversation at, xxiii; inquiry projects presentation at, 40–41; during ongoing IEI Leadership Programs, 299

Hirsch, E. D., 81
Hirschfeld, G., xxviii
Holmes Group, 261
hooks, b., 243, 248
Hord, S. M., 33, 261
Hughes, D. M., 41, 212, 216, 236,
273, 341–349
Hughes, K. H., 273
Huling-Austin, L., 261
Human conversation, the: access to
the full range of, 14–15, 76, 93–94;
or human conversations, xxv–xxvi,
xxix, 76, 77, 81; knowledge and,
98–103; origins of the idea of,
xxvi–xxviii. See also Conversations,
state leadership program
Hysterical character, the, 139–140,
149

I

IHEs. See Higher education, institutions of
Inclusiveness of education. See Access
to knowledge
Inclusiveness of stewardship, 159
Incommensurability of knowledge,
the problem of, 79–80
Inquiry projects, program participant,
166; benefits to teacher education
sites, 226, 230; fear of independent,
305–306; the four goals of, 40; by
IEI Leadership Associates, 40–41;
the IEI Leadership Program, 32,
323–326, 332; in the NNER,
323–326, 332; and partner schools,
346–348; presentations, 40–41;
state leadership program, 197–198,
210–211, 226, 229–230, 246; sustaining, 214–215; by teams, 226,
229–230. See also Research
Institute for Educational Inquiry
(IEI), 271; goals, 307–308, 334;
participation in the, 234, 236;
senior fellows, names of, 41. See
also Leadership Program (IEI)

Institutions for the education of edu-
cators: postulates on key conditions
in (#1–3), 19–20, 21, 337
Interest groups: the role of schools
and rights of, 21, 158–159, 339
Internet communication, 227, 249
Interview comments from NNER set-
ting directors, 314, 316–317, 323,
324–326, 328–331, 335n.2
Introductions of participants, first ses-
sion, xxvii, 55–57, 303–304
Introspection, 148–149; barriers to,
138
Ishiguro, K., 37
Ishler, R. E., 261
Italy, democracy in, 60–61

J

Jacobowitz, T., 243
Jefferson, T., 59
Journals, participant, 242, 277
Joyce, B. R., 33, 173
Justification, defensible, 86, 92

K

Kailua High School (Hawaii), 166
Kamehameha schools. See Hawaii
Leadership Associates Program
Keating, P., 212, 223, 261, 278
Kegan, R., 33–34
Kerr, D. H., xxiv, 41, 62, 165–166, 279
Kingston, M. H., 128–130, 132, 133,
148
Knowledge: and the human conversation, 98–103; justified true belief
(JTB), concept of, 86–89; and multiple intelligences (MI), 95–97;
performance or skill, 89–92; propositional, 85–89; and self-renewal,
329–330; standard analysis of,
85–86
Knowledge, conceptions of, 73–103;
and belief, 84–85; and cognitive
science, 95–98; difficulties with,
73–83; dualisms in, 74–75; from

Subject matters: providing disciplined encounters with all, 14–15, 77–82, 93–94; school tracking and classroom, 112–113. *See also* Content and activities, leadership program
Sugai, R., 169
Summer Institute. *See* South Carolina Summer Institute of Leaders
Superintendents, school, 268, 320
Surface, J., 167

T

Tannen, D., 209, 212, 296
Tarcov, N., 61–62
Teacher education programs: and access to knowledge, 118; connection of, to graduates (#17), 22, 340; and critical inquiry, 171; and guided practice, xxii; impact of leadership programs on, 229–230; inquiry projects on, 226; involvement of Associates in, 331; participants from, 221, 283; postulates on conditions for students in (#7–12), 20–21, 158–159, 297, 338–339; postulates on content and obligations of, 21–22, 339–340; postulates on policymaking for, 22, 331, 340; research on problems in, xxi, 260, 261, 269n.1; statewide collaboration among, 219–220, 254–257; visits to, 240
Teacher relationships with IHE faculty. *See* Faculties; Simultaneous renewal
Teachers: character of, 52–53, 147–149, 235; critical inquiry by, 170–173; meaning of being morally responsible, 175, 177, 180, 209, 312–315, 328–329, 331–332, 334; nurturing democratic dispositions, 147–149; peer coaching by, 173–174; "Portrait of a Teacher" (MSU), 234, 235; preparation of, 113–115, 155, 176–177, 179–180,

223–224, 301, 344–346; preservice, 167, 169–170, 176–177, 179–180, 197, 198, 203, 209–210, 214; professional development of, 121, 156, 173–175, 205, 230, 235, 240, 284; roles in improving access to knowledge, 116–118; socialization of, 34–35, 338; tracking and quality of, 113–115; traditional isolation of, 155–156. *See also* Education of educators
Teaching: attracting minority students into, 163–164, 197; critical inquiry into, 170–173; in a democracy, the meaning of, 175, 177, 180, 209, 312–315, 328–329, 331–332, 334; the first year of, 155–156, 159; as imparting knowledge, 100–101; the moral dimensions of, 175, 177, 180, 222, 277, 279–280, 312–315, 331–332, 334
Team-bonding activities, 226, 229–230, 262–265; action plan presentations, 266–267
Theobald, P., 167, 224
Theory and practice, educational: and Associates as change agents, 318–323; connected, 158, 299–300; partner school grounded on, 174–175; Postulate Sixteen on, 22, 340. *See also* Professional practice and education
There Are No Children Here (Kotlowitz), 37, 243, 248, 278
Thomas, B. R., 165
Time for thought, leadership program, 213, 228, 294, 302
Tocqueville, A. de, 64
Tracking, or streaming: equal access denied by, 14, 107–109, 111–113; and teacher quality, 113–115
Tripartite faculty relationships. *See* Faculties; Simultaneous renewal
"Trucking knowledge" metaphor, 100–101